MW01033920

NORDIC FOLKLORE

Recent Studies

EDITED BY

REIMUND KVIDELAND AND HENNING K. SEHMSDORF

IN COLLABORATION WITH

ELIZABETH SIMPSON

INDIANA UNIVERSITY PRESS

Bloomington and Indianapolis

©1989 by Indiana University Press

All rights reserved

No part of this book may be reproduced or utilized in any form or by
any means, electronic or mechanical, including photocopying and
recording, or by any information storage and retrieval system, without
permission in writing from the publisher. The Association of American
University Presses' Resolution on Permissions constitutes the only
exception to this prohibition.

Manufactured in the United States of America

Library of Congress Cataloging-in-Publication Data
Nordic folklore: recent studies / edited by Reimund Kvideland and
Henning K. Sehmsdorf in collaboration with Elizabeth Simpson.
    p. cm. — (Folklore studies in translation)
Bibliography: p.
Includes index.
ISBN 0-253-33125-0. — ISBN 0-253-20521-2 (pbk.)
1. Folklore—Scandinavia. 2. Folklore—Finland. 3. Folklore—
Philosophy. 4. Scandinavia—Social life and customs. 5. Finland—
Social life and customs. I. Kvideland, Reimund.
II. Sehmsdorf, Henning K. III. Series
GR205.N66 1989
398'.0948—dc20   88-45453
                                  CIP

1 2 3 4 5 93 92 91 90 89

CONTENTS

History and Legend

Folk Song and Folk Singing

Folklore and Society

FOREWORD
BY DAN BEN-AMOS

The present volume offers essays representative of current trends in Nordic folklore research. Within international scholarship Nordic folklore has a central position. Inquiry in folklore studies is commonly conducted on two levels: the national and the theoretical. National studies examine the varieties of folklore themes and forms in the context of specific cultures and languages. Such studies have historical or regional dimensions, exploring problems that have direct relevance to ethnic and national concerns. Their conclusions might affect the self-image and the identity of the specific social groups. Theoretical studies, on the other hand, address issues of the discipline of folklore itself rather than those of a specific nation or language. These studies both articulate the assumptions that underlie methodological procedures and explore the limits of what folklore texts permit readers to infer. Occasionally they include new propositions for analysis, pointing out innovative modes and models for the study of folklore in general.

A scholarly contribution on the national level, significant as it might be, does not necessarily offer new theoretical ideas or methodological principles to the discipline of folklore. The extent to which studies of the folklores of diverse nations contribute to the theory and method of the discipline varies from country to country and from one historical period to another. Nordic folklore scholarship has distinguished itself by making major theoretical and methodological contributions to the study of folklore through the explorations and discoveries in the national folklores of the individual Nordic countries. As Reimund Kvideland and Henning Sehmsdorf outline in the introduction to this volume, nineteenth- and twentieth-century Nordic folklorists laid the methodological foundations for folklore research. They were the first to uncover an oral epic, the *Kalevala*; in ballad and folktale studies they conceived of and forged the research tools that have remained indispensable in folklore studies. Their contributions to proverb, riddle, and belief studies are no less significant.

Their contributions, however, draw upon resources and trends that antedate the opening of the nineteenth century, the rise of folklore consciousness, and the formation of the discipline. In continental Europe, the Nordic countries were the last to come under the waves of Christianity that rolled up from the Mediterranean. Pre-Christian European traditions, customs, beliefs, songs, epics, and tales have continued to be part of the Nordic European traditions long after they disappeared—or became subordinate to monotheism—elsewhere on the continent. Consequently, when European intellectuals searched to the roots of their genuine ancient traditions they turned to the peoples of the North. They became Europe's own "primitive" people, who epitomized and symbolized the fundamental European culture, religion, and spirit of the folk.

In the Nordic countries themselves, the quest for national pride has been intertwined with the search for folklore. Long before other nations turned folklore into the handmaiden of nationalism, Sweden, for one, had done so through the institutionalization of folklore studies under the aegis of antiquarian research.

On May 20, 1630, the eve of his departure for the Thirty Years' War, King Gustavus Adolphus of Sweden signed a royal proclamation establishing the Council on Antiquities and outlining its research charges. These combine military goals, economic hopes, and nationalistic ideals with a disciplined research. Because of this document's significance for the history of folklore scholarship it is cited here in full.

Instructions that His Majesty graciously wishes that those who are appointed to be the antiquarians and historians of the Kingdom should follow.

1. First His Majesty wishes that they search for and collect all kinds of ancient relics and objects to glorify the fatherland. Foremost of all [they should collect] old runic inscriptions, in books as well as on stones, both broken and complete. [They should] record their locations, and give a complete account of how many of them are in each parish, writing down the old tales that exist about each stone, etcetera.

2. Next, [they should] copy and collect not only all the calendars, almanacs, and runic staves, in whatever form or shape they appear, and discover the difference between them, but also [they should] find out how their owners themselves understand them, and name the people who are knowledgeable in these matters, noting down how many of them live in each parish.

3. [They should] search for all kinds of ancient law-books like the old Wastgibtha law, the Wastmanna, Sudermanna, and Tijharad's and Smaland's laws, and others either in manuscript or print, etcetera. Also [they should collect] all kinds of ordinances and treaties, statutes, rights and regulations that might be of use to our Royal Court.

4. Likewise [they should collect] all kinds of chronicles and histories, immemorial tales and poems about dragons, dwarfs, and giants, as well as tales about famous persons, old monasteries, castles, royal residences, and towns, from which you can have some knowledge about the ancient times. [They should] not forget to find out the music of old warriors and runic songs.

5. [They should] examine and copy all kinds of old letters or excerpts of letters that can serve as a guide in the evaluation of coins, nobility, genealogies, or coats or arms and other evidence that can serve the annals of history.

6. [They should] search and collect all kinds of old coins and currencies.

7. All this information could be obtained from old farmers, burghers, and others, as well as noblemen, clergymen, bailiffs, and lawmen, and it should be looked up in churches and libraries in the towns as well as in the country.

8. Wherever they travel they should make thorough inquiries about the topographical features of the country and record the salt and fresh water lakes, the rivers, streams, and waterfalls, mountains, forests, and plains, either inhabited or uninhabited. [They should note] the distances between one place and another, [note down] the existing roads and their condition, whether suitable for travel by coach or cart. [They should record] the sources of the streams and their flow into lakes or seas. [They should comment] whether they are navigable or can be made suitable for navigation by [the construction] of locks, and what could be their use. Everything should be observed and prepared for the drawing of geographical maps of the entire kingdom of Sweden.

9. [They should] take every opportunity to list all kinds of land-measurements as mark, öre, and ortigland, . . . fields and meadows.

10. [They should] look for all kinds of boundary stones and boundary clearings. . . .

11. [They should] search for deposits of ore. . . .

12. [They should] inquire about household records and all kinds of economic matters . . . [detailed examples of agricultural work, hunting, and fishing].

13. [They should] record the different cures and search for medical books, noting down the names of herbs and trees. [They should find out about] the signs for forecasting the weather, with which those who live near the sea are usually familiar, etcetera. [They should] describe the old costumes and weapons that are used in each province and [write] about the drinking vessels, *kosor*, horns, and other objects etcetera.

14. And since the names of the tools are necessary for compiling the complete dictionary, they should record the different field tools, ship tools, and [the names of] other such objects. Likewise [they should note down] the names of hundreds of parishes, villages, forests, streams, lakes, mountains, islands, inlets, shoals, inquiring also for the origin of these names.

15. Finally [they should] find out what kind of temperament the people of each province have. As one sees, hardly anything is forgotten by the writers of history.[1]

In all likelihood Johannes Thomae Bureus (1568–1652), the antiquarian and the king's teacher, initiated and formulated this royal edict and its comprehensive set of charges. Since the purpose was to serve the royal court and not only pure knowledge, the edict targeted practical information that would serve military and economic needs, instead of addressing only linguistic, ethnographic, and folkloristic subjects. Yet the breadth of the royal edict provided a solid basis for the development of what might anachronistically be called folklore and folklife scholarship in the nineteenth and twentieth centuries, and its vigor has not abated.

Obviously there is no simple and direct line of scholarly continuity in Nordic countries from the seventeenth century to the present. Furthermore, in spite of the current scholarly cooperation and frequent communication between Nordic scholars, each of these countries—Denmark, Finland, Iceland, Norway, and Sweden—has its own scholarly tradition and research emphases. Yet in all of them, to varying degrees, popular antiquities received educated attention from clergymen and antiquarians well before the Romantic period and the post-Romantic emergence of formal folklore studies. Whether wishing to eradicate or preserve folklore, these scholars provided a solid basis for research and made the public aware of the importance of folklore as a major component of culture.

The current collection represents Nordic folklore scholarship as a mature discipline. While in other countries folklore research still requires advocacy—or worse, apology—Nordic folklorists present their modern studies with the self-assurance that an established discipline commands. Almost thirty years ago, three leading American scholars—Stith Thompson, Warren E. Roberts, and E. Edson Richmond—published surveys of folklore research in three Nordic countries, given from an American point of view.[2] The growth of folklore requires that we now become familiar with the research in these and other countries from a Nordic point of view.

NOTES

1. Quoted in Oscar Almgren, "Om tillkomsten av 1630 års antikvarie-institution," *Fornvännen* 26 (1931), 35–42. I would like to thank Mrs. Gunnil S. J. Sjoberg for rendering this document into English and for long discussions in which she clarified for me the historical background of this royal proclamation. The English translation includes a number of necessary modification, and the responsibility for the present text rests with me. For another discussion of the Swedish Antiquity Act, see Michael Roberts, *Gustavus Adolphus: A History of Sweden 1611–1632* (London: Longmans, Green, and Cc. 1953), 1:520.

2. Stith Thompson, "Folklore Trends in Scandinavia," pp. 27–34; Warren E. Roberts, "Folklore in Norway: Addendum," pp. 35–38; W. Edson Richmond, "The Study of Folklore in Finland," pp. 39–49 in *Folklore Research around the World: A North American Point of View,* ed. Richard M. Dorson (Indiana University Folklore Series No. 16); *Journal of American Folklore* 74 (no. 294) (Bloomington: Indiana University Press, 1961).

PREFACE

The articles selected for this volume present Nordic folklore studies during the last twenty-five to thirty years. The term "Nordic" indicates that the work not only of Scandinavian, but also of Finnish, scholars is included. Although Finland differs in terms of ethnic origin, language, and culture, ties to Scandinavia have been strong since the Middle Ages. Especially in folklore studies, collaboration between the neighboring regions has been fruitful, and Finnish scholars have played a major role in the development of the discipline. The articles have been chosen to reflect areas in which Nordic folklore studies have been particularly strong, as well as to demonstrate recent changes in theoretical paradigms and empirical applications. The anthology is intended for scholars and students of folklore and Scandinavian studies in the United States. It is the second volume on Nordic folklore prepared by the editors. The first volume, *Scandinavian Folk Belief and Legend,* was published by the University of Minnesota Press in 1988. A third volume, a critical edition of Scandinavian folk tale repertoires, is in preparation.

In consultation with the authors, the editors have revised most of the articles. Henning K. Sehmsdorf has translated the articles from Danish, Norwegian, Swedish, and—in one instance—German. We owe special gratitude to Elizabeth Simpson, whose unfailingly good judgment and sure sense of the American language have contributed immeasurably to the completion of this volume.

This anthology is a response to a long-standing wish on the part of the Nordic Institute of Folklore to make the results of Nordic folklore research available in English. We thank the Director of the Institute, Lauri Honko, as well as Bengt Holbek, Bengt af Klintberg, Bente G. Alver, and other colleagues in the Nordic countries and North America for their helpful suggestions. In particular, we thank Dan Ben-Amos, General Editor of the series Folklore Studies in Translation, for his encouragement. We also thank the University of Bergen and the University of Washington and especially the Faculty Exchange Committee of these universities for enabling the editors to spend leave time working on this project, as well as the Danish Research Council, the Norwegian Research Council, the Swedish Research Council, the Norwegian Emigration Fund, and the Norwegian Information Service for financial support.

REIMUND KVIDELAND
HENNING K. SEHMSDORF

The generous support of The L. J. Skaggs and Mary C. Skaggs Foundation has made the *Folklore Studies in Translation* series possible.

ABBREVIATIONS

AT   Antti Aarne and Stith Thompson. 1973. *The types of the folktale.* 2nd rev. ed. Helsinki (FFC 184).

DgF   *Danmarks gamle Folkeviser.* Svend Grundtvig et al. (eds.). 1853–1976. Vols. 1–12. Copenhagen.

EFI/   Etno-folkloristisk institutt (Department of Folklore and Ethnology),
EFA   University of Bergen, Norway.

EU   Etnologiska undersökningen, Nordiska museet, Stockholm.

FFC   Folklore Fellows Communications. Helsinki.

IFGH   Institutet för folkminnesforskning vid Göteborgs högskola (Folklore Archive, Gothenburg, Sweden).

KU   Kulturhistoriska undersökningen, Nordiska museet, Stockholm.

LUF   Folklivsarkivet, Universitetet i Lund (Folklore Archive, University of Lund, Sweden).

NFL   Norsk folkeminnelags skrifter. Oslo.

NFS   Norsk folkeminnesamling (Norwegian Folklore Archive, University of Oslo, Norway).

SKS   Suomalaisen Kirjallisuuden Seura (Finnish Literature Society, Helsinki, Finland).

SLS   Svenska litteratursällskapet i Finland (Swedish Literature Society in Finland, Helsingfors, Finland).

ULMA   Dialekt- och folkminnesarkivet i Uppsala (Folklore Archive, Uppsala, Sweden).

Introduction

NORDIC FOLKLORE STUDIES TODAY

Reimund Kvideland and Henning K. Sehmsdorf

Looking at Nordic folklore studies today, we find that there is no single methodology dominating the field. Various scholars combine a number of approaches in their work. We can trace this methodological pluralism to the very beginnings of folklore as an academic discipline in the early nineteenth century. Until approximately three decades ago Nordic folkloristics drew their inspiration from the neighboring fields of philology and comparative literary studies; since then the methodological paradigms have often come from the social sciences, occasionally in combination with literary and other humanistic approaches. Lauri Honko's influential *Geisterglaube in Ingermanland* (Spirit Beliefs in Ingria, 1962), for example, combines the methods of social psychology, perception psychology, history of religion, and frequency analysis in mapping out the belief tradition of Ingrian communities around the Gulf of Finland. On the other hand, Bengt Holbek's recent *Interpretation of Fairy Tales: Danish Folklore in a European Perspective* (1987) integrates the structuralist methodology of the literary critic Vladimir Propp with psychoanalytical and sociohistorical perspectives to arrive at an interpretative model of the folktale.*

We can distinguish two tendencies in Nordic folklore studies: on the one hand, scholars in each country have developed research traditions reflecting national interests and areas of emphasis; on the other, theoretical and methodological debates have tended to cross national boundaries and embrace the entire Nordic area. Thus, specific research projects most frequently utilize empirical data from the scholar's district or home country rather than the entire Nordic area, but the establishment of transnational research institutions such as Folklore Fellows in 1907, NEFA (Nordic Ethno-Folkloristic Student Organization) in 1963, and especially The Nordic Institute of Folklore in 1959—as well as frequent Nordic conferences—have facilitated regular contact and joint discussion of common interests. In the 1960s, for example, the

---

* In using the term "fairy tale," Bengt Holbek departs from usual practice in Nordic folkloristics. The term "fairy" usually refers to preternatural beings in legends and folk belief only.

problems of genre analysis and questions of terminology occupied folklore scholars throughout the Nordic countries. During the 1970s the problems of specialists—archivists, ballad scholars, experts on children's traditions and mass-lore, and others—were put to a general debate, along with more inclusive, theoretical questions concerning the coherence of Nordic folkloristics as a field of study. Another question recently occupying the attention of folklorists in the Nordic countries concerns the nature of "oral tradition" from which scholars interpret the cultural history of the people (Lehtipuro, 1983).

Beginnings

In the Nordic countries, as elsewhere in Europe, the first impulses toward the development of folklore study as an academic discipline came from National Romanticism. Following the example of the Grimm Brothers' *Kinder- und Hausmärchen* (Children's and Household Tales, 1812–22), Nordic collectors published the oral traditions of the rural folk. For a variety of reasons, preference was given to specific genres, primarily folktales and ballads, and to music traditions. Folklorists felt that what presumably were the oldest traditions preserved the spirit and lifestyles of the "folk" most faithfully; and if the traditions they found appeared fragmentary and deteriorated, it was the task of collectors and editors to "restore" them. The folklorists, almost all of whom belonged to the urban, intellectual elite, were less interested in the unlettered rural populations of their own day than in the supposedly glorious national past surviving in fragmentary form in folk tradition. Folklore thus became a means of defining the identity of the nation. Especially in Norway and Finland, both of which had recently become independent, the new discipline spearheaded the development of a national culture. In Sweden, by contrast, folklore served to reinforce the national self-image as a Great Power. Denmark, like Sweden, had always been independent and therefore did not need national symbols derived from folk tradition. Nevertheless, Denmark too found folklore useful in strengthening the nation's self-respect after defeat in the Napoleonic wars, and somewhat later in the national struggle against political and cultural hegemony by the German neighbor to the south.

The oldest Nordic folklore archives are those of the Finnish Literature Society, founded in 1831 by a group of young scholars, among them Elias Lönnrot, collector of the Finnish epic poem, the *Kalevala*. The archives are the central depository for all kinds of folk traditions in the Finnish language (Herranen/Saressalo, 1976). By contrast, Swedish-language materials documenting the origin and development of Swedish folk culture in Finland have been collected by the Swedish Literature Society since its inception in 1885. In 1937 a folklore archive was established at the University of Helsinki to preserve and index the Swedish-Finnish collections.

With the appointment of Svend Grundtvig as lecturer at the University of

Copenhagen in 1863, university-level folklore studies were taught for the first time in a Nordic country. When Grundtvig died twenty years later, his private collections of Danish folklore were donated to the Royal Danish Library. A permanent government grant for the maintenance of Grundtvig's and later collections led to the founding of Dansk Folkemindesamling (Danish Folklore Archives) in 1905. A nationwide collecting effort was started and the archives now encompass all kinds of Danish folklore materials dating from about 1830 to the present.

In 1886 Molkte Moe was named professor of folklore and Norwegian dialectology at the University of Oslo. He was the son of Jørgen Moe who, in collaboration with P. Chr. Asbjørnsen, had published various editions of Norwegian tales and legends during the 1840s and 1850s. The manuscripts and notes of Asbjørnsen and Moe's collections—together with parts of the ballad collections of M. B. Landstad (1853), those of Sophus Bugge, and Moltke Moe's own collections—became the basis for the Norske Folkeminnesamling (Norwegian Folk Archives), established in 1914.

In Sweden, systematic collecting of folklore materials began with the founding of Nordiska Museet (The Nordic Museum) in 1873. But folklore studies did not become an academic subject area in Sweden until 1912, when Carl Wilhelm von Sydow became a lecturer and later professor of folklore at the University of Lund. Von Sydow pioneered the development of genre-analysis and an internationally accepted folkloristic terminology.

A Turning Point

Until fairly recently, Nordic folklore studies emphasized texts found in the archives. Throughout the nineteenth and early twentieth centuries, scholars continued the labor of collecting and classifying folk traditions in their respective language areas; besides tales, ballads, and musical traditions, they gathered customs and folk beliefs, proverbs, riddles, sayings, and other forms of expressive culture. Classification involved a comparative, historical approach focused on narrative types and motifs. The Finnish scholars Julius and Kaarle Krohn developed the so-called historical-geographic method to explain the similarities of stereotyped, complex forms of folklore as the result of shared origin and migration. In 1910, Antti Aarne devised an index of tale types (revised in 1928 by the American Stith Thompson) to facilitate the labeling and ordering of narratives according to plot. Axel Olrik in Denmark and Moltke Moe and Rikard Berge in Norway developed the idea that folk narratives were autonomous, "superorganic" products of the human imagination that followed their own inherent laws, quite independent of the sociocultural milieu of the storyteller and his or her audience.

An important change began between 1920 and the 1940s, when C. W. von Sydow introduced the concept of genre analysis, distinguishing different kinds of folk narratives in terms of the function, adaptation, and dissemination of each. Von Sydow also pointed out that different tradition genres (notably legends and memorates) provide different kinds of evidence for the study of folk belief. His work was continued by several of his students, among them Albert Eskeröd, who combined von Sydow's concept of "source criticism" with the functionalist approach of Malinowski and Radcliffe-Brown in a major study of folk belief surrounding harvest practices in Sweden (Eskeröd, 1947). In Norway, Svale Solheim arrived at similar results, though less on the basis of theoretical considerations than on an intuitive understanding of the sociocultural function of tradition (Solheim, 1952).

The gradual shift from text to context engendered a new concept of tradition. Originally scholars felt that the study of the present would deepen our understanding of the traditions of the past. Soon it became obvious, however, that contemporary tradition was interesting for its own sake and important in understanding our own time. Tradition was no longer regarded as historically fixed and belonging to the past, but as an ongoing, dynamic process relevant today. By the same token, the "folk," by which in the past folklorists had usually meant the unlettered populations in agrarian, preindustrial settings, now were discovered to include all of society, including the urban middle class, the rich as well as the poor, factory workers, policemen, and professors.

From the upheavals of the 1960s the general expectation developed that research in all fields, including the humanities and social sciences, have social relevance. Scholars became aware of the political implications of their own work. Was it the task of folklorists to support existing ideologies, or should they contribute to social change, and, if so, in what direction? Looking for answers to these questions, Nordic folklorists turned their attention from comparative projects to the study of local milieux and special groups: children, women, ethnic minorities, street people and hippies, dance groups, and other performers. Just as folklore had contributed to a sense of national identity in the early nineteenth century, recent studies of communities and groups as microcosms strengthened the sense of local identity and belonging. Radio and television programs, exhibitions, and printed collections made people aware of their own traditions. In 1981, a project of the Nordic Institute of Folklore involving scholars from all Nordic countries dealt specifically with the relation of folk tradition to regional identity (Nenola-Kallio, ed., 1982).

Fieldwork

Responding to the example of cultural anthropologists in the U.S., the Organization of Ethno-Folkloristic Students in 1965 organized the first Nordic seminar in fieldwork methods, resulting in the publication of a fieldwork guide (NEFA, 1968). The seminar, which has been repeated every three years, focused on how to produce contextual data in folkloristic interviews. At first these data consisted mostly of external description of informants and their sociocultural milieu. As methodological procedures were refined, techniques were developed to reveal personal attitudes and social values and norms. Most folkloristic studies during the 1970s were thus based on empirical data newly gathered in the field, rather than on archival materials. In the 1980s, however, some scholars have returned to the archives and "do fieldwork" in older materials, i.e., combine archive data with detailed studies of nineteenth-century social history in an attempt to reconstruct the social-cultural context. Today, instruction in fieldwork theory and methods constitutes a major part of the training of folklorists at Nordic universities.

Prose Narrative

Since the late 1970s, there has been considerable debate concerning the theory and methodology of folk narrative research in Nordic folkloristics (Honko, 1979–80; Herranen, ed., 10, 1981; Leino, 1981; Holbek, 1983, 1987). Currently there are few purely textual studies of prose narrative (one exception is Sato Apo's structuralist analysis of Finnish tale tradition [1986]). In most instances, scholars feel called upon to place the narrative text in its sociocultural context. A number of historical studies of nineteenth-century tale tellers aim at reconstructing the ecology of repertoires found in the archives. R. Bjersby, for example, has described the storytellers documented by P. A. Säve on Gotland (1964); Ørnulf Hodne has analyzed the informants of Jørgen Moe (1979); G. Herranen has sketched the life history of the Swedish-Finnish storyteller known as "Blind" Strömberg in relation to his repertoire (1984); and, most recently, B. Holbek has studied E. T. Kristensen and other tale tellers in Denmark (1987).

One narrative genre that has received a great deal of attention lately in the Nordic countries is the so-called urban legend (Klintberg, 1986). The first scholarly articles about contemporary legends were written by American scholars in the 1940s, and it is from the U.S. that many of the stories traveled to other parts of the world. In 1974, the Swedish folklorist Bengt af Klintberg systematically began collecting the genre in Sweden and throughout the Nordic countries. Often macabre in subject matter, urban legends can be characterized as a kind of "collective fantasy" that mirrors the world view of modern, postindustrial society.

Klintberg and his colleagues note that the narrative structure and rhetorical style of urban legends is one of the reasons the genre is widely popular today. Other studies focus on the social realities mirrored in prose narratives, including tales, legends, memorates, personal narratives, and anecdotes, as well as interviews. Juha Pentikäinen, for example, has related the analysis of world view to a study of the repertoire and life history of the Finnish storyteller Marina Takalo (1978); Anders Gustavsson has investigated the function of gossip in resolving community conflicts in a fishing village in Sweden (1979). Personal narratives and interviews form the basis of studies by Bente Alver, Torunn Selberg, and other scholars of the reasons behind the widespread interest in alternative forms of medicine in Scandinavia today (Alver/Selberg, 1984). In a study of stories told by factory workers during their lunch breaks, Gösta Arvastson has analyzed language and the role of the storyteller as mirrors of working conditions, beliefs, and social values (1986).

Jokes and rumors are also studied as reflections of social attitudes. Bengt Holbek led the way in 1974 with his discussion of ethnic jokes as a reflection of widespread anxiety about rapid socioeconomic and cultural change in Denmark. In 1979 the Norwegian folklorist Stein Mathisen stirred a great deal of public interest with an article analyzing jokes told in Norway about Finns. He was able to show that the stereotypical depiction of Finns as hard-drinking and sexually primitive functions as a form of self-ironic criticism of an established masculine ideal. In 1983 a topical issue of the Norwegian folklore journal *Tradisjon* presented four articles along similar lines, showing how ethnic jokes about immigrants and blacks expressed and perhaps perpetuated discriminatory stereotypes among the Nordic people.

Folk Belief and Legend

The thorough revision of the theories and methods of folk belief research carried out by Lauri Honko in the early 1960s can be traced in applied studies such as Juha Pentikäinen's analysis of the dead child in Nordic tradition (1968a) and Bente G. Alver's study of the folk concepts of the human soul (1971). Further examples of the psychosociological approach are found in the work of Matti Sarmela, who in 1974 published a macroecological investigation of guardian spirits in Finland, and Jonas Frykman, whose doctoral dissertation on the unwed mother in preindustrial Sweden traces the social realities reflected in folk belief (1977).

New theoretical considerations concerning the ecology of tradition surface in a volume of essays edited by Lauri Honko and the Swedish scholar Orvar Löfgren in 1981. The essays are critical of the functionalist approach and instead propose an interpretative model that places folk belief in a larger context of traditional knowledge and socioeconomic factors. In a study of beliefs and ritual behavior, for example, Löfgren examines the interplay of magic and economics in the social system of Swedish fishing communities during the nineteenth and early twentieth centuries.

Most recently, Bengt af Klintberg has suggested that the modern urban legend serves as an indicator of folk belief in a postindustrial context (1986). Klintberg does not discuss his conclusions theoretically, but makes them empirically plausible in commentaries on legends currently circulating in the Nordic countries. Similar observations of folk belief codified in personal narratives appear in articles by various scholars describing folk medical traditions (Alver/Selberg, 1984).

History and Legend

Nordic collectors and scholars were initially more attracted to legends than to tales. As Bengt Holbek has remarked, this may be because, since the Renaissance, there had been an antiquarian interest in chronicles, legends, and myths. From the 1620s on, crown ordinances directed clergymen and other officials in Sweden and Denmark-Norway to gather historical sources, including legend materials (Holbek, 1983, 146). When Andreas Faye published *Norske Folke-Sagn* (Norwegian Folk Legends, 1833), he singled out historical legends as important to "anyone who has a sense of history, or who takes an interest in the fate of his country throughout the centuries." Faye allowed that legends may not be reliable as historical documents, but they nevertheless reveal "the people's memories of strange and wonderful deeds or events" (Faye, 1833, IV).

Until the late 1950s, both historians and folklorists tended to look at historical legends primarily as historical documents and, like Faye, found them unreliable. In 1961, however, at an ethnofolkloristic conference in Ålborg, Svale Solheim—in a discussion of the cycle of ballads about St. Margaret—suggested that their historical authenticity lies not in the accuracy of specific details (persons, events, dates) but in the depiction of "general reactions to contemporary events and social conditions" (Bødker, 1962, 125). Brynjulf Alver followed Solheim's suggestion with a methodologically important study of historical legends to show how they reveal the folk's perception of their own history. Legends thus become a significant supplement to other historical sources (Alver, 1962). A further example of this approach is Bjarne Hodne's analysis of legends about assault and murder from the seventeenth to nineteenth centuries, in which he compares the legends to legal protocols and other historical documentation (Hodne, 1973).

Another Norwegian folklorist, B. Hertzberg Johnsen, has brought a functionalist perspective to the analysis of historical legends. On the basis of fieldwork done in a community in northern Norway, she places current traditions about a soldier supposedly killed by wolves in 1612 in the context of the local milieu to demonstrate how legend functions to maintain cultural values and a sense of regional identity. The study provides empirical evidence that legend tradition is typically transmitted in the form of abbreviated comments and conversations among individuals in the community, rather than in stereotyped story form (Hertzberg Johnsen, 1980). These findings corroborate the observations made by Linda Dégh in her analysis of storytelling in rural Hungary (Dégh, 1971).

In Finland and Sweden scholars have emphasized studies of belief legends, while historical legends have received less attention there. Bengt af Klintberg, for example, justifies the emphasis on supranormal legends in his edition of *Svenska folksägner* (Swedish Folk Legends, 1972), by explaining that in Sweden historical legends are regionally limited and therefore not central to overall tradition. Norwegian scholars, by contrast, have argued that, quantitatively speaking, historical legends are at least as important as other legend genres and, furthermore, express the same supranormal world view.

Folk Song and Folk Singing

In the 1970s American scholars developed new methodological perspectives in folklore studies to emphasize "performance," by which they mean the dynamics of expression and communication in the transmission of traditional materials. "Language, oral tradition, traditional behaviors and other non-verbal means of expression are all part of human communication, symbolic competence, values and norms, identity and self-realization" (Kvideland, 1981, 56).

In Nordic folkloristics, performance studies have been particularly productive in regard to folk song and singing. In 1975 a research project in this area was proposed to the Nordic Institute of Folklore, and in 1980 scholars from Denmark, Norway, Sweden, and Finland met to present preliminary results of their investigations (*Sumlen*, 1982). Besides various theoretical discussions, major empirical studies combined performance with musicological perspectives to describe singing activities in a microculture. For example, Päivikki Suojanen (1978) published a monograph on hymn-singing among the Beseechers of Western Finland, analyzing recordings made over ten years as an in-group observer at prayer meetings. Another important work is Jan-Roar Bjørkvold's analysis (1979, 1985) of spontaneous singing among preschoolers in the Oslo area.

In addition to studying singing in a sociocultural and performance context, ballad and folk song scholars in the Nordic countries continue the tradition of literary-philological analysis and editing of texts. But text-oriented research too has taken on new dimensions to include aspects of use, function, intention, and repertoire (Kvideland, 1983).

Folklore and Society

Today the majority of Nordic folklore scholars are concerned with the ecology of folklore products. But we can further distinguish studies that focus specifically on how society is revealed in tradition rather than the other way around. Jonas Frykman, for example, has analyzed folk belief and narratives to isolate views toward sexuality in preindustrial Sweden (Frykman, 1977). Other recent studies focus on problems and patterns in contemporary society: the function of parties in creating contact and a sense of identity among teenagers

(Johnsen and Mathisen, 1979); the norms and rules governing the expression of aggressiveness in "street wars" among urban children (Sørensen, 1979); or children's use of storytelling to articulate their concern with the problem of death, which has become a taboo subject for most urban dwellers (Kvideland, 1980).

In some instances, applied folkloristic studies aim directly at solving specific social or other practical problems. For example, the results of folklore research have proven useful in community planning of childcare centers and playgrounds. Another important project concerned the investigation of how rheumatic patients experience their own illness. In 1981 two Norwegian physicians undertaking a systematic survey of rheumatic patients, asked Bente G. Alver to supplement their data with interviews utilizing folkloristic techniques. Their collaboration resulted in a study revealing the patients' views and attitudes, particularly in respect to the treatment of rheumatism by official, as well as by alternative or "folk," medicine (Larsen, Alver, Munthe, 1984).

FOLKLORE AND NATIONAL IDENTITY

Brynjulf Alver

One of the first things we learned as students of folklore was that, once the Grimm Brothers had published their famous tale collections in 1812, the Romantics set in motion the machinery that became the science of folklore. The great names identified with that school of thought come crowding up from the history of our discipline: Macpherson and Percy, Walter Scott and Jamieson, Arnim and Brentano, Herder and Goethe. As the German literary historian and philologist Wilhelm Scherer put it, the idea of a nation and a national past became "a revolution in the spirit of Rousseau against the spirit of Voltaire, of nature against culture, of feeling against reason, of genius against esthetic rules" (Moe, 1927, 18). We see this more readily in individual art than in the study of tradition; however, tradition became the handmaiden of poets whenever the spirit moved them. Nor must we forget, on the one hand, that the brutal driving force behind the Romantic "revolution" was Napoleon's imperial dream and the battles of Jena and Auerstädt; nor, on the other, that the underlying ideas had been voiced in Europe long before. To give an example from our discipline: before Macpherson made "Ossian" famous in hyperliterary circles all over Europe, Scots philosophers had already studied folk speech and oral literature in detail, using much more authentic materials than Macpherson's (Grobman, 1973).

Bourgeois Counterrevolution

This "revolution," which took up folk tradition for serious discussion and publication, occurred exclusively among the urban cultural elite. In no sense

Original title: "Nasjonalisme og identitet. Folklore og nasjonal utvikling." Published in *Tradisjon*, 1980.

was it a "folk" movement, but rather a bourgeois ideology whose object was the "folk." Moltke Moe called the waves reaching Norway "the National Breakthrough" (Moe, 1927), but today we see clearly that the term "Bourgeois Breakthrough" would be more precise. By and large even today's folklore research is dominated by bourgeois ideologies. But in contrast to the poets and scholars from the Romantic period, we do know the "folk" we are studying. In Norway, for example, the discovery of folk-cultural traditions came as a shock to the small circle of intellectuals in Christiania in the 1840s. Although nearly all of the rural traditions that caught their interest—tales, ballads, music, beliefs, and customs—were about to be replaced by new ideals and forms, the wealth in subject matter, the creative imagination and incredible symbolism, and the survivals from an older cultural period overwhelmed and astounded scholars and writers. The folk had preserved a rich cultural heritage, a heritage so completely hidden from the elite that even that most Norwegian of nationalists, Henrik Wergeland, had no idea that "folk poetry" even existed (Moe, 1927, 60f.).

Of course, the cultural elite in Norway knew about National Romanticism elsewhere in Europe, and this was finally the reason for the general interest in folk literature. But Romantic ideology influenced the collecting and publishing of folk materials only to a minor degree in Scandinavia. Now and then we encounter Herder's and the Grimms' *Volksgeist* ("folk spirit"), for example, in Geijer and Afzelius' *Svenska folkvisor* (Swedish Folk Ballads, 1814–17), mostly in Geijer's preface; but of course Geijer was no folklorist. To be sure, the texts have been edited; according to the ideology of the time it was more important to recreate something whole than print fragments. But interest in the ballad antedated the National-Romantic vogue, and Vedel's ballad edition from 1591, and Syv's from 1695, had a much greater effect on the "folk" than those that appeared in the nineteenth century.

Before long more sober ideologies made themselves felt alongside the Romantic. Hand in hand with the idealization of the "folk" went the notion that they were not creators in their own right but received their culture from the elite. In Norway, this view was quite prevalent. Moltke Moe, for example, was convinced that the creator of *Draumkvedet* (Dream Poem) must have been a "poet of high rank," a priest who perhaps lived in northern England and wrote the ballad there (Moe, 1927, 211, 279, 334).

Orientation to the Past

Romantic influence on folklore studies was felt most keenly in a pervasive enthusiasm for the past. From the early nineteenth century until quite recently scholars looked backwards in time. Whether the subject matter was building types, social life, or dancing, the focus was on the past, preferably the distant past. The background was the Romantic idea that certain groups in society had preserved traditions and lifestyles from an older stage. More than that, it was felt that in almost every country the past had somehow been greater and nobler than the present. Precisely because the present seemed impoverished, disjointed, and lacking in originality, the idea arose that folk culture preserved remnants of an ancient glory. There we could find our cultural origins, however obscured by the passage of time; and origins were equated with the "national" in our cultural heritage (Velure, 1975a, 14).

Nowhere was this more pronounced than in epic poetry and music traditions. Wasn't the epic *Kalevala*—which astonished the whole world when "discovered" by Elias Lönnrot in the 1830s or 1840s—the greatest of all Finnish poems? And didn't it (though composed by unlettered folk and transmitted in a vernacular the cultural elite looked down upon) yet bear witness to a tradition almost unfathomably rich? Small wonder that the Romantic fascination with the past enjoyed a strong position. But tradition lay in ruins; it was in need of reconstruction so that the whole of the past could be revealed. "Restoration" is what they called it.

This is how it was everywhere. The dream of a glorious past became an important source of inspiration in times of national distress as well as of national expansion, and many good collections of oral traditions and excellent studies of national subjects were published. Age itself became a test of quality. The further back in time one could trace aspects of folk culture, the more valuable and interesting they became. The very titles of various publications reveal how important the element of age was: *Danmarks gamle Folkeviser* (Denmark's Old Folk Ballads), *Altdänische Heldenlieder, Balladen und Märchen* (Ancient Danish Heroic Songs, Ballads, and Tales), *Deutsche Rechtsalterthümer* (Monuments of Ancient German Law). "I love the old legends," the Norwegian poet Simon Olaus Wolff sang in National Romantic spirit, and Andreas Faye borrowed Wolff's phrase as a motto for his edition of *Norske sagn* (Norwegian Legends, 1833; see Alver, 1980a).

Selection

Often age by itself was not a sufficient criterion. *Fula visboken* (The Book of Nasty Songs) and *Erotiske folkeeventyr* (Erotic Tales) do nothing to enhance our national pride even though the materials collected in these volumes are unquestionably old; no one would use them to argue on behalf of, or explain, our national culture. Until quite recently, the interest in oral traditions has been selective, with regard both to age and to certain esthetic criteria for what ought to be collected and preserved. Ballads were considered more valuable than children's rhymes, thus our archives contain many more recordings of the exotic ballad than of the children's rhymes still on everyone's tongue. The foremost Norwegian collector of musical tradition during the nineteenth century, Ludvig M. Lindeman, wrote in his "Report" (1850, 484):

> If you're looking for melodies worth collecting, you'll have to be willing to listen to all kinds of trash and keep on coaxing until you bring to light forgotten treasures, because the old ballads and songs are lost more and more and buried beneath recent, and largely worthless, songs.

At the same time Lindeman wrote his report, "Myllarguten" (Miller) Torgeir Augundson (1801–72) was giving concerts for the cultural elite in Christiania and Bergen. Quite possibly "Myllarguten" was the greatest musical genius ever born in Scandinavia, and he had been brought up in a rich and ancient musical tradition. But his sophisticated city audiences could not understand any of the music he played. In their eyes, his fiddle tunes from Hardanger were Norwegian "nature," not music.

Marginal Culture

One consequence of the fixation on "old" materials was that what scholars collected and studied was marginal to contemporary culture, known only in the form of "survivals" and fragments about to vanish from living tradition. As early as the time of the Grimm Brothers, tale telling was much rarer than research history leads us to believe. As far back as a century ago, Wilhelm Mannhardt found it difficult to gather sufficient data to support his fertility theories. And the ballads were nearly gone by the time collectors tramped through Telemark—the very center of balladry in Norway—in the 1840s. "It was like saving an old family heirloom from a burning house," Magnus Brostrup Landstad wrote, "or perhaps I should say, it was like snatching a brand from the fire, bearing the marks of the fire's consuming power" (1853, IV).

As a result, the collecting of traditions took on the tone of a rescue operation, and often scholars were faced with seeing materials disappear under their own eyes before they were able to save them. Because these were cultural monuments from which national identity could be developed, the age factor and the urgency of preservation became important arguments in applications for financial support for collecting and research. But nearly always it was too late. "The ethnological world is ablaze," Anton Bastian wrote some ninety years ago (Lid, 1933).

The Scholar as Idealist

Perhaps we ought to look beyond grand generalizations and focus on the scholars' premises for their own work. National-Romantic proclamations are for the most part of little use; they tend to be anecdotal and have little direct connection with folk tradition or its analysis. On the other hand, many folklorists brought a high seriousness to their life's work and saw it as a patriotic calling. When Moltke Moe said that he wished to "serve the fatherland" and "work to benefit the country," he was not making fancy speeches; he meant what he said (Liestøl, 1949, 154ff.).

Actually, folklorists today, like their nineteenth century colleagues, tend to ask why they do their chosen work. We feel obliged to prove that what we do is useful, not just some irresponsible game without obligations, research for its own sake, as was often the case during the interim period (Herranen and Saressalo, 1976, 53–94). In the nineteenth century there was general agreement on two premises for folklore studies: (1) the importance of folk tradition for research, and (2) the importance of folk tradition, through research, for the history of the homeland. The Norwegian minister Andreas Faye, in the preface to *Norske Sagn* (Norwegian Legends, 1833) brought together most of the contemporary arguments for legend study. Largely uncritical and derivative as he was, he did not add much of his own, but he became a voice for many editors and scholars (Faye, 1848, III–VI):

1. The supranormal legend tradition supplements our knowledge of pre-Christian religion and of Eddic poetry.

2. The legends explain nature and man's relationship to nature. In support, Faye refers to the findings of natural science. (I believe the argument could be of use in social planning and in environmental protection today.)

3. The legend tradition can serve "poets and lovers of poetry" both as inspiration and as a material source. This argument was found in many places until recently. It was applied not only to legend, but to all forms of folk literature. Henrik Ibsen, for example, proclaimed: "The time will come when our national poetry will turn to our ballads as an inexhaustible gold mine" (1857). When in 1958 the monumental series *Norsk folkemusik* (Norwegian Folk Music) was begun, one of the arguments was that it would provide subject matter for composers today.

4. Legends have historical interest not so much by virtue of their authenticity, but by virtue of the folk's perception of their own history. Thus legends can supplement what is revealed by conventional historical sources, and they allow us to connect local with national history. In our own day, it has been demonstrated that in times of crisis legendary tradition can serve as a model for action (Solheim, 1970).

5. The sense of local identity is strengthened when people see their own traditions in print. For travelers, too, a locality becomes more attractive when it is colored by tales of old. This point is of renewed interest today, both for pedagogical purposes in school and for the tourist industry.

6. Legends have further pedagogical use as an idealistic form of youth literature. Today we would perhaps emphasize the intrinsic value of legends as literature rather than as an apology for a given world view.

Folklore scholarship developed beyond narrowly national perspectives at an early stage, and the Andreas Faye we meet in his Preface is just as much a rationalist as he is a romantic. In his own opinion, the useful was just as important as the ideal; and I believe he is not too distant from us today. On the contrary, perhaps one of the best arguments for taking good care of the mass of data folklorists refer to as "archives" is that they contain insights and experiences society may be able to use and should therefore know about.

It would be wrong to think that the National-Romantic roots of folklore studies are an exclusively nineteenth-century European phenomenon. The underlying causes can be traced much further back in time. Only by understanding the idea of Sweden as a Great Power, for example, can we understand how Johannes Thomae Bureus (ca. A.D. 1600) was able to argue that the runic alphabet had an historical connection with the Hebraic of the Kabbala, that their common origin was Swedish and the latter therefore the most ancient of the Germanic tongues. Today we smile at Bureus' capers, as we do at Olaus Rudbeck who about a century later indulged in etymological fantasies to prove that Sweden was the lost Atlantis, the ideal country and cradle of human culture described by Plato (Boberg, 1953, 218).

No one would indulge that kind of fantasy unless his nation were strong. National research in a country that has been suppressed will tend to have different premises. In the preface to his doctoral dissertation Knut Liestøl, for example, asks:

> Would not some of the glorious poetic creations of the ancient Norsemen live on in the folk ballad and down to our own times? Would not the splendid fate of some of the personalities in our ancient history grip the people with such power that they, too, would bring forth their singer of tales? Would not the adventure of the old sagas inspire poets in secluded valleys during long dark winter nights of great deeds and heroic struggle with fearful powers of nature? (1915, 11)

Liestøl's approach is no doubt both specifically Norwegian and Romantic, but it differs radically from the position of National Romanticism. Liestøl provides an example of conscious national-programmatic scholarship based on ideologies created around 1905 from the national dream of freedom and rediscovery of an ancient cultural identity across five hundred years of humiliation. This is folklore put to political use!

In the Nordic countries that sort of ideology is very much out of place today, although since the Second World War folklore has in fact served political purposes a number of times. But in countries where folklore can help unite a nation, one might well find it used that way. For example, in the nineteenth century folklore expressed the idea of the German nation across political borders; and today, with Germany divided once again, there is a fervent search for a sense of community between East and West Germany in spite of the ironclad political border. Another variant exists in the new national states in Africa, many of whose political borders are artificial lines of separation drawn by European colonial masters. Here the task is to create a sense of national identity and statehood within the existing borders, and here experts use folklore to fashion a community in spite of linguistic, ethnic, and historical differences.

Folklore Scholarship and National Identity

There is no reason to hide the fact that European folklore research had unexpected consequences. Some of the conclusions scholars arrived at were strongly supported at the grassroots level. Emphasis on the age factor and esthetic quality as criteria of selection endeared scholars to organizations committed to cultivating the old culture as especially national. Folk dance groups, fiddlers' associations, crafts organizations, groups cultivating national customs, and so on represent a political response to folklore research; their organizational viability has been an important political argument in the search for national identity. Variation in tradition was regarded as undesirable and an obstacle to correct form; and God help the folklorist who suggested in these circles that age was not always proof of genuine national identity, or that oblivion was the only threat to the stability of tradition. Fake-lore took over from folk-lore, and national navel-gazing won the day from comparative research in the eyes of the public.

In some instances folklore and folklore scholarship actually hinder national consolidation and become a troublesome or even dangerous political force. This is particularly true of countries constituted of several ethnic groups or language groups, or populations of different national background. I will pass over our own geographical area and instead give some examples from the eastern Mediterranean.

Modern Turkey needs national consolidation emphasizing Turkish identity. Folklorists, however, are not willing to ignore the fact that the population of Turkey consists of various ethnic, language, and religious groups, and that each has its own folklore. Nor can folklorists ignore the fact that Turkish tradition is a variation of a much larger system. The political confrontation has been so difficult that folklore has been eliminated as a subject taught at the universities, folklorists have been imprisoned, while official organizations of folk singers and musical performers of Turkish traditions are given preferential treatment (Basgöz, 1972).

In the young state of Israel, where national and cultural unification is of paramount importance, it is at the same time difficult to find a common base. Folklorists feel they are under pressure when politicians decide that it is politically expedient to emphasize a hypothetical unity rather than the historical variety of national traditions.

The national desire for independence and the cultural response to that desire are related to the level of interest in folklore and folklore scholarship. It is no accident that Finland and Ireland, two countries that had to struggle for national and linguistic independence, boast the largest folklore archives

anywhere, built from systematic collecting of national traditions in the vernacular. Young states needing to develop their national identity have tended
to assign priority to folklore studies and research. And why are folklore archives
and studies relatively underdeveloped in old imperialist countries like England,
France, Spain, and Portugal? Is it because their energies have been focused on
distant lands rather than on everyday life at home?

There are aspects of culture other than folklore that have national significance. Nothing contributes more to a sense of national identity than shared
language and history. An important element in the interest in folklore has to
do with the creation of a national written language, partly because it was
thought that folklore materials contained survivals of older language forms.

But we must guard against thinking that only humanities have national
significance. The same is true of the natural sciences: geology, biology, zoology,
botany, and meteorology not only have their own folklore, but are important
to a country's national identity.

Folklore as National Symbol

We fool ourselves if we believe that folklore alone represents national culture,
whether in the nineteenth century or today, or that it can always be employed
as such. But there is one area in which folklore outstrips other cultural
expressions: as a national symbol of the folk. Both within and outside the
borders of Finland, for example, the *Kalevala* is the unquestioned symbol of
everything Finnish, in spite of the fact that most people know it only superfi-
cially at best. And what spiritual goods do we produce other than the Dream
Poem and Hardanger fiddle tunes if we want to present Norway? No one has
visited the Færoe Islands without experiencing the Færoe dances as national
symbol and as the cultural phenomenon most representative of national
identity. Sameland (Lapland) is geographically vague, but since the Norwegian
contribution to the European Grand Prix in 1980, there can be little doubt that
the *joik* (a traditional type of Lappish song) is a resounding national symbol of
what it means to be a Same (Lap). Iceland, on the other hand, has such a strong
literary tradition that nothing can compete with the sagas as national symbol.
We can take comfort in the fact that the sagas are partly rooted in folk tradition.

I pass over Denmark and Sweden because those countries have not needed
national symbols of a folk character. Both countries have always been independent, both have escaped long periods of foreign occupation, both have
recent imperialist traditions. It is not surprising that it is in these countries we
find the seeds of pan-Scandinavianism. It makes sense that it was a Swede who
in the sixteenth century wrote *Historia om de nordiska folken* (The History of the
Nordic People), that Nordiska museet (The Nordic Museum) was founded in
Stockholm in 1873, and that its collection actually became Nordic in scope.
And C. C. Rafn, a farmer's son from Fyn (in Denmark) in 1825 established

Nordisk Oldskriftselskab (Nordic Society of Ancient Letters) with the express aim of studying and publishing Icelandic manuscripts. I submit that either venture would have been unthinkable in Norway either in 1825 or 1873.

No need to be naive: certain imperialist interests did play a role in all of these undertakings. But there was more to it than that. They do bear witness to ideas that transcend narrowly national boundaries, to a vision of the Scandinavian North taken as a whole. Perhaps there was a dawning sense of a Nordic identity, something similar to the impulse that lead to the founding of Nordisk institutt for folklore (The Nordic Institute of Folklore) several generations later.

Folk Narrative

METHODS IN FOLK NARRATIVE RESEARCH

Lauri Honko

The study of folk narratives is a central part of folkloristics. During the postwar decades, the emphasis in folklore studies changed from text to context-oriented approaches. Present-day folklorists are more interested in the ecological conditions and socioeconomic structures that give meaning to folkloric acts of verbal communication and behaviors. The demand for holistic thinking has motivated intensive studies of individuals and small groups, authentic performances of tradition, and the environmental adaptation of tradition actually in use in communities. The rise (and decline) of modern sociology and the only recent success story in the humanities, modern linguistic theory, have left their imprint on folklore methodology. Trends in cultural anthropology and sociolinguistics have inspired some folklorists. Semiotic and communication studies shape the terminology of the discipline. Psychological and, to a lesser extent, psychoanalytical explanations are also being proposed. Studies of the personality, life story, and repertoires of informants are thriving, along with studies of cultural symbols. Vivid interest in myth, world view, supranormal experience, and religious genres has made the neighboring disciplines of comparative religion and phenomenology of religion important for folklorists.

Much of this newer methodology is just emerging. And much of the old prewar methodology persists—sometimes refashioned—and produces results. Any statement on folklore methods will thus have to concern itself with past, present, and future, many of the present accomplishments being the result of methods developed in the past, and many present theories still having to demonstrate their viability. To discuss trends in methodology therefore becomes an exercise in history and futurology.

The relative importance of particular methods to folk narrative research and to folklorists in general varies, but this is not the concern of the present study.

Originally published in *Ethnologia Europaea*, 1979–80.

Methodological developments, whatever branch of folkloristics they have occurred in, have usually also been felt in the study of folk narratives, and vice
versa. Concentration on folk narrative may, however, help sharpen the profile
of methodological development.

The Evergreen Historical-Geographical Method

In the introduction to a recent American survey on modern folklore theory,
William R. Bascom recognizes two major problems "which have concerned
earlier scholars and which are still important today."

> The first question is, how are we to explain the similar tales that are found in
> different societies, sometimes separated by great distances? Some of the answers
> that have been proposed are suggested by the following questions. Are these
> similar tales to be explained in terms of extreme antiquity; that is, did they spread
> with man from the cradle of mankind? Are they to be explained in terms of the
> psychological unity of mankind, or the principle of limited possibilities, or in
> terms of historical accident? Are they to be explained by diffusion or borrowing,
> or by migration, or by independent invention, perhaps inspired by common
> sources in nature? (Bascom, 1977, 2)

This is a familiar bundle of questions, not only for folklorists but also for
ethnologists and anthropologists. The answer provided by the oldest folklore
method worthy of the designation was quite definite: observable affinities are
the result of historical diffusion of and connections between tales, or more
precisely, between the variants of a migrating tale. The method originated in
Finland during the latter half of the nineteenth century through the work of
Julius and Kaarle Krohn, father and son, and has been called the "Finnish" or
"historical-geographical" method ever since. Parallel development or convergence was not taken into consideration to explain the occurrence of similarities
on the basis of factors other than genetic interdependency: each folktale had
been invented only once. Using this method, a scholar was able to pinpoint the
place, time, and language of origin for each folklore product. By way of
reconstruction it was possible to delineate the archetype or original form
(*Urform*) of the tale. The network of variants, when compared and analyzed,
could open up lines of diachronic heritage and geographical diffusion of the
folktale. Several criteria were used to sort out primary episodes, motifs, traits,
elements, and so forth, from secondary ones. General knowledge of history,
culture, and migration of populations was utilized to avoid the contradiction
of facts and to complement information derived from the comparison of
variants. The aim of the study was usually a monograph to outline the origin,
diffusion, and emergence of local redactions of the narrative (Krohn, 1926;
Anderson, 1934–40, 508–22).

Folklore monographs are still written along these lines today. In 1971, Kaarle

Krohn's "Die folkloristische Arbeitsmethode" (1926) was published in English translation (as "Folklore Methodology"), another sign of the continuing importance of the method (Krohn, 1971). Despite criticism, there is tacit agreement among folklorists that under certain circumstances the principles of the historical-geographical method are applicable. But the limitations of the method are seen more clearly now. First, the historical-geographical method works best, if it works at all, with fixed and complex forms of folklore such as long tales, stanzaic, metric ballads, formulaic riddles, and proverbs—that is, forms as complex and stereotyped as possible—to give the assumption of monogenesis some plausibility. Second, the archetype or basic form is at best little more than a handful of hypotheses as to the relative primariness of some traits (Kuusi, 1956; Dundes, 1965). Kaarle Krohn's dream of the well-balanced, poetically perfect *Urform* as the legitimate target of folklore research was abandoned long ago. Third, the idea of wavelike diffusion does not account for the observable dispersion of the material.

There are other, more fundamental doubts, which cannot be eliminated by improving the method. A folktale is handled as a unique creation on one hand, and as a typical representative of one or more folklore genres on the other. Themes cross genre boundaries, and genres have specific rules of production and different communicative functions; thus the scholar who transcends genre systems and genre-specific communication when tracing a tale is often following not a tale but a theme (which may carry different messages). The question arises whether the historical-geographical hunter is really chasing the same hare all the time. Many scholars have had difficulty drawing a line between one tale or ballad and similar tales or ballads intended only as material for comparison. Even after items have been accepted as variants of a folktale, it may be difficult to place them within one genealogy. This suggests that the similarities and differences between variants may not have originated as the historical-geographical method assumes: the idea that all folklore is produced in the same manner, and is subject to the same kind of change when used and transmitted, may be too simplistic. If this doubt is legitimate, rules of production and forms of adaptation of different genres should be given at least as much attention as the *Urform*. Perhaps this is the way out of a contradiction inherent in the historical-geographical method: the simultaneous adherence to the monogenetic origin of tales and to the polygenetic origin of themes (Honko, 1979a).

The Dilemma of Comparison and the Paradigms of Development

Folkloristics has always been based on comparison. Local motifs and themes acquire new splendor when parallels in other, sometimes ancient, cultures are disclosed. Many tales and motifs in the oral tradition of Europe have been traced back to ancient Greece, Egypt, or the Middle East. Why? Not necessarily because those literatures show a close resemblance to the tales and motifs studied, but because they are the most prestigious inheritance in European culture. Often it was a way of enhancing nations of lesser historical grandeur, simply to show that their oral tradition belonged to an "original" and common European heritage. Furthermore, it was a way of demonstrating that folklore was not backward and trivial, that it was not some antipode of civilization.

Instead, folklore was a natural resource, a warehouse of valuable documents of the past. Adherence to the cultural-historical lineage was so strict that the concept of fairy tale or *Märchen* was applied by some folklorists only to Indo-European tales (Thompson, 1946). The question of whether other linguistic groups and other parts of the world also possessed fairy tales was left open and has been debated ever since (Bascom, 1965). Today folklorists are adopting more anthropological attitudes and some Eurocentric categories are being replaced by universal ones.

Even if we avoid the unchecked comparativism of Frazer, for example, some problems still remain. Above I showed how the unit of comparison can shift from tale to theme. Single motifs can also be chased across seas and continents: when all the parallels to particular motifs and elements in a narrative are assembled for comparison, analysis may acquire impressive temporal and spatial dimensions. Such atomistic comparison, however, does not appeal to present-day folklorists, who question the fruitfulness of single-item comparisons. They want to know more about the context—the body of knowledge, the complex of behavior, or institution, of which the item is a part. They ask questions about the genre affiliation of the item. In other words, modern folkloristics is becoming systems-oriented. Comparisons now tend to focus on larger bodies of tradition in limited geographical areas and less extensive historical periods. In the future, it is probable that fewer monographs will be written on single narratives than on whole genres or interactions of genres within definable social and historical settings.

Most comparisons imply change and development in folk narratives, yet these comparisons do not result as directly from meticulous analysis as they seem to: behind them we find broad personal theories concerning folklore development. At this point it may be useful to differentiate between paradigms of evolution and devolution. Under the paradigm of evolution, a folklorist tends to see narratives as developing, becoming more complex, branching out, attaining new elements and characteristics, growing from modest beginnings to splendor and perfection. Under the paradigm of devolution, narratives are closest to perfection in the beginning, just when they have been created, and in developing lose their beauty and break to pieces. When evidence is scanty or problematic, these paradigms help scholars bridge a gap, and they invisibly play their role in systematizing research material.

It is impossible to say which paradigm has been more popular in modern folkloristics. Perhaps the paradigm of devolution made the quest for an archetype worth the trouble. But, although the founder of the historical-geographical method, Julius Krohn, was an evolutionist, his son Kaarle became a devolutionist. These paradigms belong mostly to personal theory: the choice between them is one a scholar makes intuitively, many times, in the process of sketching a line of development. The reader needs to recognize the choice, regardless its permanence or coherence, because a paradigm structures the results of a study.

Genre Systems—Real or Ideal?

Genre analysis is central to folkloristic methodology. Regardless of their theoretical, sometimes opposed, positions, most folklorists utilize the concept of genre. Genre analysis may be used for taxonomy and classification, term analysis, cross- cultural comparison of genre-systems, analysis of genre interaction, and so forth (Honko, 1968, 48–66; Pentikäinen and Juurikka, 1976, 13–74; Ben-Amos, 1976). Genre analysis is often used in combination with some other method, such as communication theory, frequency analysis, or function analysis. Generally it acts as a check on the arbitrary use of narrative materials.

The dynamism of recent writing on genre theory may derived from a basic opposition between ideal and real genres. Are genres only categories upon which scholars have agreed, or do they also exist and operate for informants and tradition communities? Ideal and real genres should not be thought of as alternative concepts, as Dan Ben-Amos seems to do (Ben-Amos, 1976, xv–xx). On the contrary, the dialectics of genre theory rest on the insight that ideal and real genres interact continuously in the making of theory. Bronislaw Malinowski was one of the first to try to delineate a real system of narrative genres in the Trobriand Islands, but in fact he was forced to hybridize native and scholarly concepts (Honko, 1970, 45–52). Similarly, folklore scholars, teachers, and archivists also develop and adjust concepts on the basis of new empirical findings. There is a constant flow from particular, empirical, and real genres toward general systems of genres as defined by folklorists. Whether the point of departure is abstract systems or raw material provided by informants, the scholar is compelled to build bridges between the two.

Most of our terms, such as tale, legend, myth, and anecdote, are general and may be inaccurate from the point of view of a particular tradition community. Pure genres are rare. Genres thought to be more or less universal emphasize certain criteria that differentiate one genre from others, but this web of distinctive characteristics cannot represent a full description of real, existing genres. Because genre concepts tend to emphasize certain qualities and exclude others, I have resorted to the concept of ideal type, which, according to Max Weber, is based on reality but is not a manifestation of it. Let me illustrate this by one possible paradigm of ideal narrative genres and their relations.

Figure 1 is a development of the scheme presented by C. Scott Littleton (1965). Two axes, "factual-fabulated" and "profane-sacred," measure the place-

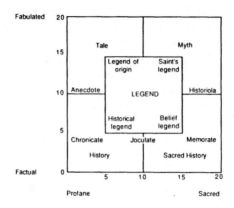

Figure 1

ment of narrative genres according to the degree of fabulation and sacredness attributed to them. Other variables could be chosen, and the map would have to be modified accordingly. The present scheme differentiates between religious and nonreligious narratives (referring to supranormal beings and events). It shows the distance of a narrative from everyday reality, whether sacred or profane. Thus, *chronicates* relate factual experiences; if the subject matter is humorous as well as historical, we label it *joculate*; if it is supranormal, we call it a *memorate.* The central category, *legend,* includes factual and profane historical legends, factual and sacred belief legends, fabulated and profane legends of origin, and fabulated and sacred saints' legends. But these are not absolute characteristics because legends represent a transitional field between everyday life and tale and myth. More genres could be added to the scheme; for example, I have included *anecdotes* (humorous tales and jokes) and *historiolas* (mythical narratives used in chants, prayers, and so forth).

Ideal types are justified as analytical tools: ideal-type genre concepts provide a common language to realize existing forms and talk about them. This use of ideal types is more useful than the observation that the genre system of a given culture does not fit neatly into our terminology. Narrative genres of a general system will always be culturally homeless or supracultural. Weber's concept of ideal type does not transform all genres into instrumentalities; instead, it helps us to understand why—in the mass of narratives—few items fully correspond to our genre definitions, and many represent incomplete or mixed forms.

The opposition "ideal vs. real" runs parallel to (but is not identical with) such pairs as "universal vs. particular," "nomothetic vs. idiographic," and "fablicated vs. native." Recent genre theory stresses the latter components of these pairs: interest focuses on the real, existing genres in particular societies and emic, native systems. Studying these genres requires thorough fieldwork and theoretical imagination.

There is, moreover, a diachronic and developmental dimension in genre analysis. The same content may appear in one period as memorate or chronicate, in another as legend, in a third as myth; or, conversely, a myth may give rise to a new memorate or legend tradition. Instead of creating better taxonomies, etic or emic, future genre research, whether historical or empirical, will have to study the development of genres and genre systems. Relating these to social development is an urgent task. The lifespan of a genre is limited in two ways: (1) a genre may die or disappear altogether, or (2) it may become inadequate or obsolete in one social group, but continue to exist in another. The cause is not usually in the genre itself, but in surrounding socioeconomic changes. The degeneration of a genre is normally a symptom of cultural and social change, which has numerous manifestations within and outside folklore. In our time, demographic changes in rural populations and the mechanization of agriculture—along with the expansion of mass media—have eliminated many of the social conditions necessary to traditional genres. Tales and some forms of legends are on the verge of extinction in many places in Europe; in their place, folklore archives are flooded with ethnohistorical memoirs and short personal narratives, materials previously regarded as nontraditional. We need to know the stratification and density of genres in a particular society, as well as the cultural centrality or marginality of given genres.

Structural Analysis and the Problem of Meaning

The story of structuralism has been told so many times that I may be brief about it. From the standpoint of folk narrative research, the fact that one of the Russian formalists of the 1920s was a folklorist is of paramount importance. That scholar, Vladimir Propp, published his most important works, *Morphology of the Folktale* and Transformations of the Folktale, in 1928, eighteen years before the publication of his doctoral dissertation, *Historical Roots of the Folktale*, in 1946. Thirty years later, an English translation of the *Morphology* appeared, generating a boom of folkloristic structuralism in the United States. Simultaneously, linguistic and anthropological structuralism, with Claude Lévi-Strauss (1955) as one of the leading scholars, was quickly gaining ground. During the 1960s, the Soviet Union, the United States, and France became the strongholds of folkloristic structuralism: Eleazar Meletinskij (1971), Yuri Lotman (1964), Alan Dundes (1964), Elli and Pierre Maranda (1971), Claude Bremond (1964), and A. J. Greimas (1966) became known as advocates of structural analysis. Folk narratives, especially the so-called ordinary folktales (tales of magic) and myths, were the main subjects of methodological experiment, only gradually did structural analysis begin to deal with other genres, such as epic and lyrical folk poetry, charms, riddles, and games.

Structuralism has taught at least one important principle to students of folk narratives; there are similarities and differences between narrative texts not manifest on the surface. Two texts may be structurally identical, although they do not have a single motif in common on the textual level. The idea of three levels—texture, text, and structure—has become familiar to analysts of folklore texts; and the actual linguistic form, the content, and the structure are accordingly regarded as requiring different analytical methods.

Defining structure always means reduction. The level of abstraction may vary, but structures are never found on the same level on which motif analysis takes place. Deep structure, the most abstract of the three levels, can be disclosed only by the use of intermediate structures. The choice of structural units is of critical importance. As a basic rule, in deep structure there are fewer units than on the level of intermediate structure; the units on these two (or more) levels may be partly or totally different.

Structures may be paradigmatic or syntagmatic. Paradigmatic structures do not follow the chronological order of elements of the text, nor do they comprise the entire text. Units for paradigmatic structures are usually abstracted from among the key events or actions in the narrative. One unit may contain one or more events; in the latter case, events are considered structurally parallel or identical.

The relationship between units is important. Sometimes the units are in opposition (binary opposition is a fairly common structure); sometimes the relationships are more complex. The definition of these relationships is a second key operation in paradigmatic structure analysis. It is here that the meaning or message of the narrative begins to take shape: the comparison of units and the delineation of their relationships may, if we are to believe Lévi-Strauss, disclose a meaning which was probably never understood in its basic form or explicitly formulated by the people who told the narrative or myth in question. Very often the message is a statement of a conflict (between life and death, nature and culture, or between some specified alternatives or elements of world order); sometimes the conflict is mediated (thus "mediator" is a common structural unit). The ambition of the structural analyst is to go beyond the unarticulated structure and find a meaning, a message. According to Lévi-Strauss, the myth of Oedipus states a conflict—without solving it—which in ancient Greek culture centered on the origin of man. By stating a real conflict innumerable times, the myth generates more and more variants of itself—none of which is more authentic or current than any other—finally consuming itself until the intellectual impulse dies and the myth (and the reality of the conflict?) disappears (Lévi-Strauss, 1955).

Syntagmatic structures are chronological and linear. They cover all essential events and elements largely in the sequence in which they appear in the text. One might expect these structures to represent the order of events on the content level more closely than paradigmatic structures do, and this is true, when the content is well developed and the number of units relatively large. But this totally depends on the units chosen. If the structure is defined as "lack—lack liquidated," then (unless we have a very short narrative) the level of abstraction remains high, and there is only a basic polarity, somewhat similar to a paradigmatic structure.

If Lévi-Strauss was the original paradigmatist, then Vladimir Propp was the syntagmatist par excellence. In his study of Russian tales of magic, he came to the conclusion that these tales had one basic and common syntagmatic structure; all existing tales in the genre were variations, mostly incomplete, of that structure. Propp distinguished thirty-one units, which he called *functions,* and listed altogether 150 structural elements in tales of magic. It becomes easier to read Propp if we recognize three levels: the level of *function* (to which all the elements on the upper levels can be reduced); the level of *forms* of functions (also a structural level, but one in which alternative manifestations of a function are preserved); the level of the *text* itself. Two tales may have different plots on the textual level but still be identical on the level of functions. Propp regarded functions and their order as a constant. Functions he based on action; acts like Absence, Interdiction, Violation, Reconnaissance, Fraud, Villainy, and so forth could be carried out by different actants. He also operated with morphological roles, of which he identified seven; their sphere of action covered up to six functions and was not regarded as a structural unit. Furthermore, Propp listed some twenty forms of transformation in tales of magic: according to these, an element could change or vary by reduction, amplification, deformation, inversion, intensification, debilitation, and by various forms of substitution and dissimilation (Propp, 1928, 70–89).

Propp has not escaped criticism. He seems to contradict himself when he maintains that the order of functions is constant, for he makes exceptions to this rule in thirty of his forty-five structural analyses of individual tales. What is worse, in some cases the location of an element in the sequence defines its relationship to function. The question of why there should be just thirty-one functions is also open to debate, as is the relevance of the "hero-pattern" studies (Taylor, 1964, 114–29, Dundes, 1964). More interesting, perhaps, is the criticism presented by Lévi-Strauss, which is by no means negative, but stresses the need to reduce the number of functions by various transformation rules: for example, the Departure and Return of the hero are equal to Disjunction of the hero, positive and negative. After such operations, a paradigmatic structure begins to emerge and the clarification of the meaning of the tales of magic becomes possible (Lévi-Strauss, 1960, 143). Lévi-Strauss thinks that syntagmatic, linear models do not reveal anything about the meanings of narratives. He does not recognize that Propp's "explanation" of structure is intended to be historical, not psychological or phenomenological.

Alan Dundes, the most prominent defender of Propp's method, prefers to replace "function" with the term *motifeme* and speaks of *allomotifs* that fill a motifemic slot on the manifest, content level. His own analysis of North American Indian folktales shows less motifeme depth, that is, fewer structural units, than Propp's, but this has been attributed to differences in the primary material, not in methodology (Dundes, 1964). The same tendency can be found elsewhere in post-Proppian methodology, which in general is occupied with the elaboration of analytic models rather than with the testing of the models on primary materials. A. J. Greimas has systematized Propp's idea of morphological roles and developed a transformational model which condenses Propp's thirty-one functions into four basic units (agreement, test, absence of the hero, and communication) (Greimas, 1966). E. Meletinskij has built the structural scheme of the folktale on two key units, "test" and "values" (Gasparov, 1974, 39–41). This is also a reduction of Propp, in the spirit of Lévi-Strauss. C. Bremond has been less interested in hybridizing syntagmatic and paradigmatic approaches; his models focus on the linear and partly parallel logical processes in the narrative and also take the role of the narrator into consideration (Bremond, 1970, 251–57). Thus he approaches what has been labeled narratology, the study of structural principles of oral and literary narration.

Structural theorists have discussed the possibility of discovering genre-typical structures, and structural cross-genre studies are oriented toward structural identification of different genres. At this point it seems that structural analysis does not contribute to clearer distinctions between genres. As far as plot structures are concerned, the same narrative structures can be found in various narrative genres and in many other genres as well. We probably need more studies which contrast folktale, legend, and other narrative genres before the question of genre-specific structures can be answered.

At present, the future of structural analysis is unclear. There is no denying the fruitfulness of the structural mode of thinking itself, but the usefulness of some of its results is problematic. For the moment, studies are being written on the basis of various mixtures of paradigmatic and syntagmatic models; folktales from a geographical region or of a language community are being analyzed along the lines of Propp and Dundes, and one may find an occasional attempt to combine structural analysis with the folktale classification of a region. Although folklorists may well continue to use structural analysis, the general trend seems to be toward semiotic and cybernetic models; that is, toward more comprehensive studies of human communication. It remains to be seen how much the dull boxes of theoretical information will improve our structural schemes. One possibility is an orientation toward processes of transmission and the problem of meaning. If, as Lévi-Strauss has insisted, structures are the bearers of the essential meaning of narratives, they should be included in the study of semantic processes. One future task may be the integration of narrative structures and narrative codes.

Performance and Production of Tradition

If structural analysis has been nonempirical, text-oriented, and highly abstract, there is another pervasive methodological trend that favors empirical, context-oriented approaches. I refer to the study of performance and affiliated methodologies where the focus of interest has been shifted from folklore texts to the performers of folklore (Ben-Amos and Goldstein, 1975). "Performance" is not to be understood here as artistic performance, although this aspect is by no means excluded. All users of folklore are performers now and then: telling a joke or uttering a proverb constitutes a performance. The key insight here is that there is no natural existence for folklore beyond the performance. Folklore archives are nothing but collections of dead artifacts, arbitrarily limited texts, that were generated under rather special, mostly nonauthentic circumstances and immediately placed outside that system of communication which maintains folklore. These limitations may be overcome by better documentation (sound film, etc.) of authentic folklore performances, but only to a degree. Archived data remain at best momentary reflections of living folklore. The other possible repository of folklore is the human mind and human memory. But this type of folklore storage is also problematic and elusive: research on the brain and memory may never disclose exactly how non-active folklore is preserved. Of the possible research strategies, what remains then is a hard look at the performance situation, where folklore becomes—for a moment—accessible to empirical observation.

We may study both the competence of the performer and his or her particular performances. With the help of repertoire analysis and life-story interview, it is possible to create a picture of the systems of cultural expression that the person commands. It becomes possible to say on which topics and in which genres he or she is likely to be a specialist, an active or a passive bearer. The gaps in knowledge of tradition emerge, and his or her cognitive maps begin to take shape. If comparative material is available concerning other individuals and performers in that culture, the tradition-bearer can be placed in a typology of cultural competence.

The study of actual performances requires not only observation of the performer in action, but also analysis of the social situation in which the performance takes place. There may be social events and backgrounds which "load" the performance with meanings and connotations difficult to detect in the text itself. The audience is of crucial importance and often plays an active role. There may be other significant roles, such as the patient in a healing act, or gods in a sacred ceremony, which influence the performance. In most cases, however, the performer is the conductor of role play and provokes, interprets, and modifies the behavior of the other actors. Nevertheless, it may be necessary to analyze some performances as sociodramas rather than performances by a single individual.

Today it is commonplace to state that problems of meaning cannot be solved without contextual information. The barrenness of a folklore text becomes obvious when one begins to list all the occurrences of a proverb, a joke, a legend. The scale of possible meanings is often very large. Many narrators are able to introduce new dramatic and semantic elements by identifying themselves or individuals in the community or the audience with the personages of the narrative. It is probably most useful to conceive of the performance situation as a mixture of reproduction and creativity. There are models, to be sure, in the mind of the narrator: memories of similar performances, structural and genre-specific rules, mnemotechnic devices, stylistic norms, and alternative ways of developing the story. There are more possibilities than can be used in one performance: in other words, there is choice. Performance is not a question of reproducing a memorized text word for word, even if some very limited examples (such as recitation of a charm) might be exceptions to this. In fact, a narrative is reborn in every performance, especially produced to fit a particular occasion. The choices that the narrator makes are not arbitrary, but are determined by circumstances to the point where the range of alternatives finally narrows down to one.

Among the methodological models important to this approach are some derived from sociolinguistics. Probably the most influential is Dell Hymes' study of speech acts (Hymes, 1962, 13–53), which Alan Dundes and others have applied to folklore studies. The psychology of perception and role theory may lead to a multidisciplinary strategy of performance analysis (Honko, 1969, 26–52; Siikala, 1978, 31–77, 319–41). Added emphasis on highly detailed fieldwork and empirical genre research is a corollary of this trend, as may be observed in most articles included in the volume *Folklore, Performance and Communication* (1975). When Linda Dégh concludes, on the basis of her tape recordings, that the auditors do not believe in legends but react to them in a number of ways which vary as the narration proceeds, she does not merely question our convention about legend genres but draws attention to the need to pursue analysis of reactive types (Dégh and Vazsonyi, 1971, 93–123; Ben-Amos and Goldstein, 1975, 207–52). To be able to deal with variation in folklore, we have to look at the processes of the production and adaptation of learned tradition to new narrators and auditors in particular situations. It may well be that the dialectic of productive types and reactive types will be one of the key elements in the analysis of narrative processes in the future.

Toward an Ecology of Oral Tradition

Modern folklore theory has for some time been extratextual. We are now at the point where contextual information is no longer regarded as mere illumination of a text and where text, context, and environment are deeply involved in the process of telling a story or producing a social drama. The roots of this movement may be seen in the Malinowskian functionalism of the twenties. Although there has been a decline of interest in functionalism in the social sciences in the past fifteen years, this trend has not been followed in folkloristics. On the contrary, folkloristic fieldwork methodology made considerable progress during the sixties, resulting in intensified interview and observation procedures in which the gathering of contextual information became the rule.

The scholar working solely on archived data became almost an object of ridicule, doomed to mere guesswork because of deficient contextual information about the data. Today archives are changing in this respect: where we used to have an abundance of folktales, ballads, proverbs, and texts in other genres with no information about the context, we are now getting vast amounts of ethnohistorical memoirs, life histories, and contextual interviews, but relatively little about traditional genres.

Fieldworkers have at least two advantages over archive scholars. First, they are not limited to fragmentary data collected by others. Instead, they can direct the quality and amount of material in a problem-oriented manner. Second, personal contact with informants and participation in the life of the community gives them an invaluable feel for the reality studied and certainly prevents many odd misunderstandings. To be sure, there are also problems in the field, such as how to restrict contextual information to "relevant context": to include information that is necessary from the point of view of the problem, and to exclude that which is extraneous.

With the shift of focus from text to tradition communities there is no doubt that empirical contact with informant and audience has become a sine qua non of folklore methodology. Normally this contact is established through fieldwork carried out by the scholar. On another occasion I have sketched the importance of interactionism on three levels: on the personal level, where ideas and emotions are exchanged and the scholar and informant share intimate details of their lives; on the instrumental level, where scholar and informant create a marginal field of interaction between their cultures and communicate their goals and knowledge; on the obligationary level, where the scholar attempts to strike a balance between moral and practical obligations to those who initiated or funded the research on one hand and to individuals and tradition community on the other (Honko, 1977, 88–89). The marginality of the folklorist should be understood by every person training to become a folklore scholar. Gradual elimination of the marked asymmetry between scholar and object of research is a long-term goal and should lead to new initiatives and increasing participation by the community in research activities.

This ideology may be new to folklorists used to climbing their ivory towers of text-comparison and diffusionistic perspectives. But it is the logical outcome of the latest development in the anthropological sciences, responding to a world where passive and introverted cultures are becoming self-conscious nations. It also implies the possibility of studying storytelling in the contexts and environments in which the narratives make sense, or from which they derive their sense. In addition to informant and tradition, the elements of community, context, and environment have become key factors of field methodology in the analysis of tradition ecology.

But what then is contextual information? In the technical sense it includes basic data about the situation in which the "text" was collected, about the informant's life, social background, and tradition teachers, the origin of particular collected items, and about the informant's reconstructions of earlier performances and comments on the meaning of the item. It also includes observations by the scholar on authentic performances and, if possible, a full description (notes, tape) and visual documentation (photo, film) of the behavior of performers and audience. Furthermore, contextual information should contain basic information about the community, its socioeconomic structure, physical setting, local history (formation of settlement, migrations), cultural geography (contacts with other groups, mobility), and the system of education (home, school, church and other institutions). Preliminary analyses and formation of hypotheses in the field are important aids to the scholar trying to define the limits of contextual information.

Richard Bauman has recently recommended a checklist of no fewer than six contexts to be remembered by the fieldworker seeking "to comprehend folklore in terms of the web of contextual interrelationships that define its essence": (1) context of meaning (What is the overall interpretation of the item by members of the community?); (2) institutional context (Where does it fit within the culture?); (3) context of cultural domain (How does it relate to other kinds of folklore?); (4) social base (What kind of people does it belong to?); (5) individual context (How does it fit into the informant's life?); and (6) context of situation (How is it useful in social situations?) (cf. Bauman, 1983). The list is useful, although the six contexts partly overlap. For example the actual meaning of a folklore item may be dependent upon the situational context and cannot be derived from the average interpretation or context of meaning.

The concept of environment is central to what I have called "tradition ecology." One may speak of perceived, effective, and total environment. The boundary between the first two is perception: a person is aware of and consciously exploits the perceived milieu, but his or her acts affect—and he or she is influenced by—the environment, perhaps unconsciously. Total milieu is an umbrella concept: it covers both perceived and effective environments plus those factors which are neither perceived nor influential. One may also speak of "habitat" (the physical milieu), "niche" (a sector of activity), and "microenvironment" (a particular behavioral situation). The last is in fact identical with the context of situation in the list above.

When we think of living folklore in a particular environment, we usually find it organized according to social roles, depending upon socioeconomic structures and natural environment. To have access to and a permanent locus in the environment, a folk narrative, for example, must adapt itself to cultural, social, economic, and physical factors. I have suggested four forms of adaptation (Honko, 1979b, 57–76). (1) In milieu-morphological or "exterior" adaptation, a narrative undergoes familiarization and localization: that is, the foreign natural setting is translated into the system of well-known features of the psychical milieu of the tradition community in question, and the story is linked to a familiar locality. Among the processes of (2) tradition-morphological or "interior" adaptation, there is the linking of role-figures of the narrative to well-known personages (tradition dominants), censorship (wherein elements which would lead to norm conflict are rejected or replaced), the adaptation of the narrative to a genre in a local or personal genre-system and to the genre-specific codes of communication. Most adaptations imply change. Changes resulting from the preceding forms of adaptation are lasting and take place only once. These changes are called "great variations." But is the actual meaning of the narrative already defined by milieu- and tradition-morphological adaptations? Obviously not. What is still required is (3) the functional or "momentary/situational" adaptation. The personality of the narrator, the composition of the audience, the focus of interest of the community, events of the recent past and fears and hopes for the future, will normally bring about changes which lend the story a meaning *hic et nunc*. It should be remembered that the story itself may have been heard many times already in different microenvironments. Nevertheless, it can convey new messages and meanings, thanks to functional adaptation. The changes brought about by adaptation do not last very long, however, and may disappear in the next narration of the story. They are therefore called "little variations."

It is obvious that theories of tradition production and adaptation meet in the analysis of function and performance situation. It is also obvious that various adaptations may take place simultaneously within one performance. But will the piecemeal analysis sketched out above lead us to some kind of synthesis? How could numerous observations on folklore adaptation and production be organized to reveal some basic characteristics and the uniqueness of a tradition community? To achieve this we must turn to the ecotype and processes of (4) ecotypification (Honko, 1979b, 71–75). The folkloristic contribution to the discussion of ecotypes probably culminated in Roger D. Abrahams's study on black ghetto traditions in Camingerly, Philadelphia. The value of his argument is the definition of ecotypification as something completely transcending genre boundaries, and including a motley collection of content elements, contextual factors, stylistic and structural features, together with a possibility of connecting the tradition with its specific social base (Abrahams, 1970, 173–81; Sarmela, 1969 and 1974). Ethnologists and anthropologists have used the term ecotype somewhat differently (Steward, 1973; Wolf, 1966; Stoklund, 1976; Löfgren, 1976), but always in relation to economic structure and natural environment. The question is whether these approaches are relevant to each other. Can one in practice combine folkloristic material (say, folk narratives) and economic behavior in the analysis of milieu adaptation and milieu exploitation? Leaving the detailed argumentation to another occasion, I submit that the answer is yes.

In short, I believe that in defining folklore ecotypes we should let cultural, social, and economic systems blend as they do in real life. Data on means of subsistence, social roles, and oral narratives should merge as we attempt to grasp the reality of the tradition community. Whatever elements we may choose to include in an ecotype, they should (1) permeate several areas, (2) be frequent and representative, (3) be able to reproduce themselves, (4) show advanced milieu adaptation, (5) resist alien divergent elements, and (6) manifest a distinctive character.

Folklore motifs are seldom unique. Nevertheless, we may sense the uniqueness of the tradition climate in a region or a social group: motifs known from elsewhere are organized in a special way and fit neatly into the lifestyle and environment of the people. The task of microstudies and regional studies in folklore is to clarify how that uniqueness comes about, and into what context the folklore has been fitted. The task may also have a practical value in our time, when the revitalization of local cultures has become a human need and a political fact.

Postscript

The preceding description of six or seven main approaches to the study of folk narratives should create a fairly full picture of the status and trends of methodology. Nevertheless, additional remarks may be needed to clarify the importance of some dimensions of methodology that were not dealt with separately, partly because these dimensions are less specific to folk narrative research than those presented above.

The first point needing comment concerns quantitative methods. Since the 1960s, quantification, sampling, and statistical presentation of findings have played a significant role in folklore research. One important aspect of this trend is modern cartography. Though qualitative methodology has once again been gaining ground in anthropological studies, and the "hard data" which quantification produces are not currently pursued, these trends should not keep us from seeing the importance of quantification to folklore methodology. It has put a stop to the purely arbitrary choice of "examples" and has drawn attention to the analysis of frequency, distribution, and density of folklore products. One aspect of tradition ecology depends strictly upon quantification: the study of "tradition in use" as something different from the "stored tradition." The differentiation between collective, individual, and idiosyncratic elements in various bodies of tradition (as in repertoires) is actually a purely folkloristic contribution to the methodology of quantification. Furthermore, there is no danger of overquantification of folklore research: the case that could be made against hard data sociology is not valid here.

A second concern is the indexing and cataloging of folklore. This part of methodology is closely linked to archiving techniques and is likely to preserve its strategic importance for research regardless of the fate of comparative studies. Originally, the need to provide scholars with all the available variants of a folktale for comparative geographical-historical study called for extensive preparation of type-catalogs, a trend which continues even though the monograph is not as popular as it used to be. Ever since, methods of cataloging and indexing have been based on genres, types, and motifs; now a change is underway in this area. Genre-based indexing is growing increasingly ineffective in the face of the flood of everyday stories and memoirs that fill the archives. At the Nordic Institute of Folklore a group is preparing recommendations for indexation; the topic was discussed at the second and third Nordic Conferences on Folklore Archiving and Documentation (1978, 1982), and possibilities are being examined for the establishment of central archives with coordination of data search and retrieval.

A final matter needing comment is the use and revitalization of folklore. Here we find a vivid spectrum of spontaneous, more or less commercial folklore movements, which may well have prolonged the life of folkloristics by decades. They have been studied very little and should be given more attention in the future. The use of folklore in mass media, in advertising, in comics, and so on is another important aspect of modern life which imposes increasing demands on folklorists. It is a multidisciplinary field, and very little has been done so far to create an adequate material base for it. What we need are archives concentrating on popular culture. The heroes of folk narratives are very relevant to the study of popular lore and mass lore.

The use of folklore in nation-building has played a conspicuous role in many European countries, and a recent NIF symposium was devoted to the subject, with the focus on the Nordic countries (NIF Newsletter, June 1979). The role of folklore identity as an index of identity (national, regional, sub-cultural, and so forth) and as an element in the dialectic of nationalism and conservatism versus internationalism and liberalism is an interesting issue both in European ethnology and in development studies of the Third World. Much of the methodology will be applicable to the study of present-day tradition communities and culture areas.

THE LANGUAGE OF FAIRY TALES

Bengt Holbek

1

The term fairy tale will be used in the following to denote a category of tale in which a hero or heroine is subjected to a series of trials and tribulations characterized by the occurrence of "marvelous" beings, phenomena, and events, finally to marry the princess or prince in splendor and glory. Tales of this kind have existed in oral tradition in Europe and most adjacent areas, and they are occasionally reflected or referred to in literary monuments from antiquity and the Middle Ages, after which time they become more frequent. They have been recorded in vast numbers during the nineteenth and twentieth centuries. The present study is based primarily on fairy tales recorded in Denmark in the last third of the nineteenth century, but it is contended that the conclusions reached are largely valid for European fairy tale tradition in general.

The "marvelous" elements characteristic of this genre cannot be theoretically defined at the present stage, but an enumeration of instances will serve to indicate their nature. They include such beings as ogres, giants, witches, dragons, speaking animals, powerful but strange helpers in the guise of old men and women, fairies (for whom the genre is named), dwarfs, spirits, saints, angels, and devils, the latter figures being almost devoid of specifically Christian characteristics; such phenomena as seven-league boots, invisibility cloaks, magic tablecloths, flutes and violins with spell-binding powers, invincible swords, glass mountains, forests of copper, silver, and gold, castles in the air, ships that will sail over land and water, inexhaustible purses, healing and resuscitating salves; and such events as incredible feats of running, jumping, eating, fighting, traveling vast distances in moments, being transformed into an animal or stone and back again, being killed and magically resuscitated or put under a spell and released, receiving magical help in the nick of time.

Adapted by the author from his *Interpretation of Fairy Tales*, FFC 239 [Helsinki 1987], pp. 404–48.

The purpose of the present exposition is to expound a method of interpreting such "marvelous" narrative elements. There is considerable literature on the topic, but it will be passed over here; the reader is referred to my book-length study of the subject (Holbek, 1987).

Fairy tales were a regular part of the traditional peasant cultures of Europe and adjacent areas. A limited number of fairy tales have been documented in European and Oriental literatures from the eighteenth and earlier centuries, but the question whether the literary tales derive from folklore or vice versa has never been settled. In the following, the tales recorded from oral tradition will be regarded as primary sources, whereas literary collections of tales—those of Perrault, the Grimms, and the Arabian Nights, for example—will be disregarded. This is not an arbitrary decision. It is based on the view that literary collections of fairy tales may be explained without difficulty as recordings from folklore embellished and adapted by individual writers, whereas it is exceedingly difficult to explain the rich variability, broad distribution, and close links to other folklore of the oral fairy tales under the assumption of ultimate dependence on literary sources.

The number of fairy tales recorded from oral tradition is vast, but far from all records are good. (In former times, when these tales flourished, recording techniques were poor, and many questions that modern collectors would regard as indispensable were not asked. The interpreter of fairy tales has to disregard much source material because of the poor quality of the recording itself or the insufficiency of contextual data, or both.) The following summary of observations on fairy tales in oral tradition is therefore based exclusively on material recorded by highly skilled collectors who have provided contextual data sufficient for an analysis of the social setting of this traditional art form. I have relied principally on the work of Evald Tang Kristensen (1843–1929), who recorded folktales from nearly all parts of Jutland from 1868 to 1908. His collection is one of the largest ever assembled by a single collector, sufficient for observation of salient characteristics, and of fairly good quality despite the fact that modern recording techniques were not available in his time. The following trends were found:

1. The number of people who specialized in the telling of fairy tales was—and probably always had been—strictly limited. They were not "folk" tales in the sense of "tales told by everyone"; on the contrary, they were told only by skilled specialists.

2. Nearly all those who told and listened to fairy tales belonged to the lower strata of traditional communities. Members of higher strata might occasionally listen to them, but usually regarded them with condescension or even contempt.

3. Fairy tales were told by and for adults. Children might listen, but they were not the primary audience. There were special tales for children: animal tales, chain tales, jingles, a subgroup of the genre under scrutiny which may be called "children's fairy tales" (see below); but the adaptations of full-scale fairy tales

for children's reading is a characteristic of the modern world that should not be projected onto the traditional communities in which the tales were originally recorded.

4. Male and female repertoires differed. There was a strong tendency for men to prefer masculine tales (tales with a male protagonist), whereas women's repertoires were more evenly distributed between masculine and feminine fairy tales. This may be associated with the fact that men would often tell fairy tales away from home, for all-male audiences (at work, in the army, on hunting and fishing expeditions), whereas women would normally perform only in domestic circles.

5. Fairy tales were regarded as "lies" (that is, as fiction). This was signaled by opening and closing formulas emphasizing their distance in space and time and was confirmed by metafolkloristic utterances by the storytellers themselves. There is no doubt that they distinguished them clearly from other narrative genres, as may be seen from the fact that different storytellers often specialized in different genres or subgenres. The view of fairy tales as "lies" did not prevent storytellers from emphasizing their complete truthfulness.

6. There were many indications that storytellers identified themselves with the protagonists of the tales (the "I" of the storyteller) and that the listeners did much the same thing. There was agreement between the sex of the storyteller and the "gender" of the tale in many cases; most of the protagonists began their careers in circumstances exactly like those of the storytellers and their audiences; when the traditional communities began changing radically, fairy tales began disappearing, undoubtedly because they no longer offered adequate patterns for projection. In other words, in traditional communities, fairy tales provided a means of collective daydreaming. The word "daydreaming" is not to be taken in a pejorative sense. The tales were escape fantasies inasmuch as they offered temporary relief from the intrusive awareness of poverty and oppression that was the storyteller's usual lot, but at the same time, they depicted a world in which wrongs were righted and the poor and powerless were justly recognized for their true worth. They thus kept alive a keen sense of justice and rightness; they depicted a true world, that is, a world in which the audience's norms were validated.

Most of these observations may be confirmed by studies of the fairy-tale tradition in other parts of Europe. There is one exception: in some areas, the position of male storytellers was considerably less prominent than in rural, preindustrial Jutland. The reason may be that public storytelling as an exclusively male art form disappeared from some areas before it could be documented, whereas domestic storytelling, which was carried on by both sexes, continued to exist well into the present century; but there may have been regional differences as well. Regrettably, such questions attracted few collectors' attention at a time when European folklore was still teeming with fairy tales.

In the following discussion, I propose to show that fairy tales may be read as expressions of the thoughts, feelings, and norms of traditional storytellers and their audiences; more specifically, that the "marvelous" elements referred to above may be read as expressions of emotional impressions associated with experiences in their own lives. If a link can be shown to exist between these narrative elements and the facts of the storytellers' own lives, there is no need to assume that fairy tales retain traces of ancient beliefs or that they have "sunk down" from literary sources, from higher social strata, or from higher cultures. Instead, they may be perceived as an integral part of the rural population's own traditional culture, a perpective which will open the way for interpreting fairy tales as expressions of that culture.

My contention is that the telling of fairy tales is a traditional art form comparable to the singing of epic songs, the playing of musical instruments, or the exercising of traditional crafts like those of joiners, shoemakers, and locksmiths. This view of storytelling as a traditional craft is founded on Bogatyrev and Jacobson's view of folklore (oral verbal art) as a special kind of language (1929). Such a definition of storytelling implies that it is based upon traditional techniques that can be acquired by training, and that the relation between these techniques and individual tales is analogous to that between Saussure's concepts of *langue* and *parole*, or, perhaps better, Noam Chomsky's concepts of *competence* and *performance*. It should be stressed that these concepts are analogies. A folktale—specifically, a fairy tale—is neither a piece of music, nor an object shaped by a craftsman, nor a speech act in the general sense, but the analogy is justified if fairy tales can be described as products of an analogous technique.

The structure of fairy tales has been the subject of investigation and debate ever since Propp's (1928) *Morphology* appeared in English in 1958. Among the numerous ideas in that line of research, two in particular stand out: (1) Propp's own model of the narrative sequence, which may be likened to a syntax and has since been modified by Meletinskij (1969), and (2) Köngäs Maranda's model of tale roles, which may be likened to a morphological paradigm (1971). These models were developed independently, but it is possible to combine them. The combination provides a structure which may be regarded as the "grammar" for the telling of fairy tales.

Symbols are "polyvalent," that is, they evoke all sorts of associations in the listener's mind. If the "marvelous" narrative elements referred to earlier are regarded as symbolic expressions, they must be perceived as carrying many meanings or aspects of meanings. They will appear in a different light to different interpreters, unless it can be shown that their meaning is, to some extent, "kept in place" by a common framework. And this is where the syntagmatic and paradigmatic models mentioned above come into the picture. They provide a framework which permits only a certain range of interpretations in each case. The study of a number of fairy tales by this method reveals that symbols are formed in a regular way according to rules which can be formulated. Therefore, the following exposition has three ingredients: (1) a description of the syntagmatic pattern, (2) a description of the paradigmatic pattern,

(3) an account of the rules for the formation of symbolic expressions within these patterns.

2

The basic unit of Propp's syntagmatic model, the function, is defined as "an act of a tale role, defined from the point of view of its significance for the course of the action." Different acts are expressions of the same function if their significance for the course of the action is the same; likewise, different characters perform the same function if they embody the same tale role. The functions follow one another in a specific order, rather like the various syntactic units of a sentence. Propp thinks that the order of concatenation is governed by a logical principle: one cannot rob the house before breaking and entering, and the theft has to be committed before the perpetrator can be hunted, apprehended, brought to trial, sentenced, and put in jail. A similar sequential logic may be applied in the analysis of fairy tales. Moreover, it may be applied not only at the level of individual functions, but also at the level of larger syntactic segments, moves, as defined by Meletinskij as well as at the level of the tale as a whole. It is actually preferable to start at the level mentioned last because the units of lower orders are easier to comprehend when seen as parts of the whole.

The total movement of the fairy tale pattern may be seen by a comparison of the initial situation with the final one. The former was designated by Propp and the latter will be designated here.

In the initial situation, the hero(ine) is dependent, often abused or ridiculed, poor, unrecognized, deprived of friendship and love; in the final situation, the hero(ine) is independent of parental authority, fully recognized, rich and powerful, and has found a spouse. The wedding is the crowning achievement of efforts at three levels: that of gaining independence from parents and other authorities of the preceding generation; that of winning the love of a person of the opposite sex; and that of securing the future of the new family. These efforts are, then, dominated by three sets of thematic oppositions: (1) that of the conflict between generations, (2) that of the meeting of the sexes, and (3) that of the social opposition between the "haves" and the "have-nots." This explains the central position of the wedding that concludes fairy tales in nine cases out of ten.

The pattern of the fairy tale explains how these changes come about, as may be shown by analyzing the tale twice. First backwards, from Ω to A, in order to expose the underlying narrative logic and thematic organization; this exposition will be based on the masculine version of the pattern because that version is the foundation of Propp's model. After that, the model will be worked through from A to Ω with a view to placing the "marvelous" elements in their context; they will then explain each other to a considerable extent. In between, the paradigmatic system of tale roles will be explained.

The wedding is our point of departure in the first leg of the analysis. What is so special about it?

It is a misalliance: against all probability, the poor stableboy or shepherd in filthy rags marries the princess, or Cinderella marries the prince. There may have been other obstacles: the prince or princess may have been under some sort of spell, abducted, or transformed into an animal, but such obstacles are usually of secondary importance at this point in the tale. The hero is sometimes "really" a prince in disguise, but he is in disguise and no one knows of his noble descent or of his riches or marvelous prowess at the time when he confronts the false hero, the princess, and her father. The transfiguration (Propp's function No. 29, henceforth referred to by the abbreviation Pf + no.) takes place after the confrontation, when he has already proven himself. He is recognized by his qualities, not by his appearance.

The final part of the tale which leads to the wedding begins when the hero arrives in humble disguise (Pf 23). It will be designated as move V (Pf 23–31). It may contain a test of the hero (Pf 25–26), but it need not be a task disclosing his true power, prowess, or riches. Usually the main point is to get the hero into the castle so that a confrontation—a showdown with the false hero—may be staged. The hero is frequently rather passive in this move, whereas the princess may have an active role: she gets the hero into the castle and sets the stage: she refuses to marry the false hero, she poses a task which can be solved only by the true hero, or she helps him solve a task posed by her father.

Comparing the initial positions of hero and spouse in this move with their final positions will show that both of them succeed in effecting a movement. He arrives in humble disguise and is elevated to power and glory. She is under her parents' dominance at the beginning, they are on the verge of marrying her off to a suitor who is to their liking, but she rebels against their wish as soon as she learns of the hero's arrival and ends up having her own way. The movement is defined in his case by the thematic opposition between low and high, in her case by that between young and adult.

Why does the princess choose the hero instead of the false hero who has her parents' approval and who appears to be a better match than the dirty stableboy, tramp, or gardener she prefers? The answer to this is found in the preceding part of the tale pattern, move III (Pf 15–22; for the time being, move IV—which may be inserted between Pf 22 and 23 but is not indispensable—may be disregarded). In that move, the princess is liberated from the ogre's cave, fetched down from the glass mountain, awakened from her deathlike trance in a coffin in the church, or delivered from the dragon to whom she was to be given.

A comparison of the initial and final solutions of this move will show that at the beginning of the move the hero and the princess do not know each other; at the end, they have fallen in love. The dominant theme of the move is therefore that of the meeting of the sexes.

This contradicts the customary interpretation, which emphasizes the exploits of the hero. He has to overcome an obstacle: a vigilant troll, a terrible dragon, an enchantment, an unimaginable distance, a hedge of briars, cruel tests of his wit, skill, prowess, and endurance. The princess is regarded as a mere object, a prize to be won. This interpretation cannot, however, explain the logical connection between moves III and V (which is undoubtedly why some have thought of the latter as an "additional test" of no structural significance). The fact is that the love relation established in move III explains why the princess chooses the true hero instead of the false one in move V. There is a logical, irreversible organization of moves in the fairy tale pattern.

The next question is this: How could the hero win or "liberate" the princess when no one else could? There is a throng of knights at the foot of the glass mountain; countless young men have perished in the briars surrounding Sleeping Beauty; the king has beheaded all the suitors who could not answer his daughter's questions.

The answer is to be found in the preceding part of the pattern, move II (Pf 9–14), which contains the "preliminary" test. Upon leaving home, the hero is challenged in some way. He must help an old woman carry her firewood home, give an old man something to eat, give his last three pennies to wicked men who are maltreating the body of a dead man who could not pay his debts, divide booty equally between fighting animals, serve an ogre for three years, or defend the sheep he has been sent out to look after. The assistance he receives in return—be it a "magic" property of his body, a "magic" implement or weapon, "magic" advice, or a "magic" helper—is the reward for having proven his worth in this test. The rules of the game, of which he must prove his mastery, summarize the behavior expected from a mature, responsible member of the community. There is evidently some sort of connection between the gift and the test. The test reveals an inner quality and the gift is the outward sign of its presence or, to put it another way, the qualities he proves himself to possess are literally changed into the "magic" which enables him to win the love of the princess. There is thus a logical, irreversible connection between moves II and III as well.

In the initial situation of move II, the hero is a good-for-nothing, a lazybones, a rebel, or an object of abuse and ridicule; he is under the care (and the power) of his parents or a tyrannical master. At the end, he is independent and powerful. It is difficult to see this as anything but an initiation test dominated by the opposition between young and adult. And in fact, the testers, who are usually also the donors, very often ostensibly represent the older generation. In some cases, the hero explicitly receives his gifts from his parents, from a dying father, for example (correspondingly, a heroine may receive her gifts from her dead mother from beyond the grave).

One question is left: how did the princess get into her desperate plight? Far from all tales offer any explanation. In some tales it is merely said that a dragon demands her or that a monster has abducted her, but some tales give the reason, which constitutes move I of the narrative pattern (Pf 1–8). The princess is subjected to—and fails—a test: to obey an injunction or interdiction, not to speak to strangers, not to reveal secrets, not to leave home, and so forth. In many cases, the fatal act is transferred to a member of the preceding generation, but the consequences are nevertheless visited upon the princess: she is struck dumb or cannot laugh, or falls into a deathlike sleep, or she is put under a spell or abducted, or a dragon demands her. In other words, the situation is created which is presupposed in move III.

It should be noted that there is no direct relation between moves I and II. Both are prerequisites for move III, but independently, and their order of presentation may in fact be reversed.

A comparison of the initial and final solutions of move I shows that the thematic opposition dominating this move is the same as in move II. The characters who expose the young people to tests represent the world of adults and its searching question: Is this young person mature, ready to assume the status and responsibilities of an adult? The test may have a negative and a positive outcome; and it is worth noting at this point that the negative outcome is found at the high level of the princess, whereas the positive outcome is found at the low level of the hero. There is thus an opposition between moves I and II, one dominated by the opposition between high and low.

A study of the larger segments and of the pattern as a whole thus discloses a logical and thematic organization that cannot be reached by an analysis of individual functions, much less even smaller elements.

The oppositions young vs. adult, male vs. female, and high vs. low have already been referred to several times. They were first defined by Köngäs Maranda, who used them to construct a model of tale roles in the form of a cube (Figure 1); while Maranda opposes "young" to "old," "adult" seems preferable to "old" (Köngäs Maranda and Maranda, 1971, 23).

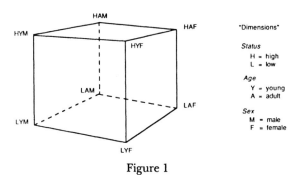

Figure 1

It should be noted that this model differs from the syntagmatic models devised by Propp and some of his successors in which the tale roles are defined on the basis of mutual relations (opponent, helper, etc.). In the paradigmatic model devised by Köngäs Maranda, which may be described as a three-dimensional conceptual matrix affording the thematic framework for three categories of conflict or opposition, the relations of or interaction between the two tale roles will be referred to as a theme.

All of the tale roles defined by this model may be found in fairy tales and all principal characters in fairy tales may be shown to occupy these roles. Each of the characters may be doubled, trebled, or split into a "good" and "bad" or a "strong" and "weak" or an "active" and "passive" aspect, each aspect then appearing as an independent figure. A character may fill one role to begin with and later assume another—actually, the unit called "move" above may often be described as the attempt of a character to leave one role and assume another— and a character may be dispossessed of any tale role; that character then dies or is of no further importance. There may, finally, be fierce competition between different characters aspiring to the same role; sibling rivalry and contest between a true hero(ine) and a false one are examples.

The distinction between masculine and feminine introduced above may be explained in terms of this model: in a masculine tale, the two main characters are the low-born young male (LYM) and the high-born young female (HYF). Conversely, the two main characters of the feminine tale pattern are the low-born young female (LYF) and the high-born young male (HYM).

The parents at L level (LAM and LAF) fill the tale role of the donor, as defined by Propp. If hero and donor are of opposite sexes (LYM + LAF or LYF + LAM), the relation between them is as a rule friendly; it may have sexual overtones. If they are of the same sex (LYM + LAM or LYF + LAF), their relation is often hostile; the donors are then frequently represented as witches, trolls, ogres, and such like, and there may be a fight. Sometimes the character filling the LAM role in masculine tales seems to be a master rather than a father, the man whom the hero serves as an apprentice or as a farmhand; in such cases, the LAM and HAM roles may merge. In some feminine tales where the heroine has to ward off the incestuous advances of her father, he fills the donor's role.

The parents at H level are the guardians and masters of their children and therefore, by implication, hostile toward the low-born intruders. Here, too, illicit sexual relations sometimes occur. The roles of HAM and HAF are frequently filled by hideous, frightening beings, but when they are overcome, the parents in their own guise appear as less frightening but still formidable opponents.

The six tale roles mentioned up to now form the stable nucleus of fairy-tale tradition as it is known in Northern Europe; most of these roles are filled in nearly all tales from this area. In addition to the young couple and their parents (in various guises), there may be more characters filling the last two tale roles.

In masculine tales, the roles LYM and HYF are always filled, but the LYF role does not seem ever to be filled, at least not in Danish tradition. Heroes may have brothers, but not sisters. The HYM role, on the other hand, is regularly filled by a negative character: a courtier (the Red Knight), one or several treacherous companions, the hero's older brothers, and so forth. The competition between the true hero and the pretenders may then be a leitmotif throughout the tale.

In feminine tales, the LYM role is filled by brothers in several tale types. The relation between sister and brother is characterized by love and helpfulness, even if fear and rivalry may also be an aspect in some tales (for example, in several versions of AT 451). The brothers may function as helpers in the same way as the male hero's helpers. The tale role LYF is frequently filled by the heroine's stepsister, who sometimes reappears at H level as the false bride (HYF). She is the counterpart of the older brothers or the Red Knight in masculine tales.

The three thematic oppositions define the three categories of crises and conflicts that occur in fairy tales:

1. Those of the young in their parental home: incestuous attraction, the rebellion of the young against the tyranny and abuse of their parents, the desire of the young to obtain independence; or, conversely, their being sent away from home prematurely. Sibling rivalry does not appear as a crisis, but as a state: the older brothers maltreat and ridicule the hero, the stepsister abuses the heroine. It is only when the hero(ine) attempts to break free of his/her subordinate role that sibling rivalry comes to a head.

2. Those associated with the meeting of the sexes: learning to appreciate and love a person of the opposite sex; winning that other person's love; his/her liberation from attachment to the parent of the opposite sex.

3. Those associated with establishing a secure basis for the married life of the new couple, which implies the recognition of the low-born partner by the high-born partner's family and the older generation's relinquishing its hold on the "kingdom" to the younger generation.

All of these problems are real or possible events in the communities in which fairy tales are told. At the same time, all of them are sensitive, even painful, subjects that cannot easily be brought into the open. The potential conflicts with actual relatives and in-laws are only too obvious. The tales solve the problem of dealing with these matters by treating them as if they were events in a purely fictitious world and by disguising the participants, whereas the nature of the conflicts is hardly disguised at all.

The sequential order of these crises corresponds to what Danish storytellers knew from their own culture: a young man could not court a girl unless he was well on his way to independence, and he could not marry until he had won her acceptance, her parents' consent, and some sort of "kingdom," be it ever so small. This order is clearly reflected in the fairy-tale pattern described above. Feminine tales may follow the same pattern, but a common alternative is one in which the heroine's real fight begins only after the wedding.

This exposition has left no room for witches or dragons, and the reason has already been implied at several places: they represent aspects of real persons, aspects produced by the narrative technique known as the split (see below). If, for instance, the HAM role is filled by the father and the dragon, the two figures may be regarded as different embodiments of the same character—with and without mask, so to speak.

It is now possible to trace the narrative pattern once more, this time from alpha to omega.

Fairy tales have two main characters, the young couple who are joined in marriage. In the masculine "gender" of fairy tales, the protagonist is the hero, and the role of his future spouse is secondary (although still important). In the feminine "gender," these roles are reversed. The fact that there are two main characters means that, theoretically speaking, there should be two points of departure. Usually, however, only the fate of the protagonist is followed from beginning to end—thus, the prince in Cinderella has no history before the girl meets him in church or at the ball. The economy of storytelling insists on following a single strand as far as possible (Olrik, 1909). There is, however, a limit to these reductions: if the princess is to be given to a dragon, or the prince is transformed into a serpent, this fact—the Villainy (Pf 8)—must be mentioned, even if it does not need to be elaborated. The history of the Villainy may be given as a flashback (the hero comes to a city clad in black and is told that the princess is to be given to a dragon).

Köngäs Maranda's graphic model may be used to illustrate this. In move I, the conflict is between the prince (HYM) or princess (HYF) and his/her parents (HAM/HAF). In move II, the conflict is likewise on the Y-A axis, but at L level; the two conflicts are not related—there is no coincidence of tale roles.

In move I, the young person unsuccessfully attempts a rebellion. The lack of success is expressed as immobility: being under a spell, being unable to speak or laugh, being transformed into a stone, condemned to sleep, imprisoned or abducted and placed in a subterranean cave. There are two reasons for this. On the one hand, the parents' authority is strong: they do not permit their daughter to "come into the open air," to speak to strangers, or whatever the prohibition may be. On the other hand, the young people themselves are immature, they act irresponsibly and often bring their misfortune upon themselves. As a result of the conflict, they remain in their respective HYM and HYF roles, but are estranged from their family. This kind of situation is common enough in the real world; it only appears to be strange because of the "language" of fairy tales.

In move II, there may be a similar confrontation between the generations, but the outcome is different. The young hero(ine) is put to a test, which he or she passes with flying colors. There is an intriguing difference between masculine and feminine tales with respect to this move: many heroines do not have to pass a test, whereas few heroes avoid it. If a heroine is tested, her reward will, as a rule, be good advice; in some cases, she receives golden apples, a golden spindle and distaff or the like, or fine dresses. The hero's gifts may be properties (ability to change shape, great strength), objects (weapons, musical instruments), or helpers in human or animal shape.

The donor test of move II is worth analyzing with an eye to the nature of the response. The protagonist must show kindness, gratitude, helpfulness, generosity, courage, faithfulness in service, truthfulness, willingness to follow good advice and to care for the dead, the infirm, and animals. On the other hand, protagonists also take what is their due, they break prohibitions which deny their basic needs, and they know how to trick or fight evil opponents. A detailed analysis of behavior rewarded in fairy tales will be a good indication of the norms accepted by the communities in which they are told.

There is a close connection between tests and gifts, akin to the connection between test and punishment ("villainy") in move I. The test proves the protagonist a worthy adult member of the community, but it concerns inner qualities. The gifts may be seen as (in many cases visible) expressions of these qualities. A hero who has proven himself is permitted freedom of movement (seven league boots, as opposed to an immobilizing spell or imprisonment). It is not surprising, seen in this light, that the gifts acquired by young men—such as swords, clubs, guns, and flutes—often have sexual connotations. Something similar may be said of the numerous animal helpers: bears, lions, horses, or foxes, for example, as well as the hero's ability to transform himself into such animals. They may be regarded as symbolic expressions of the body, of the hero's control of his own body. It is significant that the wooing of the princess follows upon the acquisition of these gifts. It has been suggested (see Jockel, 1939) that the gold received by the successful heroine similarly indicates sexual maturity and fertility, and the same is surely true of the beautiful clothes.

The contrast between the rigidity of the Y-A opposition at H level and its flexibility at L level should be seen in conjunction with the fact that the storytellers themselves as well as their listeners would normally belong to L level. Their own stratum is positively evaluated as opposed to that of their social superiors.

Children's fairy tales (such as AT 480, the Good and the Bad Girl) end at this point. They concentrate on a test where children are opposed to frightful monsters, but the dimensions of sexuality and social opposition are absent. The moral and didactic aspects of moves I and II are usually emphasized in tales of this kind. Characteristically, the sex of the protagonist is unimportant. There are masculine as well as feminine versions of AT 328 (The Boy Steals the Giant's Treasure), and in the Danish versions of Hansel and Gretel (AT 327A)—all of which seem to be derived from the Grimm tale—the structure is altered in some cases so as to turn the boy into the protagonist.

The testers/villains of move I and testers/donors of move II represent the preceding generation, often quite openly: the boy receives an old sword from his dying father, the girl good advice from the mother in her grave. Sometimes only the aspect "old" is retained: the heroine must care for an old man, the hero must help an old woman from the forest. In cases where the encounter is hostile, the power of the donor is emphasized: the hero must trick two fighting giants or steal treasures from a troll, the heroine must serve a witch who heaps impossible tasks on her.

The events of move III become easier to understand with the realization that the two who are to meet have different relations to their parents: one is free of them, the other is still in their power. They are as distant from each other as can be expressed in terms of the three "dimensions" of status, age, and sex, which is in accordance with the general character of fairy tales. Olrik was the first to define the epic law that the encounter in oral narrative art is always between two and only two characters, and that the opposition between them tends toward the extreme (1909). (The "age" difference between the two young people who meet in move III refers to their belonging to different age groups, "young" and "adult," not to an absolute age difference measured in years.) The hero who woos a princess must overcome several kinds of obstacles. In the first place, she is immature in many cases: the tale says that she is "asleep" or "under a spell" or "hidden." In the second place, she is guarded: the tale says that she is in the power of a monster, troll, ogre, or dragon. A study of twenty-three Danish versions of The Princess on the Glass Mountain showed that one version did not tell how she got to be there; in nine versions the villain was a troll, dragon, or the like; in the remaining thirteen versions she had been put on top of the glass mountain by her father—which means that fathers and monsters are "motifemically equivalent" (Dundes, 1982). In the third place, finally, the princess is somewhere inaccessible—a castle, glass mountain, tower, cave, distant island, or whatever—and the hero has to gain access in spite of the guardians or the princess herself.

This last point is important. The princess herself is sometimes opposed to the hero at this stage. In the tales of The Danced-Out Shoes (AT 306) and The Monster's Bride (AT 507A), for instance, she visits a monster every night, and the hero or his helper must expose this illicit relation. If the monster is again interpreted as her father, the problem in tales of this kind is clearly that the princess is secretly infatuated with him. This is the "secret" the hero guesses when he hands her the monster's head in plain daylight.

The meeting of princess and lover sometimes takes the form of a secret tryst. The suitor dons a feathered disguise and arrives at her window at night, or he finds her in the distant castle or in the church at midnight. The two young people meet and fall in love, but the meeting is secret. One is reminded of the ancient custom of bundling which was still known in many parts of Europe in the nineteenth century when these tales were taken down.

Customary interpretations of move III emphasize the hero's prowess, strength, or ability. It is of course true that he kills dragons and scales glass mountains; nevertheless, that sort of interpretation is wrong because it is onesided—it does not take the acts of the princess into account—and because it misses the significance of these events for the course of action, the basic principle defined by Propp. Only a Proppian analysis will make it clear that slaying the dragon and scaling the mountain are the motifemic equivalents of less dramatic forms of move III. In the tale of The Lazy Boy (AT 675), the hero catches a fish which he sets free when it promises him that all his wishes will come true; this is of course a form of the donor sequence (move II), and one cannot help remembering that Freudian analysts long ago observed the phallic significance of fish. The hero uses his power to wish the princess pregnant. In the course of events, this corresponds to move III.

In some tales, the princess is in animal shape; this is the case, for example, in AT 402, The Mouse (Cat, Frog, etc.) as Bride. Her transformation into a human being takes place in move III. In feminine tales, the prince correspondingly appears on the stage in the guise of a serpent, frog, or other animal, and the heroine must liberate him from this fate (AT 433, 440, etc.). If these transformations are seen as various expressions of the theme dominant in move III, boy-meets-girl, they make very good sense: they tell of a representative of the opposite sex as monstrous and animal-like. At the same time, the taming transformation of the serpent in AT 433 expresses another aspect, the "civilizing" of the unrestrained sexuality of the prince. (Symbols with more or less explicit sexual significance may be found at several places in fairy tales, but they are usually concentrated in move III, which is not surprising, considering the dominant theme of love.)

Move III may assume countless forms, but all have the love theme in common. It is, however, a clandestine love, the realization of which will meet with great difficulties further on, as is sometimes stated explicitly in the tales. The hero has slain the dragon on the beach, but he does not accompany the princess to the castle. Cinderella has danced with the prince all night, but she returns secretly to her kitchen. The reason is not far to seek: the parents of the prince or the princess have other plans for their child's future, plans which are embodied in the figure of the false hero or the false bride. Or the hero(ine) has powerful rivals, the older brothers or stepsisters at home or the ladies or knights at court. In move IV, the secret love relation is discovered, and the adversaries step in to prevent the young couple from meeting in the future. The hero is cast into a dungeon or killed (to be revived by his animal helpers) or sent on an impossible task or marooned on a distant shore. In Cupid and Psyche (AT 425), the heroine, Psyche, is abused by Venus, Cupid's mother, who gives her impossible tasks and finally sends her off to Styx. Her reasons for persecuting the girl are given in no uncertain terms: she will not accept a lowly mortal as her daughter-in-law and besides, she does not want that useless son of hers to love anyone but his mother, who is anything but old; in fact, she could easily still have other—and better—sons. Jealousy, fear of being ousted by the younger generation, and pride are nicely mixed in Apuleius' tale, the oldest extant version of AT 425.

In many tales with the feminine version of the fairy tale pattern, though the bride actually marries her prince in move III, he is still under his mother's domination, and the girl is mercilessly persecuted in her new home. The mother-in-law slanders her; in a number of tales, the children she bears are replaced by puppies, or blood is smeared round her mouth, and she is accused of eating them. She is then imprisoned or expelled from the castle, or condemned to be burned at the stake.

An interesting example of the mother's domination is found in The Forgotten Fiancée (AT 313): the heroine has helped her friend perform impossible tasks and saved their lives when they fled from the ogre, but he must enter his parents' home on his own. The heroine beseeches him not to kiss his mother, but the mother kisses him while he sleeps, and he immediately forgets his fiancée.

Fathers' domination of their daughters is expressed through barring the heroes from access in the usual way. When the hero insists on making his relations with the girl known in AT 400, she is removed to the Castle East of the Sun and West of the Moon, or he has to travel for seven years or until he has worn out seven pairs of iron shoes. These symbols may be read as various expressions of the huge distance the low-born hero(ine) has to overcome to win his/her spouse. The glass mountain expresses the same idea.

The hero(ine) is not, however, without helpers. Sometimes they are the same as in move II; often the advice given in move II is put to use in move IV; in other cases, move IV contains a (second) donor sequence. It is therefore difficult to describe the structure of this move in detail, whereas the general direction is clear enough: no obstacle is too great to be overcome by the couple who became lovers in move III.

By contrast, the events in move V follow a rather regular pattern. There may be a difficult task as in Propp's model (Pf 25–26). In such cases, the hero is secretly aided by the princess (he is, for example, to recognize her among twelve girls who look exactly alike) and the heroine by her prince (in AT 425, he gives her good advice and helps her when she is overcome by a spell). In a great many tales, however, the hero(ine) does nothing in this move. He has killed the dragon or fought his way through other dangers, or she has worn out seven pairs of shoes or spent three nights calling the prince's name (he has been drugged by his mother, the "witch"). It is the task of the future spouse to take over at this point and that is the main event in move V. In masculine tales, the princess invites the hero into the castle, or she makes the king summon him, or she has all the men in the kingdom pass muster in order to identify her secret lover, or searches for him all over the country, or tells the truth about the Red Knight who boasted that he killed the dragon—its heads are indeed hanging on the wall in the royal hall, but the tongues are missing (incidentally, this is probably a sexual symbol; if that is correct, little good can be said about the Red Knight's maleness, whereas the hero has his pocket full). In feminine tales, the hero wakes up from his lethargy. The heroine has made her way into the kitchen through the gutter (AT 403) or she has tricked her former lover into inviting her to the wedding (AT 313). Heroines often serve at the castle already so that it is primarily a question of recognition, of overcoming the social distance between the kitchen and the hall. But the prince must take the initiative. In AT 510A (Cinderella) he must search the whole country to find the girl who will fit the lost slipper, and in AT 433B he also travels far to find the girl who was driven forth by his mother, but the main problems are often simply recognizing the true identity of a girl who is already close—and standing up to his mother.

Then comes the final hurdle: the parents do not want to be deposed, and they fight their inevitable fate as long as possible. In some tales the parent of the same sex as the hero(ine) is killed. The social conflict and the generation conflict are the two main themes of move V, and they are inextricably interwoven. It is the intrusion of the low-born hero(ine) that makes the high-born partner rebel against his/her subordinate position in the nuclear family at H level. Since the love relation is of course also present in this move as an undercurrent, all the main themes contribute to the poignancy of the final conflict and to the glory of the harmonious resolution.

The main events may be graphically depicted as movements from one position to another within Köngäs Maranda's cube. In the masculine version of the pattern, the hero moves from LYM to LAM (move II) and establishes contact with his future spouse, who is in the HYF position (move III). They move to positions HAM and HAF respectively (move V). In the feminine version, the heroine moves from LYF to LAF (move II) if she is not already there at the outset, after which she establishes contact with her future spouse, who is in the HYM position (move III). They move to positions HAF and HAM respectively (move V). It is important to emphasize that both move. The fully fledged fairy tale is about the fate of two young people. Most earlier studies of the structure of fairy tales viewed them as biographies of one protagonist, stories in which the role of the other is merely that of a prize. In such interpretations (and in Propp's model), crucial narrative events are not accounted for.

3

After the "grammar" there is the "dictionary." In this case, however, what follows is not a dictionary in the proper sense of the word, not even a dictionary of symbols. It must be stressed that fairy tales can only be described as the utterances of a language in an analogous sense. The "words" are ordinary ones that have a meaning (or a cluster of meanings) outside the context of the fairy tales. Take the witch, for instance. There is a witch belief in folk tradition, and the word "witch" is used either to denote such a person or, in a metaphorical sense, a hag. But the witch in fairy tales is something else, a being whose character can be defined only in the context of the fairy-tale tradition itself. Witches (as well as other beings, phenomena, and events characteristic of fairy tales) are deprived of their usual connotations—sublimated, as Lüthi says (1947)—and given new ones which depend on the context of the fairy tales.

What is needed here is therefore not a dictionary, but an account of the ways in which the "marvelous" or symbolic elements of fairy tales acquire the specific meaning they have here.

The basic premise is that symbolic elements refer to features of the real world as experienced by the storytellers and their audiences. The foregoing has shown that there are intimate relations between living conditions and the content of the tales, but the nature of these relations has not been explored. It may be described in the form of a thesis: *The symbolic elements of fairy tales convey emotional impressions of beings, phenomena, and events in the real world, organized in the form of fictional narrative sequences which allow the narrator to speak of the problems, hopes, and ideals of the community.*

How are emotional impressions metamorphosed into symbolic expressions? This process is governed by a principle that may be specified in the form of a number of rules, some of which have already been described by other writers, principally Rank (1909) and Lüthi (1947). Seven rules have been found so far:

(1) The split. Conflicting aspects of a character are distributed upon different figures in the tale. The identity between them may be deduced from the fact that they occupy the same tale and do not interact. The split occurs in several forms: between the "good" and the "bad" aspects of a character (Dr. Jekyll and Mr. Hyde), between the active and passive aspects, and between the spiritual and bodily aspects.

The split between "good" and "bad" occurs principally in the compass of generation conflicts (the Y-A axis). Male adversaries appear as trolls, giants, ogres, cannibals, dragons, devils, wild men, and so forth, whereas female adversaries appear as stepmothers and witches. The split between the spiritual and bodily aspects occurs primarily on the M-F axis. Heroes experience their future spouses as dogs, cats, birds, and such like; heroines conversely encounter birds, serpents, frogs, and other wild animals. The split between the active and passive aspects occur in the protagonist in tales where he/she has a helper. The helper performs functions which would normally belong to the sphere of action of the hero. This split has several forms. Helpers in human shape seem to act on their own, whereas helpers in animal shape usually act as the hero's emissaries. There is a less "absolute" form of the split, in which the hero transforms himself into an animal on certain occasions; in yet another form, the hero(ine) is a despised person in daily life—the gardener's scurvy-headed boy, the scullery maid—who on certain occasions puts on a fine dress or suit of clothes to appear in all his/her splendor and glory: Cinderella is a well-known example. The same idea is known in modern comics—for example, Superman, the shy newspaperman who is really a mighty hero in disguise. Figures of this kind are perfectly suited for daydreaming.

(2) Particularization *(pars pro toto)*. Aspects of persons, phenomena, and events appear as independent symbolic elements. This rule is closely related to that of the split, but the element of dichotomy (Dr. Jekyll and Mr. Hyde) is absent.

An example: The opposition between dry and wet may express the opposition between death and life, but it assumes a special form in fairy tales where water is regularly associated with the life force of women. In a sense, water is the female principle. Rank (1909) found that birth is often associated with water in myths—with floating in or being taken out of water—and this is a common motif in fairy tales; but the same association appears at other points as well. In AT 611, the hero may receive his gifts from a mermaid; the princess may live in an underwater castle; in AT 707, the heroine liberates her brothers, who have been transformed into boulders, by sprinkling them with the water of life; in the transformation flight in AT 313, the heroine turns herself into a well (and the boy into a dipper) or into a lake (and the boy into a drake swimming on it); in one version of AT 325, the hero has been transformed into a horse, and the magician has strictly forbidden his daughters to water it (when they do so anyway, it turns into a fish). Clearly the water represents the girl, often in her sexual aspect. (Note that the boy appears as the dipper, drake, fish, or some other obviously phallic symbol.)

Far from all the symbols produced in this way are associated with sex. In the version of AT 707 known from the Arabian Nights, two brothers are instructed to look for the water of life, the speaking bird, and the singing tree. These treasures are to be found on top of a mountain, and their adviser tells them not to turn around while climbing it. The brothers hear voices shouting insults or threats at them, turn around, and are transformed into boulders. Then their sister follows them. She plugs her ears so she cannot hear the voices, reaches the treasures safely, and revives her brothers. Every element may be read as pertaining to real life. The climbing of the mountain is a common enough symbol of development and growth, where the aspect of arduous ascent is singled out. The phenomenon of petrification, which has been mentioned above, refers to the arresting of a young person's development. The voices probably refer to the authorities whom the young people must learn to ignore if heeding them means turning away from the ascent. In this, the girl is wiser. She will not let herself be shut off from the water of life. This sequence is clearly concerned with development, with moves I and II of our syntagmatic model, and its symbols are dominated by the thematic opposition Y-A. It would be a mistake to interpret them in a sexual sense.

(3) Projection. Feelings and reactions in the protagonist's mind are presented as phenomena occurring in the surrounding world. The prince and princess were not the cause of their own misfortune—their parents were (move I). The hero is not immature—the partner is an animal. The girl did not desire her father—he desired her (AT 706). The hero does not feel lonely—the castle is deserted.

An example: The father unwittingly promises his son to "a little grey man." In danger at sea or having lost his way in the wilderness, he falls prey to the little man's cunning: he must give him the first living thing that meets him when he returns to his home (the Jephthah's daughter motif). This turns out to be his son. What is reflected in this motif, which is a common one in fairy tales, seems to be the fact that in traditional peasant communities children were often sent away from home at an early age to serve at a farm. Naturally they were unhappy, but it was not easy to blame their parents for their misfortune; the cunning of the little gray man was an explanation that would permit them to hate without guilt. Their life at the foreign place is often described in a way that lays the possibility of projection near at hand: they serve at a desolate castle (they feel lonely) in the wilderness (they feel lost) or with a troll (a stern master) who heaps impossible tasks on their shoulders (they feel small and weak) and does not permit them to eat (the growing child is hungry).

(4) Externalization. Inner qualities are expressed by attributes or through action. Fairy tales do not possess a vocabulary for the description in abstract form of such qualities as generosity, valor, and kindness or their opposites, stinginess, cowardice, cruelty, and so forth. This rule is particularly visible in moves I and II. A characteristic example is The Girls in the Well (AT 480), one of the best known of all fairy tales. Two girls are sent away to serve with a witch and are rewarded according to the quality of their work. The good girl is given gifts: pearls will drop from her hair when she combs it, gold from her mouth when she speaks, roses and lilies will grow where she walks. The bad girl is punished: snakes will drop from her hair when she combs it, toads and frogs jump from her mouth when she speaks, and she will break wind at every step. A survey of the donor sequences (move II) of a number of tales will provide a veritable catalog of examples.

Similarly, the properties of the adversaries encountered at various stages really describe their inner qualities: they are gigantic or many-headed or fire-spewing or ugly or accompanied by loathsome animals. An intriguing example is the ogre whose heart is external, hidden in an egg (AT 301). The hero must get hold of it, and either he or the ogre's daughter must break it. The association of the breaking of the egg-heart with the girl's falling in love with the hero leads to an interpretation of the heart as an expression of the ogre's desire for the girl. The relation between them is not clear in all versions, but she is manifestly his daughter in several of them. The hidden, external heart may then be interpreted as a father's hidden desire for his daughter.

The rules of particularization, projection, and externalization cannot always be kept completely apart. In a common subtype of AT 425, the heroine's fiancé appears in the shape of a dog. This may be interpreted as an indication of the immature girl's feelings (projection) or as an indictment of his subservient role in his own mother's house (externalization).

(5) Hyperbole. Intensity of feeling is expressed by exaggeration of the phenomena eliciting the feeling. The opponent is not just large, he is a giant. The hag is not just old, her back is bent into a circle. The master is not just stern, his orders are issued on pain of death. The palace is not merely rich, it is golden and encrusted with diamonds. The girl is not merely beautiful, her face is more radiant than the sun. These examples might be multiplied endless-

ly. Fairy tales use extremes to an extreme extent. This also appears from the narrative organization, the heroine is saved from a threat in the nick of time, for example. The split may be viewed as an example in that conflicting qualities or properties of a character (as seen from another character's point of view) are carried to opposite extremes embodied in two figures. The paradigmatic model of the fairy tale itself is based on contrasting extremes.

The "magic" gifts may often be regarded as hyperbolic expressions of the range and power of the adult: the flying carpet, the invisibility cloak, the invincible sword, the fastest and strongest horse in the world, and so on. The position of the hero(ine) is also described in hyperbolic terms: first the hero is in the snake pit or dungeon, next he ascends the throne; the heroine, transformed into a duck, first enters the kitchen through the gutter as the lowest of the low, next she sleeps on the king's arm. Hyperbole is a device for clarifying the ideal. Details and modifications are neither needed nor wanted; they would signify an attempt at verisimilitude which is totally foreign to fairy tales.

(6) Quantification. Quality is often expressed as quantity. The impressive being, phenomenon, or event is multiplied, usually by three. Also, extension in space or time may be enormously augmented (serving the Devil for three times seven years, traveling through nine times nine kingdoms, etc.). The hero fights the dragon three times or he fights three successive dragons of increasing fearfulness. This is in agreement with Olrik's (1909) observation that fairy tales do not resort to description (cf. also rule No. 4). Instead, the action is repeated and often intensified.

(7) Contraction. Developments extended in space or time are contracted so as to appear as instantaneous changes, often by three stages. The slow change, the long and weary journey, the endless routine work, and the gradual transition are never described, as has already been said. An example: in the introduction to AT 650, the hero nurses at his mother's breast for six years, after which he tries his strength; it is insufficient. He nurses at her breast for another six years, and tries again, but only the third time, at the age of eighteen, has he obtained the extraordinary strength he wants. The process of growing is thus described in three static blocks, each followed by a test. It is the same with work: the boy's service with the troll in AT 313 is described as three successive tests, and his service with the cat in AT 402 is described as three eventless years interspersed with visits to his parents.

The rule of contraction is combined with that of projection in tales where instantaneous transformations (other than those associated with work) take place. Instead of gradually growing up, familiarizing himself with the farm where he serves and getting acquainted with the farmer's daughter, finally to fall in love with her, the hero serves three times one year at an empty castle, after which he "disenchants" a cat by beheading her. At that very instant she is transformed into a princess and the gloomy, subterranean castle into a magnificent kingdom.

Further rules may have to be defined. For example, the phenomenon Freud calls "upwards displacement," which is also found in fairy tales (the queen eats a fish and becomes pregnant), cannot easily be described by the rules as they stand, and other minor difficulties may turn up. It is, however, more important to emphasize that the seven rules defined so far constitute a coherent system, as may be seen from the fact that many symbols conform to more than one rule. All of them are, as was said at the outset, governed by a common principle, which can now be formulated: certain important beings, phenomena, and events are presented under the aspect of their emotional impact, but in the manner and style of factual reporting—of "marvels," however. This technique creates the strange impression of detachment, of keeping vital matters at arm's length. The purpose seems to be to permit a vicarious working through of emotional problems that cannot be openly vented.

In a number of cases, symbols have been "translated" as if they were in fact parts of a dictionary. Does that not contradict the view expressed at the beginning of this section? Yes and no. A series of symbols referring to sexual organs and activities has been elicited. They are probably universal (with modifications having to do with cultural history). Freudian analysts observed many of these symbols in dreams and others have confirmed their occurrence in literature and the arts. One should not balk at such observations. Fairy tales deal with sexual relations and there are limits to the forms symbols expressing this can assume. What has brought the approach of the psychoanalysts in disrepute is part excess, part the reluctance of the general reader to accept that tales that today are treated as literature for children were in fact entertainment for adults.

But sex is not all. Fairy tales deal with painful experiences and feelings that must at all costs be prevented from being openly expressed. The difficult relations between siblings, between parents and children, between daughter-in-law and mother-in-law, also have to be dealt with in this cautious manner. It would therefore be a mistake to read sexual meanings into all symbols. An example: Golden balls are mentioned in many fairy tales. If the hero scales the glass mountain on his mighty steed, swings his sword three times over the princess's head (an upwards displacement if ever there was one), and in return receives a golden apple or three golden apples, it is justified to interpret these apples as symbols of fertility and the sequence as a sexual event. The context indicates it. At the same time, however, the apples are golden; the princess is, after all, rich, and golden apples have been an imperial ensign since Antiquity. The symbol is overdetermined. In the tale of the Frog Prince, the princess's golden ball drops into a well, whence it is retrieved by a frog. It is still possible to think of the ball as an expression of the girl's sexuality which gets into the power of the frog, but some writers have thought otherwise. It has been suggested that the golden ball may be a symbol of her innocent childhood. In AT 502, a prince similarly plays with a golden ball that rolls into the cage of a wild man; in this case, the sexual interpretation becomes meaningless. In several tales, heroes or heroines are advised by strange old men or women to follow a ball that rolls along by itself until it reaches the goal they are seeking. There is some sort of association between the young person and the ball, but it hardly expresses sexuality in those tales.

The example shows that symbols should not be interpreted as expressions of a single, unalterable meaning. The meaning depends on the context in which they appear.

The context may in part be described by means of the syntagmatic and paradigmatic models presented above, but there is yet another determining factor: the symbols of a given tale often influence each other. They constitute a coherent whole, which may be called imagery. If for instance the phallic aspect of the hero is to be stressed, he may be equipped with a sword, spear, club, gun, hammer, or flute, or he may appear as a serpent, frog, cock, or the like, or he may be able to transform himself into a lion, bear, bull, horse, or bird of prey. The choice depends on the imagery as a whole. Thus, a series of masculine images is dominated by chivalrous imagery (AT 300, 301, 303, 314, 502, 530, 550, 581, 590, etc.) and the hero has a sword or spear. This would be incongruent with the imagery in AT 570 in which the hero is a herdsman and his attribute is a flute, or with that in AT 650 where he may be a farmhand or journeyman smith and his attribute a club or hammer. In numerous feminine tales, the future spouse's sexual aspect is seen from her point of view, from the outside, so to speak; his maleness may appear to her as loathsome or as a physical threat, and this may result in his appearing in the guise of a reptile, for example.

To this should be added that individual symbols may influence one another, as may be shown by two examples: in many versions of AT 425, the heroine lights a candle to see who her lover is; this may be followed by a scene in which she must hold a candle for the false bride. In AT 433B, part of the serpent's disenchantment is that he is bathed in milk; later on the expelled heroine, who is nursing twins, has to empty her breasts, and two birds are transformed by drinking her milk. The choice of symbols is thus not only directed by the narrative pattern, but is also influenced by the imagery through which the narrator's intentions are realized.

The three analytic tools described above—the syntagmatic pattern, the paradigmatic model, and the rules for the production of symbols—have been applied to a random selection of twenty-six Danish records of fairy tales, one of which was studied in depth (Holbek, 1987). The results cannot be summarized here, but a few salient points may be mentioned.

First, all the tales selected—with one exception (see below)—conformed to the patterns described above, and they not only had numerous symbols in common, but also turned out to be susceptible to the same kind of analysis. In several cases, indications could be found that the storytellers themselves were well aware of the meaning of the symbols brought out by the analysis.

Second, a single tale, a humorous version of AT 571B, which had been selected along with the others because it was catalogued in the bracket reserved for fairy tales (AT 300–749), did not conform to the pattern. This shows that the method described above is genre-specific and, by implication, that the genre of fairy tales possesses characteristics that distinguish it from other kinds of oral prose narratives.

Third, it appeared that the five storytellers whose tales had been selected for analysis differed both with regard to sex and personality. There were sex-based preferences in the choice of subject matter and to some extent in underlying attitudes, but apart from that, it also turned out that different individuals handled similar narrative ideas differently. For instance, one female storyteller built her tales schematically and put great stress on the performance of one's duties, whereas a male storyteller's tales were a little vague and meandering with regard to syntagmatic structure, and his heroes were regularly put into desperate situations where they needed outside help. One storyteller was dignified and a little distant, another humorous and insistent. One male storyteller, who had never been married, accorded his female characters very little room for independent action, whereas his heroes were impetuous and headstrong, not to say male chauvinist pigs; he had been a blacksmith and this may explain his predilection for horses—all of his tales featured horses, even at points where records of the same tale types from other storytellers had none. These and similar observations show that the patterns and rules defined above were anything but straitjackets. The same may, of course, be said about the grammatical rules of ordinary speech.

The main point is, however, that the genre of fairy tales did in fact turn out to possess a series of specific characteristics, to be the products of a technique, or·way of narrating, that had been mastered by several storytellers. Their tales had individual traits, but a common basis—just as the utterances of different individuals carry their individual stamp even though they are all expressed in the same language.

Future students of fairy tales will have to take this into account. It will no longer be possible to rely on general statements as to the nature of the fairy tale. One will have to be specific as to the level of generalization.

A BLIND STORYTELLER'S REPERTOIRE

Gun Herranen

The tendency during the 1960s and 1970s was to declare old archive materials devoid of interest and text-based studies hopelessly passé. Lack of sociocultural context has been regarded as the most serious flaw of archive materials—this is no doubt true for a regrettably large amount of what has accumulated in folklore archives. But there are perhaps exceptions to this situation. Can a storyteller who has been in his grave for more than seventy years be an interesting object for research? Can the collection of his folktales in the archives tell us something about the folktale-producing individual and genre-specific rules?

Source Criticism

In 1981 I made a discovery in the folklore archives of the Swedish Literature Society in Finland. Among V. E. V. Wessman's collections of Swedish folklore in Finland, I found a richly detailed description, dated 1909, of the blind storyteller Berndt Strömberg (1822–1910). This description of a tradition bearer attracted my attention for more than one reason. First of all, most of his contemporaries were characterized only by brief remarks about their names, ages, professions. But here was a full portrait of an informant who was a narrator of folktales. Furthermore, he was old and blind and deaf when Wessman noted down 120 tales from his repertoire; he died a year later (SLS 202, II). The editors of the folktale volumes in the series *Finlands svenska folkdiktning* (Allardt and Hackman, 1917–20) had hidden the narrator behind the system of classification in keeping with the geographical-historical method (Aarne, 1910; Hackman, 1911). My own method in studying Blind Stromberg and his repertoire began with tracing the folktales to their printed sources. My reaction, again,

---

Original title: "Aspects of a Blind Storyteller's Repertoire: Auditive Learning—Oral Tradition." Published in G. Calame-Griaule et al. (eds.), 1982.

was one of surprise: Did the printed sources really contain so many folktales from the same narrator without its being noted anywhere? Thirty tales printed *in extenso* stemmed from Blind Strömberg; seventy abstracts could also be traced back to him.

In the first decades of this century, collecting for the Swedish Literature Society in Finland was done by scholarship recipients; in that capacity, Wessman had delivered eighty-two folktales and three legends, plus the description of the narrator, Blind Strömberg, to the society. He did not turn over an additional thirty-five texts that he had collected from Strömberg, saying that they were of literary origin. The present study is based on the entire collection, including the latter thirty-five texts.

In 1893, sixteen years before Wessman rediscovered Blind Strömberg, another collector, L. W. Öholm, had interviewed him. It is probable that Wessman did not know of Öholm's interviews with Strömberg until he started to copy out his own notes and compare them with tales in a regional collection published in 1896 (Allardt and Perklén, 1896). Öholm had documented twenty-six tales told by Strömberg in 1893, eight of which eventually found their way into *Finlands svenska folkdiktning in extenso* (Allardt, 1917–20), while abstracts were printed of seventeen texts (Hackman, 1917–20) on the basis of the Nyland volume. After many twists and turns I finally found Öholm's manuscripts, which had been lent out and forgotten in the 1930s.

As a result I ended up with a total of 137 tales by Blind Strömberg. Among them are some he had told to both collectors, which makes it possible to study changes in the tales over a period of sixteen years. Study of the texts also makes clear that Öholm was an amateur collector, whereas Wessman was an expert with long experience in fieldwork and a thorough knowledge of dialectological documentation.

Classification

From source criticism, I proceeded to classification in keeping with the AT-system in order to get an overall picture of Blind Strömberg's repertoire. According to what Strömberg told Wessman, he knew 366 folktales—"one for each day of the year"—and a couple of hundred songs. His songs were not documented by either collector. Their interest focused on his tales, and the repertoire of Blind Strömberg as it was documented by Öholm in 1893 and Wessman in 1909 contains:

Animal tales	4	(Öholm	1,	Wessman	3)
Tales of Magic	62	(Öholm	9,	Wessman	53)
Religious tales	4	(Öholm	1,	Wessman	3)
Romantic tales	19	(Öholm	4,	Wessman	15)
Stupid Ogre tales	2	(Öholm	1,	Wessman	1)
Anecdotes	15	(Öholm	5,	Wessman	10)

Legends	4	(Öholm	1, Wessman	3)
Unclassified	27	(Öholm	5, Wessman	22)
Totals	**137**		**27**	**110**

Although Wessman documented many more of Strömberg's tales than Öholm, the tale types represented in their collections show the same outline—tales of magic and romantic tales dominate, anecdotes and a few legends are equally represented in both. Wessman's method of interviewing was adapted to Strömberg's deafness: after Wessman had transcribed part of Strömberg's dictation, he would touch the old man's foot with his own to indicate that he could go on.

Who Was Blind Strömberg and How Did He Learn His Tales?

Blind Strömberg was born in 1822, the second child of a crofter in a village on the south coast of Finland. He lost his sight as an infant, when smallpox caused scarring of the cornea. As the number of children increased, the family moved frequently from place to place within the region around the town of Ekenäs. When he came of age, Strömberg received a small sum of money from the parish and, as a pauper, stayed with different families in the town.

Wessman found Strömberg extremely interesting. That is why—as an exception to common practice—he included so much of Strömberg's life history. Wessman was puzzled by the great number of tales in Strömberg's repertoire (cf. Dégh 1969): Where and from whom had he learned them? Wessman mentions a tailor and various sailors, as well as the local library. Though he could not read himself, Strömberg asked schoolboys to borrow books of folktales and read them aloud to him. The local library was fairly modest: by 1872 it contained only 834 books, among them Topelius, v. Becker, Asbjørnsen and Moe, and Hans Christian Andersen. Another possible source, very difficult to document, is broadsheets containing folktales by, for example, the Grimm Brothers. Certain tales in Strömberg's repertoire seem to prove that broadsheets printed in Sweden from the first half of the nineteenth century had found their way to the Finnish coastal districts where Swedish was spoken. Contacts across the sea with Sweden were common among the fishermen of the district in question. The bulk of Strömberg's repertoire, however, seems to have derived from oral sources.

The Storytelling Event—Context in the Text

Wessman gives some information about where and to whom Blind Strömberg told his tales. When he was younger he would tell his stories in the marketplace; after he became too old to walk the six or seven kilometers from his village to the nearby town, young people would visit him on weekends to listen to his stories (SLS 202, II,3). I was lucky to find three people who could still remember Strömberg. From a man born in 1892 I learned that Strömberg told his stories whenever asked by young people assembled for Saturday evening dances. What one of these sessions may have been like is reflected in one of his tales, "The Boy Who Came to the Pancake Mountain" (AT 727):

> Nils, fifty-two years old . . . would sing and tell fairy tales. On Sunday evenings between All Saints' Day and Christmas, the boys and girls of the village gathered around him, and they gave him money so that he could buy tobacco. They came on Sunday evenings, when Nils was at his best. Now, on the evening of the fourth day of Christmas, they were dancing and singing. . . . But the farmer's wife did not like Nils; she scolded him for his songs and his fairy tales, and all the other rubbish. . . ." (Allardt, 1917–20, No. 258)

Here context is revealed in the text: Strömberg characterizes himself in the setting of the storytelling event. Another informant, a woman now seventy-nine years old, said that young people and children gathered around Strömberg every Sunday to listen to his tales. When he had finished a story with the usual "And this was the end," the children knew that he liked them to say, "It was a beautiful story." And his standard answer was, "Did you think so?"

Blindness and Memory

Sensory deprivation is often perceived as a trigger for compensatory sensory hyperfunction. Blindness, however, is individually experienced, and generalizations about connections between "good memory" and blindness tend to be exaggerated: blindness does not automatically produce acuteness in other senses, as so many people assume. A comparison of the sensory acuteness of blind and seeing individuals in hearing, touch, smell, and taste has not revealed any significant differences in favor of one group or the other. The same thing can be said of the memory of blind individuals. If a blind person shows greater sensory efficiency, it is due to "more frequent use, increased effort, and enforced concentration, but not to any automatic 'sensory compensation.' Blind persons must use their nonvisual senses and interpret whatever they can gain by hearing, touch, smell and taste" (Lowenfeld, 1964, 88f.). Strömberg's blindness seems to have equipped him with increased receptive and storage competence, probably because he used a combination of mechanical, logical, and associative techniques. Frequent retellings, added, of course, to the stability of his tales.

Expansion and Adaptation

Along with stability, expansion and adaptation are also evident in

Strömberg's repertoire. If we compare a version of "The Faithless Wife" (AT 1380) told in 1893 with a version told in 1909, we find that the latter is somewhat longer. Although, according to Wessman, Strömberg was "meticulous, as old storytellers tend to be" (SLS 202, II), in his stories he elaborated the details of everyday life. The main plot is stable, but connectives and lexical realization vary. The following example illustrates the striking exactness with which Strömberg repeated descriptive details in the two versions:

1893	1909
(Och så går hon in efter fat att tappa bloden i och vispel och salt)	(Gumman gick in efter ett fat, salt och kräkla för bloden)
And then she went in to get a vessel for the blood and whisk and salt	The wife went in to get a vessel, salt, and whisk for the blood

Strömberg also expanded his stories by combining segments from different tale types. For example, in 1893 he told a story that combines AT 503 and AT 103, which he told as separate stories in 1909. Another story that demonstrates Strömberg's use of expansion and variation has a literary origin. The printed source is a broadsheet published in several editions in 1809, 1825, 1827, and 1833 (see Bäckström, 1845). The broadsheet, entitled "A Suitor's Speech," is a joking conversation between two neighbors. Strömberg uses the conversation and its joking devices—a tail connected to every line creates a humorous effect—but he adds a frame story around the conversation about the "two neighbors who live in a village. Both were rich but they were tight-fisted, too, and neither allowed himself any servants." In other words, he molds the conversation of the broadsheet into a folktale pattern.

In his study of AT 480, "The Kind and the Unkind Girls," and "The Twelve Months' Form," the tale of which he reports forty-four versions, Warren E. Roberts states that this form "is confined, with a few exceptions, to Southeastern Europe, being found in Italy, Russia, Poland, Slovakia, Yugoslavia, Bulgaria, and Greece. There is also *one version from the Swedes in Finland*" (Roberts, 1958, 99, italics mine). This odd version was actually told by Strömberg, noted down by Wessman, and printed in *Finlands svenska folkdiktning*. How did Strömberg come to possess this unusual form of the tale?

In Roberts's brief outline, "The Twelve Months' Form" (AT 480) goes thus: "A mistreated stepdaughter is sent out to gather strawberries in mid-winter. She comes upon the twelve months sitting around the fire and is polite to them or guesses their names. Most commonly, strawberries are made to ripen as a reward, but in many versions the heroine is given gold. The bad girl is frozen" (Roberts, 1958, 99).

Strömberg's version follows this outline: first the kind girl is sent out to pick flowers, then strawberries, then apples. The flowers referred to are "nattvioler" (butterfly orchids); in Finland these bloom in June. When the kind girl visits the twelve months sitting around the fire, "each on his stick," January changes places with June, July, and September so that she succeeds in gathering all three—the flowers in June, the strawberries in July, the apples in September. The unkind girl tries the same thing, but is impolite to the personified months and consequently fails. The evil stepmother goes out to look for her daughter, and both freeze to death (Allardt, 1917–20, No. 168).

Blind Strömberg learned the tale from a translation of Edouard Laboulaye's *Contes Bleus* (1867), which was in the local library in 1872. Strömberg took the central theme of the Laboulaye story, adapted it according to tradition-ecological demands, and included it in his repertoire. When Lauri Honko speaks about the adaptation of tradition, he uses the terms "familiarization" and "localization" as milieu-morphological variables (Honko, 1981, 31f.). In this case Strömberg has used familiarization: instead of Laboulaye's names for the girls, Dobrunka and Zloboga, Strömberg calls them Maria and Helena. In Laboulaye, the months that change place with January are March for violets, June for strawberries, and September for apples. This does not accord with Finland's climate, so Strömberg naturally told the story according to his and his listeners' world. When the Laboulaye version speaks of "violets," Strömberg speaks of "nattvioler," literally, "night violets."

Strömberg adapted two more of Laboulaye's tales: "The Lazy Girl" and "Yvon and Finette." The latter has an interesting background, which Reidar Th. Christiansen has disclosed. His conclusion is that Laboulaye had read Dasent's translation of Asbjørnsen and Moe's collection (1858–59), in which the Norwegian folktale "Mestermø" (Mastermaid) is included. Laboulaye's "conte breton" actually comes from Seljord in the Telemark district in Norway! Christiansen has also noted the "Yvon and Finette" version collected by Wessman and points out that there is hardly more than one intermediary between the translation and this version: "One could assume that it was noted down according to one who had once read the printed story" (Christiansen, 1946, 60ff.). This observation is modified when we know that the narrator was Blind Strömberg. Where the literary version has "Framåt, riddare av Kerver" (Forward, knight Kerver) Strömberg has "Framåt, riddare djärver"; here the mishearing is obvious, but the interpretation is logical: "djärver" means bold. The literary version is long, and so is Strömberg's version, which runs to ten pages in print. On the whole, Strömberg's version of "Yvon and Finette" is very close to the literary original. The traces of his personal stamp can be seen in forms of contraction and familiarization (see also Swahn, 1971).

Tradition and Creativity

Blind Strömberg's repertoire shows that he knew bawdy anecdotes (AT 1360B, AT 1730) and religious tales (AT 710, AT 755), but he preferred tales of magic and romantic tales. He told stories with male and female heroes (for instance,"Katie Woodencloak" or "Cap o' Rushes," AT 510B). He seems to have been extremely receptive and eager to enlarge his repertoire. He was a very conscientious storyteller, but like the Hungarian storyteller György Andrasfalvi (Dégh, 1969, 235f.), Strömberg elaborated his tales with realistic details. The familiar environment, the details of everyday life, and the setting or introduction to the stories are deployed in order to slow down the transition to the world of the tale. To a reader some of the tales seem tedious. Blind Strömberg is not one for colorful ornaments—his style is rather meager in this respect. Wessman reports, however, that he acted out the dialogs of some tales, using archaic dialectical pronunciation for what an old man, a husband, or a troll says. This undoubtedly added color to his narrative style.

Even without detailed analysis, we can assume that Albert Lord's oral formulaic theory (Lord, 1964) can cast light on the threefold process of listening/learning, adaptation/memorizing, recreating/telling. Within this system, Strömberg can be labeled a "creative producer" (Honko, 1981a, 39f.). Motivation is a key concept in each of the steps from listening to telling. Strömberg's blindness, which destined him to remain a pauper all his life, also caused his great interest in learning stories, since storytelling was his only way of winning people's approval and, in his old age, gaining the company of young people and children.

LEGENDS TODAY

Bengt af Klintberg

Ever since the days of the Brothers Grimm, folklorists have used the terms *folktale* and *legend* to designate the two most conspicuous genres in oral narrative tradition. Those who have tried to define these two genres have often contrasted them to each other. The folktale takes place in a fictional world and is not believed by the audience; the legend takes place in the real world and is told as if relating a real occurrence. The primary function of the folktale is to entertain, while the legend's function is to inform and reinforce belief and norms. In style the folktale is more artful and detailed, the legend more ordinary and brief.

For a detailed study of folktale and legend the above distinctions are altogether too schematic. But they help in circumscribing two genres that seem to have been differentiated also by the people who told and listened to them. In other words, folktale and legend constitute two natural genres. When it comes to the quantitative relationship between them, our folklore archives show clearly that the recorded number of legends is much greater than that of folktales. This is mainly because the folktale was a demanding genre mastered only by a few people in peasant society. Legends, on the other hand, could be told by anyone.

It is a fact that folktales, at least the multiepisodic tales of magic, ceased being told when traditional peasant society disintegrated. The descendents of people who used to sit around the storyteller now sit in front of the TV watching tales projected on the screen. Legends, however, are told as much in our society as they were in traditional peasant society. Just as the old legendary tradition gives us invaluable information about our forebears' world view, beliefs, and concept of history, so folk legends today tell us a great deal about what goes on under the surface of our own society.

Original title: "Folksägner idag." Published in *Fataburen,* 1976.

Legend and Rumor

In the 1930s C. W. von Sydow introduced the term *memorate* to denote a genre related to the legend. Memorates are narratives about people's real experiences. Their form is often traditional, since the experiences are generally interpreted on the basis of the collective tradition, but the plot of the memorate is not as firmly constructed as that of the legend. Scandinavian folklorists have devoted a great deal of attention to the memorate, primarily because it gives descriptions of supranormal experiences—descriptions which can be a valuable source for the study of folk belief. On the other hand, recent research has not supported von Sydow's contention that the memorate constitutes an early phase of the development of the legend. To be sure, it is possible to detect real supranormal experiences behind certain local legends, but on the whole it is more precise to say that legend and memorate are two genres that exist side by side in tradition and constantly influence each other.

The lively debate in Scandinavia about legend and memorate is one reason why so little has been written about another set of closely related genres, namely legend and rumor. Many of the legends told, for instance, about witches and wise folk in preindustrial society were probably preceded by rumors about these individuals. In studying contemporary narrative tradition in which the genesis of legends is much closer to us in time, it becomes imperative to consider how rumor and legend relate to each other.

The theory of rumors has been developed by sociologists. A fundamental work—albeit much criticized—is Allport and Postman's *The Psychology of Rumor* (1947). It has been pointed out that their model for how a rumor changes as it spreads has only limited validity because it is based on laboratory experiments. It is only in the process of unilinear dissemination that a rumor is stylized in the manner they have outlined; in reality, dissemination occurs as a collective process and the possible variations are legion (Peterson and Gist, 1951). But the sociological study of what happens as rumors spread has produced results that are directly relevant to folkloristic study of contemporary legends in specific cultural contexts. There exist methodologically useful analyses of concrete examples (e.g., Festinger et al., 1948) as well as theoretical discussions of the dissemination of rumors (e.g., Buckner, 1965). A volume summarizing research concerning rumors to date is Shibutani's *Improvised News* (1966). The author emphasizes the function of rumor as a collective solution to given problems.

In an important article entitled "Modern Legend and Rumor Theory" (1972), the American folklorist Patrick B. Mullen has related the theory of rumor to the study of contemporary legends. According to Mullen, the difference between a rumor and a legend lies mostly in the traditional content and more stereotyped epic form of the legend. There is no direct connection between rumors and older tradition. The core of a rumor is usually a brief assertion surrounded by various kinds of supplemental information. Rumor and legend both have a cognitive function in a context where there is no official information. Another function shared by the two genres is emotional, namely to dissipate the feeling of uncertainty and tension in a given situation. Above all, folklorists can learn from the sociological study of rumor that every legend constitutes a dynamic process. It is important to realize that collected legend texts are artifacts. In reality, legends are a continuously changing, oral form of communication between people.

This essay will present some of the legend tradition current today. In it I shall deal with a partial selection only, since the overall scope of the material has not yet been established. My preliminary outline should not be understood as a finished system of classification. However, I should point out that the legends are not grouped merely according to their content, but also according to their manner of dissemination. A major portion of the legends accounted for here spread in the same way as rumors: suddenly they are heard everywhere in a given locality until they are denied and disappear. After a while they might appear in some other place, and the process of dissemination is repeated. As we discover, these legends concern matters that touch directly upon the audience's own existence, that is, something they might experience themselves. Later in the essay I will deal with legends that spread in a quieter, more relaxed manner. Their content may well be startling and even frightening, but the audience feels that the risk of experiencing something similar is small. There- fore these legends are told mostly for entertainment.

There are certain questions about contemporary migratory legends that have no unequivocal answers. These are: Has this actually happened? If so, when did it happen, and where? A more fruitful question is: Why do people tell these legends? Why not some other stories? We need to keep in mind that the range of possible stories is infinite. Every day newspapers and other media report countless dramatic real-life events, and every day legend material is produced in written and oral forms. Nevertheless only a few stories survive and circulate among thousands, even millions, of individuals. What is it about a particular legend that proves so fascinating to people? Two factors may be especially important here. One is the form of the legend. The story at first glance seems realistic, but a second look shows that it is in fact very stylized. The action is simple and highly visual, easy to remember and to pass on to third parties. The other factor is social. The spreading of legends is often a sign of social unrest. They are disseminated because they reinforce people's more or less tacit view of reality. It is imperative for the scholar to map out the social background of a given story at the earliest stage possible, because later it may prove impossible to reconstruct.

Ethnocentric Legends

Folk legends often contain information about the unknown and foreign. In depicting strangers or minority groups legends usually reflect the values, norms, and lifestyle of the majority; in other words, they are ethnocentric. In preindustrial Sweden, for instance, there existed a wealth of ethnocentric legends about the alleged supranormal powers of Lapps and Finns (Tillhagen, 1969). It is typical for ethnocentric folklore to be based on ethnic stereotypes, that is, on generalizations concerning characteristics and attributes of people belonging to some other nationality or having a different ethnic origin. Some of these stereotypes are positive, others negative. When, for instance, Magne Velure entitles his article dealing with stereotypical Swedish conceptions about Finns "Kniv, sprit och sisu" (Knives, Alcohol, and Endurance, 1975), he combines two negative stereotypes with a positive one.

During the last decade there has been a rash of legends about immigrants in Sweden, legends built on a handful of stereotypical motifs. The economic boom of the 1960s brought about an increased need for industrial workers from abroad. The immigrants moved to new housing developments in industrial areas throughout the country. The legends describe how they brought their primitive lifestyle to the modern apartments assigned to them in Sweden. The Nordic Museum has collected a tremendous amount of material showing that Swedes of all ages and throughout the country are familiar with these legends. The following was collected from a woman, aged seventy, who lives in Stockholm (KU 5376,2):

> In 1964 I visited a niece in Köping. On my way back to Stockholm I met a lady on the train. We started talking about immigrants, and she told me about two Yugoslavs working at a large factory where her husband was employed. They had gotten apartments in the same building for their families. But their neighbors thought they heard strange noises and there was an awful smell. An investigation was made, it turned out that they kept chickens and had put down soil on the floor in one of the rooms. They came from a small town and were used to having chickens. They also had cut a hole through the wall connecting their apartments and were sharing the same telephone.

The story might appear fairly believable at first. What it says is not altogether sensational and reminds us of ordinary gossip. But it taxes our credulity when we hear the same accusations from hundreds of towns throughout Sweden. These rumors are not, as one might think, limited to immigrants from remote countries such as Yugoslavia, Greece, and Turkey. They are told just as frequently about Finns, which is really surprising considering that the lifestyle of Swedes and our neighbors to the east is not all that different. From a high-school class in Södertalje comes this story:

> About Finnish immigrants I have heard that some of them have torn up the hardwood floor and put down sand so they won't have to take their kids to the playground, that they made their kitchen into a sauna, and cut a hole into the wall between two apartments in order to share the expense of having a telephone. This is supposed to have happened in a new housing development. (KU 5766,18)

One can ask to what degree these stories have been looked upon as true. The material itself does not permit an unequivocal answer, but in some instances one suspects that the stories were passed on not because they were thought to be true, but because they appealed to the sense of humor of the storyteller—this is especially true among younger people. But most of the informants nevertheless present the story as if it had really happened, sometimes adding realistic details to strengthen this impression. The story most frequently told about Finns is that they have made their kitchen into a sauna—that Finns take sauna baths a lot is a widely accepted stereotype. Supposedly it was discovered when a neighbor's wall started peeling. However, the same story is also told about other immigrants, which demonstrates that many Swedes tend to think of immigrants as an undifferentiated group.

The material collected so far generally documents that the stereotypes we find in legends strengthen popular prejudices against immigrants. However, there is no indication that they lead to any discriminatory acts. They are passed on among Swedes, and many immigrants are quite ignorant of their existence. All the rumors and legends flourishing about immigrants are also told about Swedish gypsies. During the 1960s the gypsies received from the state the means to move into permanent homes. The legends about how they behave in their apartments are a shade more aggressive than legends about immigrants. For instance, there are reports about gypsies making a fire in the middle of the floor and burning the furniture bought with money given them by the state.

The following motifs all appear regularly in legends about immigrants and gypsies living in modern apartments: they break up the hardwood floor and grow potatoes; they break up the hardwood floor and make a sand-pit for their children; they cut a hole in the floor for the Christmas tree; they cut a hole into the wall between two apartments and share the same telephone; they take sauna baths in the kitchen; they call the manager to come and empty their toilets; they have a salted pig in their bathtub; they have chickens, goats, or pigs in their apartment or on the balcony; they slaughter their livestock on the balcony; they build a fire on the floor. There is a tendency among informants to combine a number of motifs to make a story; one can speak of a kind of conglomerate legend. When the story consists of a single motif, then it is fleshed out with greater detail and thus appears more realistic and believable.

The material collected in Scandinavia shows that nearly all the motifs listed above existed already in Swedish tradition before the wave of immigration in the 1960s. But earlier on the stories were told about people moving to urban areas from sparsely populated areas or about Lapps moving into modern apartments or about some village original moving into a retirement home. Here is just one example. A woman informant who was visiting in Luleå during the summer of 1958 tells of a rumor about people from an outlying district moving into a new area at the edge of town:

They came from primitive huts with a dirt floor to modern apartments which were quickly run down. Rumor had it that they had cut holes into the walls to get back and forth between the rooms more easily. At first they didn't know that one has to flush the toilet and when the toilet bowl was full they called the manager to come and empty it out. They pickled salt pork in the bathtub and hung up their laundry inside. They are also supposed to have cut holes in the floor for the Christmas tree. (KU 6192, 95)

Of course there are differences in lifestyle between immigrants and their Swedish neighbors. But on that point the legends give us little information of real value. In effect they tell more about Swedes than about the immigrants. Negative ethnic stereotypes tend to be the opposite of characteristics and modes of behavior valued in one's own culture. By talking about the transgression of norms on the part of immigrants—for instance, their abusing an accepted status symbol such as hardwood floors—people express what they themselves find normal. The notion that immigrants are primitive and find it difficult to adjust to the Swedish lifestyle expresses the self-identification of most Swedes with a modern, urban culture.

The legends tend to be believed most readily among people who already are prejudiced against immigrants. As one would expect, prejudices are more prevalent among the less educated than the educated, and more among older people than the young (Trankell, 1974), in other words among those people who are threatened by immigration inasmuch as it increases competition for jobs. The legends reinforce their self-concept as better adapted and more worthy than immigrants.

Another category of ethnocentric legends includes stories that in recent years have been connected with a number of foreign restaurants. In Stockholm during the summer and autumn of 1973 there was a widely circulated story about someone who went to a pizzeria and got something sharp stuck in his teeth. A dentist removed it and it turned out to be the tooth of a rat. When the health department inspected the restaurant, a great many skinned rats were found in the freezer. The storyteller often emphasized that he had heard the story from an acquaintance of the victim, the dentist, the health inspector, etc.—a trait regularly found in contemporary folk legends.

The same story surfaced in subsequent years about several pizzerias in towns outside Stockholm. Another version, more or less the same as the pizzeria story, told what had happened to a Swedish tourist in Rhodes. It was reported by a provincial newspaper on 29 October 1973. The next day the story was repeated uncritically on the front page of *Dagens Nyheter,* and by the end of the week it could be read in many Scandinavian newspapers.

Both of these two versions neither of which apparently had any basis in fact—were offshoots of a Western European legend tradition that had reached Scandinavia the year before (Klintberg, 1974). During the summer of 1972 a Chinese restaurant in Borås lost so much business because of rumors that had begun circulating that spring that it had to close its doors. The most common of the rumors was that a garbage collector had found a large number of empty cat food cans in the restaurant's trash. But the rat's tooth story was also reported (e.g., *Vastgötksa Demokraten*, 21 June 1972). Shortly thereafter, both the rat's tooth legend and the rumor about empty cat and dog food cans started appearing in Göteborg, where they were linked to Chinese restaurants. During the spring of 1973 Chinese restaurants in Copenhagen and other Danish cities were accused of putting rat meat into the food. One restaurant guest was supposed to have gotten a rat's bone in his throat while eating an eggroll (*Weekendavisen*, 25 May 1973).

The dissemination of this tradition outside Scandinavia can only be suggested with a number of selected examples. There are, as the examples above indicate, two basic types, both of them with a number of offshoots. Several Scandinavian informants have testified that the legend about the rat's tooth was a hot topic in Paris in 1971 (KU 6192, 15, 22, 99). At approximately the same time or shortly thereafter the story was applied to Chinese and Yugoslavian restaurants in Germany (Lore and language 2:3, 30) and to Chinese restaurants in England. As early as the 1960s the legend appeared in England in a version in which skinned cats were found in the refrigerator (KU 6192, 121, 122). This version is also documented in Canada.

The motif of the empty pet food tins is also widely extant. In the 1950s it circulated in New York. The tins are supposed to have revealed that Chinese restaurants were putting cat food into their chop suey (KU 6198, 1). In 1969 an English newspaper reported that a lady living near the kitchen entrance of an Indian restaurant became suspicious about the great number of Kit-e-kat tins in the restaurant's garbage cans. She called the police who informed the health authorities, and the restaurant was forced to close. The fact that no customers had complained about the food was explained by the large amount of curry used (KU 6192, 127). This rumor was also reported in France (KU 6192, 81) and in Germany. In Germany it was told that a foreign restaurant famous for its oxtail soup lost all its customers after a neighbor one day looked over the fence to the restaurant's backyard and there saw a mound of empty Chappi (dog food) cans (KU 6192, 131). It is a consistent trait of the legends that the brand of pet food is mentioned. This makes the legends more believable, while at the same time lending them a kind of grim humor. In December 1973, I collected the following story from a male ethnology student in Göteborg:

> An acquaintance of mine who's a salesman for Pripp's Breweries had the job of visiting all the restaurants in Göteborg to get orders, leave advertising signs, etc. He said that in the Chinese restaurants he saw a lot of VOV-cans on the shelves. It was well known that Chinese restaurants were serving dog food. (KU 6192, 38)

The latest but probably not last case was reported in a newspaper in Trondheim: "Groundless Rumors about VOV-Wuff in Pizza." In this instance, too, janitors were rumored to have found dog food tins in the trash cans (*Adresseavisen*, 20 May 1976).

What all these legends have in common is that they are tied to restaurants serving foreign foods. In Sweden, Chinese and southern European restaurants were a rarity as recently as the 1950s. There were a few in the big cities, and they were considered luxury restaurants. The big breakthrough for inexpensive foreign restaurants came sometime in the 1960s. From 1968 on, pizzerias multiplied in Stockholm in remarkable numbers. Until that year there was only one restaurant serving pizza, while by 1973 there were around twenty (Byström, 1973). Therefore it was no accident that the rat story in Stockholm was connected with a pizzeria and not with Chinese restaurants as it was in Göteborg and Copenhagen.

Just as in the case of the rumors about immigrants, there is an older tradition behind the recent legends about restaurants. During the crisis years of the 1940s there were rumors about local restaurants serving dogs, cats, foxes, and other animals considered unfit for human consumption. But above all, these older legends were about industrially produced food. The growth of the food industry in the twentieth century has given rise to an abundance of legends. Internationally disseminated traditions include, for instance, stories about rats in the meat grinders at sausage factories and about a human thumb found in a can of corned beef. What these legends have in common with stories about restaurants is a distrust of food with unknown ingredients. This distrust is reinforced by today's increased hygienic expectations. The attitude toward rats today can be characterized as a full-blown phobia. It is interesting to note that in the old peasant society, when people were self-sufficient, attitudes toward food were precisely the opposite. When all phases of growing and preparing foodstuffs were visible to everyone and when, furthermore, everybody understood what it meant not to have enough food, it was important to maintain the norm of not wasting anything. Peasant folklore teaches, for example, that one should not discard food just because a rat had nibbled from it or a mouse had dipped into the milk.

Among ethnocentric legends we can also count some of the narratives about dangerous small animals and pests. Often the stories emphasize that these animals come from southern countries. In the fall of 1975 many people in Stockholm got rather nervous about the following story. A family was on an outing in a car; the father was driving the car, the mother sat next to him, the two children were in the back. The children got hungry and were given a banana. Suddenly one of them said: "Mama, my banana bit me!" At first the parents didn't pay any attention, but when they turned around a little later, the child was lying there unconscious. They raced to a hospital, but too late; the child died. The physician told them that there had been similar accidents involving poisonous snakes in bananas (e.g., KU 6192, 124). Earlier, in 1973, the same story had spread like an epidemic in various parts of Sweden. The background to the story is that, earlier on, poisonous insects and spiders were in fact found in banana shipments. However, there are no documented cases of snakes or similar animals inside individual bananas. Primarily mothers and other persons responsible for the care of children, as in day-care centers, have told and believed the story about the snake in the banana. Advice circulated regarding safety precautions one should take: for instance, one should cut the banana in two or cut off the two ends before eating it.

A similar legend reported from the United States tells about a housewife who was taken to a hospital after being bitten on the hand by a snake. She had been shopping at a department store and picked up a double-folded blanket, and the snake was lying inside the fold. The blanket had been imported from Hong Kong (Mullen, 1970). Here too the ethnocentric character of the story is obvious.

A legend that spread like wildfire in 1975 could be entitled "Spider Boil." In September 1975, this was reported by a female informant in Täby (KU 6192, 114):

> A young girl told me this story, and she insists that it is true. A girl was on vacation in Gambia, and when she came home she had a boil on her cheek. She went to see a physician, but he didn't do anything and said that it would have to open by itself. The boil grew and grew, and finally she went to another physician but he gave her the same advice. The boil got even bigger, and one night when she was in bed she felt it start to open. She got up and turned on the light to look in a mirror. Out of the boil a whole mess of small spiders were crawling all over her cheek. The girl is now in a mental hospital.

In other variants, Mallorca, the Canary Islands, Italy, or Rumania is named as the vacation spot where the Swedish tourist got the boil. In all variants the tourist is always a woman, the boil appears on the cheek, and she goes insane when the boil opens. The background might be found in an article published in *Dagens Nyheter* on 22 January 1976 about Swedish tourists to Gambia, Kenya, and Tanzania who were treated at a hospital for boils infested with larvae they apparently picked up while sunbathing on the beach. In oral tradition the story has been stylized into a much more dramatic narrative than the original report. In comparison to the legend about the snake in the banana, the story about the spiders in the boil has a far more realistic basis. But both legends function as warnings about dangers associated with foreign countries to the south.

Sociocentric Legends

The norms of the cultural group with which we identify not only shape our views about people and events in foreign societies, we likewise respond to subcultures in our own society with stereotypes and value judgments that give rise to legends about those groups. These so-called sociocentric legends have always been part of oral tradition. For instance, in nineteenth-century rural Sweden there were stories about human sacrifice and other horrifying practices among Freemasons. The middle class background of the Freemasons and their secret ceremonies made them seem a frightening, dangerous organization in the eyes of the rural population (Bergstrand, 1956). In contemporary society most sociocentric legends describe subcultures that are in conflict with the norms of mainstream culture, such as hot-rodders (*raggare*) and hippies. A legend that appeared in various places in Sweden for a number of years is "The Hot-Rodder and the Bicycle Chain." It tells about a woman driving a car, usually on her way home and late at night, who is attacked by some young toughs. She stops at a traffic light when a hot rod drives up. One of the youths strikes her car with a chain he has wound around his hand. When the light changes to green, the woman pushes her gas pedal to the floor and gets away. At home she makes a horrible discovery. The youth's chain got stuck on the car and on the other end hang a couple of torn-off, bloody fingers.

These are the main elements of the legend; other details vary considerably. Variously the chain may be stuck in the side window, on the luggagge rack, or on the back fender. The number of torn-off fingers ranges from one to four; sometimes they are inside a glove stuck to the end of the chain. Some of the variants have a continuation: the woman (or her husband) alerts the police, and the police in turn notify the hospitals in the area. In one of them the authorities find a young man who has lost some of his fingers.

In a number of instances the story was reported as fact by the Swedish press. The following headlines could be read in *Blekinge Läns Tidning* on 23 March 1973: "Hot-rodder drove after woman in car and threw a chain that got stuck in luggage rack. Gruesome discovery at home: Three torn-off fingers lying on the roof." The next day the whole thing was gleefully denied by the local competition, *Sydöstra Sveriges Dagblad*, informing their readers that the story had circulated as early as 1960. The date correlates with the first appearance of the "long-haired" car gangs in Sweden; previously, motorized youth gangs had consisted of "leather-jacket" motorcyclists. Press reports from 1959 and the following years had much to say about trouble with the car gangs: reportedly they push other drivers against the curb; they invade a town for a car meet and have a run-in with the police; a youth goes berserk swinging a bicycle chain; car gangs from different towns fight each other with knuckle-rings, lead pipes, and bicycle chains. Press reports about youth gang violence must have fueled latent fears in other social groups and stimulated the dissemination of legends. Some people, especially the young, discounted them as mere horror stories. But others took them as confirmation of their suspicions about hot-rodders attacking ordinary folk. What fascinated listeners more than anything else was the shocking conclusion about the torn-off fingers. It is as explicitly moralizing as the morality tales of old, permitting at the same time dismay and feelings of secret satisfaction that the violence this time fell back on the perpetrator. The story emphasizes that the woman is law-abiding: she waits until the light changes before she makes her getaway.

"The Hot-Rodder and the Bicycle Chain" is a Swedish oicotype of a modern folk legend that has been widely disseminated throughout the Western world.

In Denmark it has been reported in roughly the same form as in Sweden (KU 6192, 64). In England the story was reported in several places in 1961–62 (Sanderson 1969, 250).

Another variant documented in England (at a considerably later date) tells about a man who stops to pick up a hitchhiker by the side of the road. But when he sees several more people rise out of the ditch, he quickly drives off. Arriving home he discovers a bicycle chain dangling from the bumper and at the other end three torn-off fingers (KU 5549, 1–2). The same version was reported in Canada in 1971 (KU 5533, 1–2). An article in the *Stuttgarter Zeitung* ("Die schreckliche Moritat von der toten Hand," dated 1 October 1971, sent to the author by Hermann Bausinger) shows that the hitchhiker version had spread to West Germany the same year. The German version of this legend is still alive, if we are to judge from an article in *Expressen* dated 15 February 1976. A motor columnist mentions a traffic accident in which a twenty-one-year-old man died after being trapped in a car wreck along a major highway for a long time because no one would stop and come to his aid. The columnist writes that he, too, would not have dared to stop "because it might be a trap. I might be ambushed, beaten, robbed." As an example, he then cites the legend discussed here, and concludes:

> This is an absolutely true story. Ever since the BMW driver himself told me about it, I have not stopped along the highway unless absolutely necessary. I drive with my trunk and car doors locked from the inside. Well, I leave the driver's door open but lock it before I talk to anyone I don't know.

There could hardly be a more striking example of the effect of modern legends on a credulous listener. It demonstrates how certain sociocentric legends can widen the abyss between different groups in society.

Drug abuse among teenagers is mirrored in a number of modern folk legends. One legend well known in the United States (e.g., Hall 1973, 158, 165) and which circulated in Helsinki in the autumn of 1971 (Nyman 1974, 70–73) is "The Grilled Baby." It is one of many horror stories about what can happen if one takes LSD. A young couple has asked a hippie to babysit their infant, and when they return they find the babysitter high on LSD and the child grilled in the oven.

In Sweden, drug abuse has contributed to a legend which in its earliest form described white slavery. I heard the legend the first time from a friend of my sister-in-law, and the friend got very upset when I expressed doubt about the truth of the story. Her aunt and two other ladies had gotten on the subway to go visit a fourth lady and play bridge. There were a lot of people on the train, so one of the ladies had to sit separate from her friends. When the two others got up to get off the train they found that their friend had collapsed on her seat. She appeared to be drugged, almost unconscious. They went up to her and shook her. Then a stranger, a man sitting next to her, said that they didn't need to worry. She was traveling with him and had gotten ill, but he was going to take care of her. "But she isn't traveling with you," the two women protested. Just then the train stopped and the man disappeared. The two ladies got their friend to a hospital where it was discovered that she had been given an injection in the thigh.

In this version there is no indication why the stranger anaesthetizes the woman. The oldest recorded versions of the story—dated from the 1930s and localized in the Paris Metro—all give the same explanation: the woman has run into a white slave trader and will be taken to some brothel abroad. White slavery was a concept already known in Sweden at the beginning of this century. An old woman informant in Skåne said that in 1916 she answered a newspaper advertisement for household help, but her father would not let her take the job—he was afraid she might fall prey to white slavers (KU 5256, 4). But today when the legend is told about someone traveling on the subway in Stockholm there is another explanation. The injection contains narcotics and is designed to make the women drug dependent, to make her into an addict. Swedish mass media have reported several times about teenage drug users hanging out at subway stations in central Stockholm. In other words, we find that a real social problem reactivates a narrative that is at least forty years old (Klintberg, 1976).

Legends about white slavery have for many years been widespread in France. Most often they tell about a young girl disappearing from the changing room of a boutique. Afterwards it is discovered that she has been anaesthetized and abducted through a trapdoor in the floor of the changing room. In 1969, Orléans was so rife with rumors that several boutique owners were threatened with lynching—in spite of the fact that the chief of police made a public announcement that no young woman had been reported missing. The sociologist Edgar Morin has shown that these events can be connected to the fact that the boutique owners were all Jews: the rumors served to activate a latent antisemitism (Morin, 1971).

Not surprisingly, the above-mentioned stories are told predominantly among women of all ages. The legends give expression to female fears. Without being literally true they nevertheless have a real basis: there is much violence against women in many forms, and it is a fact that young women disappear and end up as drug addicts and prostitutes. The stories are cautionary tales teaching that one should be on guard and avoid strangers and unfamiliar places. They also show that sociocentric and ethnocentric legends tend to go hand in hand: the subway legend mirrors as much the fear of criminal youths as of suspicious foreigners.

Entertainment Legends in the Press

One day in March 1973, this headline appeared in *Bergens Arbeiderblad*: "Terrible Revenge on Lover." The article was about a cement-truck driver in

Bergen. One day this man was passing by his house when he happened to see his best friend's car, a Volkswagen with a sunroof, parked outside. The man stopped the truck to go inside and say hello to his friend. Then he heard sounds coming from the bedroom that revealed that his wife and friend were having sex. He quietly went out again, backed the cement truck up to his friend's car, pushed back the sunroof, and filled the Volkswagen with cement. When the lover came out later, the cement had already set.

The story was sent over the Norwegian Wire Service, and the next day it was repeated by several dailies in Norway. During the following days the story was carried by papers in neighboring Scandinavian countries; by the end of the week it had traveled all the way to the *Daily Nation* in Nairobi. But by that time it had already been debunked in Norway. The narrative is a migratory legend (Kvideland, 1973). In 1960, the Associated Press disseminated the story all over the United States: the event was supposed to have happened in Denver, Colorado. An older version had already been recorded in the U.S. in the 1920s. In that variant the husband avenges himself by dumping the contents of a garbage truck into his friend's Stutz Bearcat (Smart, 1970, 7).

Clearly the story has a more humorous tone than many of the modern legends we have looked at above. It is probably right to say that the newspapers picked up the item because it was a "good story." But even if its function is primarily entertainment, the story nevertheless underscores that marital infidelity is in fact an infraction against accepted norms. Our sympathy lies with the cuckolded husband; he is morally entitled to his revenge. The fascination of the story lies also in the analogy between the bedroom scene and the nature of the revenge.

Obviously the cement-truck story was told most frequently right after it appeared in the press. Later, too, it stayed alive in tradition, but some of the external details were replaced by more local ones. The folklore collector H. Anstrin sent me the following variant from Östergötland in the summer of 1975 (KU 6192, 109):

This happened last winter at the gas station in Malexander. There were three young men in addition to the owner of the gas station (who is fifty-five years old) and another customer of the same age. The latter two I know well. Just as I came in to buy the evening paper, I heard the young men tell the conclusion of a story. I heard the words "the whole car was filled with cement." Since I had heard the story myself and seemed to remember having read in Expressen something about a VW filled with cement, I got interested. I asked the older customer who was standing to one side what they were talking about. One of the youths heard my question and began telling the story:
"This was about a rural mailman in Mjölby. He screwed with a married woman some place. It wasn't the first time, so her husband was on to them. He was a truck driver and was on his way to a building site with a load of cement. But now he drove up to the mailman's car and emptied the whole load of cement through the roof into the car."

"What make of a car was it?" I asked.

"It was a VW with a sunroof."

To see how they would react I told them that I had read a story just like it in *Expressen*. But they said that they had never heard it before. They emphatically pointed out that the story was true. They also said that the driver was a "tough devil." The gas station owner and the other customer also believed the story.

One press legend that has aroused more folkloristic interest than most is the story about the stolen mother-in-law (Dégh, 1968b; Bregenhøj 1969; Sanderson 1969, 251f.; Kvideland 1973, 9ff.). To this day the story is widespread both in Europe and the U.S. The earliest documentation in print is apparently the report of a Danish journalist in *Politikken* in 1944. When Paris was threatened by the Germans in 1940, the journalist fled, together with a Swede who had been living in Paris, the latter's French wife, and his mother-in-law—all in the Swede's car. On the luggage rack they had secured a mahogany chest containing the family silver. During the trip the mother-in-law died, and they decided to put the body into the mahogony chest. But the next morning the box was gone; somebody had stolen it during the night. Because they weren't able to prove that the mother-in-law was dead, the family could not claim their inheritance.

The existing variants of this oldest version are few in number and consistently have short-story form. By the time the legend resurfaced in oral tradition during the 1960s, its content reflected the increase in foreign tourism during this period of steep economic growth. The Swedish variants describe a Swedish family on vacation in Spain or Italy. Grandmother, who sits in the back seat, dies in the heat and they wrap her in a tarp and put her on top of the luggage rack. Later the family leaves the car in order to report the death, and in the meantime the car is stolen—along with Grandmother. The legend has been interpreted by Alan Dundes (Dundes, 1971, 33ff.) as an expression of wishful thinking in modern Western society, where families have no place for grandparents. Most likely the story owes its popularity to the fact that the macabre content appeals to the popular imagination.

In April 1966 several Swedish newspapers reported an episode that supposedly happened at a supermarket in northwest Skåne. A woman had stolen a frozen chicken and hidden it under her hat. When she went through the checkout she passed out from the cold, and the chicken rolled out from under her hat. The same story was repeated several times in the press, but by then the shoplifter was a man. According to the reports the thievery was supposed to have happened in Halmstad (1968), Säffle (1973), and Eskiltuna (1974). In oral tradition the story has been located in many Swedish towns and is also known outside Sweden.

A sort of forerunner of the story was published in the Swedish edition of *Readers' Digest, Det Bästa,* in 1964:

The other day a supervisor in a convenience store saw a man lift up his hat, put a chicken on top of his head and replace the hat. He thought he was seeing things, but it turned out he was right when he later, in the presence of the store manager, asked the man to take off his hat.

In this instance the discovery of the theft is rather trivial, and this version is not repeated in any later recording. Not until the motif of the shoplifter passing out at the checkout was added did the legend become sufficiently dramatic to live on in oral tradition (Ohlsson, 1974).

A fantastic photograph appeared on the last page of *Expressen* on 15 September 1975—that of an elephant sitting on a Volkswagen at the crossing of Valhalla Street and Sture Street in Stockholm. The caption, however, makes it clear that the picture was arranged by the Scott Circus to call attention to their arrival in town. But the event which, in Stockholm, is staged as an advertising coup, exists in the U.S. as a modern legend. An ethnology student in Stockholm told me the story as follows:

> I heard from American friends about a circus that had elephants and was parading through a town. One of the elephants was trained to sit on a red stool at a given signal from a whistle. Suddenly that kind of a whistle was heard in the traffic noise. The elephant saw a red VW and sat on it—among all the things around it looked most like a stool. (KU 6192, 113)

This version is only one of several stories about an elephant sitting on a VW, stories that have circulated since the 1950s and found their way into the papers. It seems that the entertainment value of the story is the primary reason for its dissemination. The contrast between the huge elephant and the small VW is comical in itself and has been utilized in other folklore genres as well. When the so-called elephant jokes became a craze in the entire Western world in 1963–64, the following was one of the most popular: "How do you get four elephants into a VW?—Two in front and two in back" (Klintberg, 1971, 128f.).

Another example for a typical newspaper legend is the story about a Swiss couple whose dog is cooked when a waiter misunderstands their request that he give the animal something to eat. The story raced through the world press like wildfire during the summer of 1971. Apparently that was enough for it to take root in oral tradition—in Sweden it is often told spontaneously when one asks about contemporary folk legends.

Horror Stories among Young People

The legends presented so far do not belong to any given age group but can be heard among adults as well as among teenagers. But there are certain kinds of legends which circulate only within certain age groups. Perhaps the best example is the internationally known horror stories told among teenagers. They have commanded considerable attention among American folklorists (e.g., Parochetti, 1965; Barnes, 1966; Roemer, 1971; Thigpen, 1971). Typically they are told at teenage gatherings. In American colleges men and women usually live in separate dormitories, and they become members of fraternities and sororities by undergoing certain ceremonies. These often become the stage for bloodcurdling stories about crazed murderers or pranks that end tragically. Most of these stories have never taken hold in Sweden because the corresponding institutions do not exist there. This is true, for instance, of legends about fraternity initiation rituals that end in the novice being literally scared to death (Baughman, 1945b; Dorson 1959, 258f.). Other legends, such as those based on American dating practices, have reached many other countries, including Sweden. One of the most popular horror stories among Swedish youth in recent years is the one about "The Boyfriend's Death." The following is a variant told in May 1975 by a ninth-grade girl at Gylle School in Borlange (KU 5715, 155–56):

> I've heard a story about a boy and a girl. It's supposed to be true. This happened in Germany, they were out driving. In the middle of the woods they ran out of gas, and he took off looking for some gas. Before he left he told her not to open the car for anyone. As she was sitting there in the car, she heard a bulletin about a madman on the radio. He had escaped from an asylum close by. She sat there waiting for a long time. Suddenly she heard scraping sounds at the back of the car. It got quiet for a while but then she heard a rhythmic thumping on the car roof. Just then she saw a police car with its sirens going. The policemen got out. They shouted to her through a megaphone that she should get out of the car and walk over to them. But under no circumstances must she turn around. She opened the door and climbed out while the thumping on the roof continued. But when she had gotten a little ways away from the car, she did what she wasn't supposed to. She turned around, and there on top of the car she saw the madman. Between his hands he held the head of her boyfriend which he kept banging down on the roof. I heard this story the first time from a buddy, but I've heard it many times since then. It doesn't matter where they are from, when they say that they're going to tell something awful, you always get this story. I don't think it is so awful, but that's only because I've heard it so many times. When I heard it the first time, I thought it was the worst story I'd ever heard, and everybody insists that it is true.

This horror story was largely unknown in Sweden in the early 1970s. The version above is the most common, but beginning in 1975 the story would often contain a special introductory motif. A Swedish girl had a German (English, Turkish) pen pal who suddenly stopped writing. There was no news for a couple of years. Then came a letter from the friend saying that she had been confined to a mental hospital. She had suffered shock when she had been driving with her boyfriend and he was murdered by a madman. This introduction strengthens the believability of the story even further, especially when the storyteller hints that the pen pal is an acquaintance of his/hers.

In the United States, "The Boyfriend's Death" was collected as early as 1964, and by the end of the 1960s it was one of the most popular horror stories (Dégh, 1968). The American version differs in a number of respects from the Swedish. The girl sitting in the car falls asleep and when she wakes up she hears a weak scraping sound on the roof which returns intermittently during the night. When the police car eventually comes and the girl follows the instructions to leave the car, she discovers the horrible truth: she sees the dead boyfriend hanging from a tree above the car. He has become a victim of the madman. Now and then his feet reached the roof of the car, and this is what she heard all night.

A legend that has much in common with "The Boyfriend's Death" and which also almost certainly reached Sweden from the United States is the one called "The Hook." It has been well known among U.S. college youths since the middle of the 1950s (Dégh, 1968a). In this instance too a boy and a girl have gone for a drive. They have parked the car in an out-of-the-way place and are sitting there with their arms around each other when the music suddenly breaks off for an announcement: a sex offender has escaped from a nearby mental hospital. He can be recognized by his missing right hand which has been replaced by an iron hook. The girl gets scared and asks the boy to drive home. Reluctantly the boy does what she asks and takes off with a flying start. When they eventually stop and get out of the car, there is an iron hook hanging from one of the door handles. From the American college circuit have come reports that boys have told the legend to girls when they are out driving and parking some place. The idea is to make the girl get scared so that the boy can put his arm around her for protection. The folklorists who have commented on the legend agree that there are strong sexual overtones (Dégh, 1971, 65–66; Dundes 1971, 29ff.). It also has a striking resemblance to "The Hot-Rodder and the Bicycle Chain." Both describe a violent attack upon someone in a car. The driver takes off suddenly and doesn't notice until later that he/she has accidentally torn off the attacker's hand. The macabre proof is the metal item stuck on the car. It is entirely possible that the horror story about the hot-rodder and the chain was modeled on the legend about the iron hook. On the other hand, maiming is a common motif in contemporary legends and can easily appear independently.

One of the most common legends in the U.S. and in Sweden, appearing as early as the 1920s, has been entitled "The Cadaver Arm" (Baughman, 1945a; KU 5965, 5978, 6084). Some buddies of a girl (often a nurse or a medical student) get irritated at her professed self-confidence and decide to scare her. They put the arm of a corpse in her bed and wait outside to see her reaction. The girl enters her room and locks the door, but much to their disappointment the friends outside hear nothing. Finally they look in. There sits the girl in her bed, gnawing on the arm. She had gone mad from shock. The story is reminiscent of legends about someone scared to death in an initiation ceremony. In either instance the story functions as a cautionary tale.

In the majority of cases, it is difficult to prove that particular modern legends are told under specific circumstances. In principle they are transmitted whenever and wherever people congregate. But horror stories told among adolescents are different in this regard. They constitute a form of collective narrative that belongs to the late-night hour. Camping, parties, overnight stays at the summer cottage are occasions named by informants for telling horror stories. Horror stories alternate with ghost stories. The intended effect of both types is to scare the listeners.

Legends about the Supernatural

In traditional rural society a large proportion of folk legends dealt with the supernatural—trolls, nature sprites, the walking dead, witches, and magicians. The legends mirrored a world view in which the belief in nature beings and magic was still very much alive. In comparison to this older legend tradition, stories about the supernatural are relatively rare in contemporary tradition. But that is only to be expected—most people in Scandinavia today harbor a pronounced skepticism toward anything having to do with the supernatural.

Stories about ghosts and the dead are the most viable. Belief in ghosts has survived the belief in witches and nature beings. Today we talk about ghost stories as a separate genre that is particularly popular among adolescents. Legends about the walking dead found in traditional rural society were based upon the Christian belief in the continued existence of the human soul after death, and their primary function was to inculcate certain social norms. Today ghost stories survive in spite of the fact that they are not supported by the modern world view; their function seems to be primarily to entertain. They are rooted in fright and a timeless fascination with the phenomenon of death.

Among the many legends about the walking dead probably none is as widespread as "The Vanishing Hitchhiker." Since first coming to the attention of folklorists in the 1940s (Beardsley and Hankey, 1942, 1943), it has been the subject of dozens of dissertations and papers. The earliest study divides the recorded texts into four groups (Beardsley and Hankey, 1942, 306–307). Version A is the most widely known. It describes a motorist who picks up a young female hitchhiker. She gets into the back of the car and he drives her to the address she gives as her home. But when he gets there and turns around, she is gone. Shaken by this, he rings the bell at the house and informs the person who comes to the door about his experience. He finds out that a girl identical with the hitchhiker used to live in the house, but that she died at precisely the spot where he gave her a lift. In version B the hitchhiker—who is not always a young girl—prophesies something that later happens. In version C the young girl complains that she is cold and borrows a coat from the man who is driving. They separate without her leaving the coat, and when he comes to her house the next day, he finds out that she died several years earlier. The coat is found draped over her gravestone. In version D the vanishing hitchhiker is identified with a supernatural being from local folk-belief.

It is doubtful that we can postulate a common origin for the stories known collectively as "The Vanishing Hitchhiker." What we can determine is that they share a motif that appears practically throughout the world. Version A (which, like version B, was probably developed in the U.S.) is the best known. The mass media have contributed substantially to its dissemination. In the 1960s, for instance, it was spread in comic strip form in a volume entitled "Ghosts" in the international series *Illustrated Classics* (which was translated into various languages). In the Swedish magazine *Hemmets Journal* (no. 30, 1974) the story is reported as fact, with the story citing an English source and including a photograph of the dead hitchhiker as evidence.

What makes this legend especially interesting is that the simple and suggestive plot structure has resurfaced in recent years in a number of new contexts. In June 1975 I heard the Norwegian folklorist Reimund Kvideland tell the following version (KU 6192, 100):

> There were two women out driving a car. Along the road they saw a young girl who was hitchhiking. These women never picked up hitchhikers, but the girl looked unusually sweet and friendly, and on a sudden impulse they stopped and took her along. She sat in the back and they drove for a while in silence. Suddenly the girl bent forward to the other two in the front seat and said: "Jesus is coming soon." The two women turned around and found the back seat empty.
>
> This event made a deep impression on the two women, and in the version told to me by an aunt, a teacher in her fifties, it is emphasized that the women were religious. The story became very popular and was told widely in Norway during the summer of 1973. In religious circles in Norway it was interpreted as a sign that the end of time was near, and it was taken as a true story, as a religious message from heaven.

A similar version was told to me at about the same time by a Danish museum lecturer, a woman from southern Jutland. A married couple from her area picked up a hitchhiker, a barefoot youth, bearded, long-haired, with a friendly face, obviously a hippie. After driving for a while in silence, he suddenly asked: "Do you know Jesus?" They answered yes, a little uneasy. "That's good," said the young man, "because Jesus, that's me." When they turned around to look at him, the back seat was empty. They were quite shaken by their experience and couldn't resist telling about it when they came to a gas station. The man filling their tank listened to their story and then said: "You are the tenth family today to come and tell me the same thing" (KU 6192, 103).

This variant of "The Vanishing Hitchhiker" also seems to have originated in the U.S. To judge by the three variants published so far, the story began circulating in 1972 (Mathais, Lynch, and Miller; 1972; cf. Wilson, 1975a, 89). The appearance of the legend coincides with the development of the so-called Jesus People, a Christian revivalist movement in Western youth culture. We can assume that the spread of the legend is connected with that movement, whose members caused attention by taking directly to the streets with their message.

Among more recent variations on the theme we can mention a story about a driver who identifies the hitchhiker as a Martian. In 1971 the legend appeared in Finland, where it spread quickly (Nyman, 1974, 64ff.). In 1975 southern German newspapers reported a lady dressed in black who was picked up by several drivers and suddenly disappeared.

There exist also, side by side with stories about one's own or one's acquaintances' inexplicable experiences, more or less stereotyped legends about UFOs (Unidentified Flying Objects) and parapsychological occurrences. They are not as widely spread as ethnocentric or sociocentric legends. The reason for this is that their content contradicts the world view of the majority of people today. One might almost call it a sectarian legend tradition in the case of, for example, narratives circulating in newsletters of UFO or para-psychology enthusiasts, or "counterculture" stories told among the young in protest against the establishment. UFO stories reveal the idea of the Messiah in new form: the extraterrestrial visitors represent a culture that is more highly developed than our own and will save the earth from disaster (cf. Dégh, 1971, 59). The Norwegian folklorist Velle Espeland reported the following episode from his fieldwork in Rogaland in 1969–70 (KU 6192, 102):

> One evening I was sitting and talking with some of my informants to get to know them better. It turned out that two brothers, each living on his own farm, were very interested in UFOs and that kind of thing. One of them was a member in a UFO club and subscribed to a number of Danish UFO journals. The other one, who told this story, was not interested in written materials. The conversation turned to the alleged official policy of suppressing all information about UFOs; for one reason or another the authorities did not want this kind of news to reach the public. A spaceship had landed outside Washington and an extraterrestrial being had come into the city and appeared before the Senate. There he had warned the senators not to continue with atomic testing because it upset the whole balance of the cosmos. Then he left and disappeared into the spaceship. The Senate had agreed that no one was to talk about what had happened under any circumstances. He told this in all seriousness, and I remember that his brother sat there nodding approval, so quite clearly both of them took the story at face value.

Folk Belief and Legend

NORDIC FOLK BELIEF RESEARCH

Magne Velure

Evolutionism, Devolutionism, and the Historical Approach

For much of its early history, Nordic folk belief research echoed international studies of the history of religion and continental *Volkskunde*. Evolutionist theory was dominant, and Scandinavian scholars joined in the dance around this doctrine, finding in their own cultural areas evidence that fit the paradigm. By the 1860s, Gunnar Hyltén-Cavallius, for example, had isolated the main principles of folk belief research:

1. Contemporary "customs" and notions about supranormal beings were regarded as survivals from the religious milieux of earlier times.

2. The tradition process was presumed to be destructive: cultural phenomena were believed to have been richer, both qualitatively and quantitatively, at an earlier period in history. Contemporary tradition was a priori fragmentary.

Although nearly everyone accepted these two principles, disagreement arose concerning the source of belief phenomena. In Scandinavia the most influential theory of origins was developed by Wilhelm Mannhardt, who asserted that primitive fertility cults were the basis of religious ideas and behavior. N. E. Hammarstedt (1923), Hilding Celander (1925), and Martin Persson Nilsson (1921) in Sweden, Nils Lid (1928) in Norway, Gunnar Landtman (1922), Gabriel Nikander (1916), and A. V. Rantaslo (1919–25) in Finland, and Hans Ellekilde (1938) in Denmark all adopted this theory, tracing fragmentary nineteenth century materials back to origins in fertility cults in an indeterminate past. The other major school—inspired by Herbert Spencer's manistic theory and developed in Denmark by H. F. Feilberg, and in Finland by Kaarle Krohn and Uno Harva—perceived ancestor and death cults as the origin of all religious activity.

Both schools employed comparative methods. On the basis of linguistic similarities and formal analogies, survival theorists isolated details to fit a

---

Originally published in *Studia Fennica*, 1983.

developmental scheme constructed in advance. Phenomena were detached from environmental and social contexts. Since cultural elements were by definition survivals, their contemporary use and context were disregarded: the overriding aim was reconstruction of primordial origins.

A Finnish variant of the comparative approach, the historic-geographical method, was developed by Julius and Kaarle Krohn in studies of *Kalevala* and of *Märchen*. At the time, the historic-geographic method achieved less prominence in the study of folk belief than the (d)evolutionist approach, even though Uno Harva, for example, adapted it in his doctoral dissertation, "Die Wassergottheiten der finnisch-ugrischen Völker" (*The Water Divinities of the Finnic-Ugric Peoples,* Holmberg [Harva], 1913). This method plays an important role, however, in several recent Nordic research projects on folk belief (see Pentikäinen 1968a; Wall, 1977, 1979).

Inherent in historic-genetic theories is the presupposition that to understand cultural phenomena one must find their origin. (D)evolutionists forget to ask, "How and why do survivals survive?" (Marett, 1920, 1). *Continuity* is assumed to be self-evident. Considering the problem of source materials over a few hundred years old, we realize how glibly survival theorists ignore the problem of continuity of tradition over several thousand years (see Bausinger, 1969, 17ff.).

A third characteristic of the (d)evolutionist approach is that the most important source material is *behavior* (folk customs), not concepts and ideas of the supranormal. The classic model assumes that religious rites degenerate through time and often end up as jests or games. But this is a problematic assumption, to say the least. We can understand Åke Campbell's lament:

> But is there then no ancient, original tradition of teasing, pranks and games? Are there no creative forms in ancient times expressing the human predelection for play and mockery? Where is that tradition? Have the forms of our jests, tricks and mocking games flowed from the solemn rites of a solemn past? Are play and jest merely symptoms of degeneration? (1925, 42)

Origin versus Function

Until forty or fifty years ago, survival theory dominated folk belief research, and serious conflict arose at the first criticism of this approach. In Scandinavia, the opposition to Mannhardt's doctrines was led by two scholars: Carl Wilhelm von Sydow and Albert Eskeröd. Von Sydow introduced the concept of genre analysis and stressed that tradition materials comprise different categories having different value as evidence for research of folk belief. Second, von Sydow attacked the devolutionistic model. Third, he emphasized that play and jesting are perpetual factors in human culture, just as primordial as magic and religious cults. Put another way, *homo ludens* is not necessarily a degenerate *homo religiosus* (1948).

Albert Eskeröd further developed von Sydow's ideas. But above all, Eskeröd deserves notice as the first scholar to apply Malinowski's and Radcliffe-Brown's functional theories to Scandinavian material. In his dissertation, "Årets äring" (The Year's Harvest, 1947), Eskeröd analyzed an extensive body of concepts and customs associated with everyday work in the community. One of his primary goals was to disprove the theories of Mannhardt, of the English anthropologist James Frazer, and of their followers. Like von Sydow, he wished to replace survivalist theories with psychological and functional analysis of tradition. However, Eskeröd attacked the primitive form of associational psychology employed by both Frazer and von Sydow, arguing that using associations based on similarity and psychical contact to analyze supranormal concepts only partially explains *how* people think; it says nothing about *why* people think as they do. Eskeröd introduces the term *interessedominans* (dominant interest) to the psychological explanations of people's notions about supranormal contexts:

> When ideas about supranormal relations and forces arise this is not due [to the mind's] associating isolated observations in agreement with the laws of similarity and physical contact. Rather, questions fill the mind—dominant interests, in other words, constitute the mirrors in which the external world is observed or, more concretely, through which observations are interpreted and acquire meaning. (1947, 71)

Eskeröd's bold thesis was immediately challenged. K. Rob. V. Wikman (1947) claimed that Eskeröd's analysis reflected a reductionist attitude toward folk belief. He supported Eskeröd's explaining custom and belief from the standpoint of the technology and context of everyday work; however, he claimed that functional analysis is limited by the period the material represents, and by the regional and social boundaries of the material. Wikman was therefore critical of the notion that functional analysis on the basis of contemporary material can be transferred to the study of cultural history.

Wikman's point illustrates a basic difference between Eskeröd and other researchers. Survival theorists assume that present-day tradition represents a radical change from earlier times and that this change has been negative. Eskeröd, on the other hand, postulates a continuity in beliefs and customs to justify the use of contemporary material to explain history.

This is a fundamental objection to Eskeröd's work. Even though he is critical of speculations about the origin of folk belief, he proposes a universal theory of origin based on psychological factors such as dominant interest and stress (1947, 70; 1964). Doubtless stress, fear, anger, and other emotions arise when people come in contact with the supranormal. While such psychological factors can tell us something about the actualization of a tradition complex, however, they say nothing about its origin. An explanatory model that reduces culturally contingent phenomena to the level of individual emotion is as speculative as evolution models (Evans-Pritchard, 1965, 43–47; Hultkrantz, 1973, 101–12; Keesing and Keesing, 1971, 387–91).

In hindsight, Eskeröd should have avoided entering the discussion on the premises of evolutionism. He should have refrained from claiming that functional analysis explains origin. The useful aspect of his work—regarding contact between people and the supranormal as part of the social and cultural context—has not had the effect on subsequent research it deserved. But one result is clear: the debate of the 1940s ended the use of nineteenth- and twentieth-century descriptions of customs as a basis for the study of folk belief.

Psychology of Tradition, Genre Analysis, and Functional Analysis

The next major breakthrough in folk belief research came with Lauri Honko's "Geisterglaube in Ingermanland" (Spirit Belief in Ingria, 1962), which employed psychology of tradition, genre analysis, and functional analysis. His goal was to show how and why traditions of the supranormal are an integral part of daily life. Honko asked many questions about the tradition material, questions not previously posed in Honko's systematic way: What is the social context of beliefs and narratives about supranormal beings and forces? How is a concept or rite actualized, and why? Who experiences contact with the supranormal, and how? What kinds of consequences does the concrete actualizing have for the person or persons involved? What problems are solved and what needs are satisfied through belief in the supranormal? What are the functional alternatives to actualization of the supranormal? (Honko, 1962, 150–58; 1965, 168).

Honko uses genre analysis as a major part of his functional analysis, extending the efforts of von Sydow, Granberg, and Eskeröd. He deftly avoids the problem of whether genres are "real" by defining them as ideal types:

> The primary function of the ideal type is not the most exact description of reality; rather it provides an opportunity for understanding reality better. This determines the instrumental value of the ideal type, which is the main criterion of its usefulness. (1968, 61)

Today, functional analysis—which I consider Honko's primary contribution—has receded into the background: There is relatively little research being done in the same vein. This is in part because, by and large, folk belief material in our archives does not yield to the questions of the type posed by Honko. But an equally important reason is that in Scandinavia research has largely been text-oriented. As a result, many scholars have problems when they attempt to stir beyond "the textual context" (Bausinger, 1980, 274).

Honko's revival of the problems of genre has stimulated much greater response than his use of functional analysis. Genre analysis is central to folkloristic research and has been the focus of lively debate. We must remember that the basis for von Sydow's "flora" of genres was archive material, collected in atypical narrative situations. It is possible that this factor does not influence stereotyped epic genres to any decisive degree, but I would suggest that existing genre systems contain categories that should be called archive genres, which are not found in natural narrative situations.

As an instrument for source criticism of archive material, genre analysis is invaluable. But existing genre systems become problematic when applied to narrative situations. Consider, for example, the conversation Linda Dégh reports in "Legend and Belief" (1971): any attempt to classify bits of the larger communicative whole as various epic and non-epic genres becomes meaningless. There are more important factors than genre analysis to consider when interpreting spontaneous, direct communication. To date no one has managed to adapt genre analysis to the study of narrative situations where supranormal beliefs are verbalized as stories, arguments, protests, or hints. Therefore genre analysis in its existing form remains primarily a tool to be used with archive material. On the other hand, we might turn the problem around and ask whether genre analysis can contribute to the study of concrete actualizations where sentiments and attitudes toward the supranormal are integrated in a greater communicative whole.

There has been relatively little methodological innovation in Scandinavian folk belief research since "Geisterglaube." Predictably, the most important contributions have come from the group around Lauri Honko, notably Juha Pentikäinen and Anna-Leena Siikala. In *The Nordic Dead Child Tradition* (1968), Pentikäinen primarily uses the historical-geographical approach of functional analysis. Siikala combines functional analysis with process analysis in a work on Siberian shamanism (1978). Process analysis should be useful for the study of other types of situations in which supranormal beliefs, narratives, and events are actualized.

In Sweden, Orvar Löfgren and Jonas Frykman have used folk belief material to discuss social relations (Löfgren, 1975; Frykman, 1977). In reality both assume a reductionist stance; they are not interested in folk belief as a system, but as it mirrors social realities. They represent a classic anthropological attitude toward religious phenomena (compare Hultkrantz, 1977). Also of note is Jan Wall's study of theft-milking, in which he depends heavily on the historic-geographic method (1977, 1979).

Folk Belief in Contemporary Society

Most scholars publishing folk belief research employ historical material or material from agrarian settings. In relation to the rest of folklore research—which shows an increasing interest in urban and postindustrial phenomena—it is striking that the study of the supranormal is conducted largely with historical material.

It would be unjust to claim that there is no research concerning folk belief in our urbanized environment. Several university departments are conducting fieldwork on this topic. But the work published to date is largely preliminary folk belief research grounded in contemporary concepts (see Klintberg, 1976a; Kvideland, 1976, 1980; Rørbye, 1978a; Virtanen 1976, 1980). To my knowledge, no work has yet been presented concerning the modern person's relationship to the supranormal. There are certain factors inhibiting such research. The concept "folk belief" is itself problematic. Survival theorists such as Nils Lid stressed the criterion of continuity in defining folk belief:

> Folk beliefs are inherited magical and mythical notions, found in true beliefs, and crystallized in folk customs and folk legends. Customs are the most stable of these elements. They are a fixed midpoint about which popular customs revolve. (1935, 1)

Albert Eskeröd's definition, by contrast, was completely ahistoric: "Folk belief is taken to mean beliefs in supranormal beings, powers, and relations" (1947, 44). Even though most people today would concur with this definition, the term "folk belief" involves other legacies from (d)evolutionism. First, "folk belief" often connoted conditions in preindustrial society, and social groups associated with primary economic sectors. Second, "folk belief" often suggests a distinction between institutionalized religion and folk beliefs (see Blehr, 1974). Within a framework of origins and chronology, such a distinction is meaningful. But in the interest of clarifying the role of the supranormal in social life, a division between "folk belief" and "official religion" is irrelevant, even misleading.

For example, I have an extensive collection of letters written by Swedes to a healer, with a weekly magazine acting as intermediary. Among the contributors are believing Christians, that is, they have an active relationship to the official Swedish church. For them there is no conflict between being a Christian and contacting a healer for help. A similar example is the recent discussion of the charismatic laity of western Norway. Over several years, young women were subjected to exorcism because they were believed to be possessed by devils. In these congregations, exorcism is accepted as a Christian practice. If this had happened outside a Christian group, however, it would undoubtedly have been characterized as magic and folk belief (see Apollon et al., 1981).

We must accept that people's relation to the supranormal is often syncretistic. Therefore it is the total context of ideas, feelings, and actions which is of interest, without regard to possible origin. Perhaps "folk belief" should be replaced by another term, such as "folk religion," as Don Yoder has done (1974; see also Gustavson, 1976). To be consistent, the term ought to be simply "religion," to embrace all concepts and beliefs about, and contact with, the supranormal. Of course, such use of the concept "religion" would find limited response: few problems can be solved simply by introducing new terms. What is important is the statement of the problem, and the materials and methods used.

One recent development is the study of folk medicine or ethnomedicine, as it is called today. Where researchers formerly spoke of magic and "witch medicine," the expression today is "healers" (Alver et al., 1980). Where folk medicine was previously analyzed as part of a belief system, there is today increasing interest in the healer as an agent of social interaction (Alver, 1978, 1980; Honko, 1978; af Klintberg, 1980; Siikala, 1980; Rørbye, 1976, 1978a, 1980). There is a tendency to reduce the supranormal belief content to a minimum; Birgitte Rørbye asserts that the phenomenon of healing appears as a demystified miracle (1980, 202). Concurrently, we can see a change in research attitude: explanation is replaced by understanding. Instead of seeking rational explanations of what ethnomedical healing "really" is, we strive to understand why people seek help from unofficial medicine.

Even though there are tentative beginnings of research on contemporary folk belief, there are still major gaps. We know too little about concepts and beliefs, about the group settings in which beliefs, concepts, narratives, and actions are realized, about the situations where the supranormal plays a part.

The need for research in contemporary belief systems does not preclude continuing research from a historical perspective. However, existing archive materials have clear limitations both for functional analysis and for the study of the supranormal. In terms of Hermann Bausinger's four levels of context (1980), traditional archives contain a great deal of information about "textual context," much less about "social context." We must in any case reconstruct what Bausinger calls "societal context," and, in a study of contemporary culture, we can observe and analyze "situational contexts." After more than one hundred years of research into beliefs, attitudes, and behaviors in preindustrial society, we ought to allow ourselves the luxury of research into the supranormal in our own time.

MEMORATES AND THE STUDY OF FOLK BELIEF

Lauri Honko

In the study of folk beliefs, anthropologists and sociologists investigating primitive religion become involved with the same material as folklorists investigating folk narratives. Both parties would probably profit from an exchange of ideas, from knowing each other's methods and research results. Yet there is ample evidence that no such exchange occurs. In this respect, scholarly communication functions very poorly. It might be useful to consider what deficiencies and errors result from one-sided training in practical research work.

Let me illustrate with a hypothetical example. Let us suppose that more than thirty years ago two scholars, one an anthropologist, the other a folklorist, arrived in the Finnish village of Sääskelä in the Spankkova district of Ingria (the area around Leningrad). Without meeting one another they interviewed the same informant, Maria Savolainen, who was born in 1882. This woman told them about a supernatural being, a "barn spirit" or "hobgoblin," who lived in the barn. In the autumn, grain is dried in the barn in intense heat, after which it is threshed by hand. Each scholar recorded the following information in his notebook:

A. Sometimes, if the barn spirit was in a bad mood, he caused the barn to burn; if he was in a good mood, he helped extinguish the fire.

B. The old man of Tääkeli, my mother's father, told this. When he was sleeping in the barn, someone came and moved his leg and said, "Go away from here; this is your Aunt Anni's place!" The old man said, "Did Aunt Anni have this barn built?" The old man fell asleep again and straightened his leg. Again his leg was moved to another place. He asked the boy who was with him, "Did you lift my leg?" The boy answered, "I didn't; I was sleeping." The old man said, "Well, I guess I'll have to move; I seem to be in someone's way." Then when he moved to another place, he was left in peace.

Originally published in *Journal of the Folklore Institute,* 1964.

C. The barn was warmed late in the evening. The master of the house was baking turnips on the oven stones. He sat on the threshold of the barn, looking out the door. At his side appeared someone who had a black face but whose nose was as red as fire. The master asked, "Who are you?" He answered, "I am the spirit of this building." The master said, "If you are, then why do I find you so amusing?" The master took a stick used for stirring the fire, gave it to the spirit, and asked him to squeeze it. When he squeezed it, sparks flew. The master took a baked turnip, squeezed it until water trickled out, and said, "Look, I am even stronger; I can squeeze water from a rock." The spirit said, "Give it to me!" He squeezed, but no water came; only sparks flew. The master was smarter, because he tricked the barn spirit. The baked turnip was as black as a rock; the spirit didn't notice the difference (nos. 1070, 976, 1034, Virolainen collection, Folklore Archives of the Finnish Literary Society).

In his report the anthropologist would probably tell how "Ingrian Finns believe" that the barn spirit is a capricious being who can do either good or bad. He can help extinguish a burning barn; but when he is in a bad mood, he can burn down the barn, disturb the sleep of anyone spending the night there, and so on. Because the creature is cruel and feared, the Ingrians augment their courage with certain anti-stories emphasizing the wit of the farmer or "barn-warmer." The anthropologist would perhaps continue by delineating the social context of the beliefs, in order to learn what role and function the barn spirit has in the Ingrian religious system. Altogether, the anthropologist would handle his material as one body in which different kinds of information have about the same value as evidence.

In this respect a well-trained folklorist would be more cautious. First of all, he or she would notice that the three pieces of information represent different genres. "A" is a *belief* (it could also be called a *dite*). "B" is a *memorate*. In respect to "C," the folklorist would note that the same theme appears in the Aarne-Thompson folktale index under the heading "Contest between Man and Ogre" (AT 1060), and perhaps ask whether "C," in this case, should be listed as a *legend* at all. Realizing that variants of "C" are found throughout Europe, the folklorist might be tempted to make a comparative study of Maria Savolainen's repertoire and publish a monograph, "An Ingrian Storyteller," depicting the narrator's personality and role as a tradition bearer in the community. The problem of the barn spirit, on the other hand, might not be of interest because the folklorist would be better trained to operate with the stereotyped products of popular verbal art than with loosely structured memorates and beliefs.

In folk belief study, genre analysis is above all auxiliary to source criticism. Before making any generalizations about what "Ingrians believe," one must know which tradition genre provides the most valuable evidence and which are secondary. As C. W. von Sydow emphasized in his essay "Kategorien der Prosa-Überlieferung" (Categories of Prose Transmission, 1936), the character, function, adaptation, and dissemination of genres differ; they "are subject to different laws" (1948, 60). In his article "Comparative Religion and Popular Tradition," von Sydow criticized the scholarship of primitive religion:

> The school of Comparative Religion is incapable of seeing independently which categories of tradition are of importance for the study of religion and which have nothing to do with religion at all; they have contented themselves, in good faith, with the material prepared by former scholarship, and have now and then added some detail which might seem relevant. Reliable scholarship in the field of primitive religion presupposes broadly based studies of popular tradition and a thorough knowledge of its several categories. (1948, 169; contrast Malinowski, 1954, 100–108)

With some modification, this criticism still holds true. Not even folklorists, however, have accepted von Sydow's system of traditional genres unanimously. There is room for pruning, and folklorists themselves are to blame for lack of progress in this area. Works appear constantly in which the concept of legend is handled as though categories of the legend did not exist (see Schmidt, 1963, 107–12; Leyen, 1934; Wesselski, 1934, 203–48; Peuckert, 1938, 95–150; Röhrich, 1958, 664–91). In the papers given at the 1959 congress in Kiel, the term memorate appeared only once (Ranke, 1961, 3). This was not due to the term's not being publicized in, for example, the German language area (see Peuckert, 1938, 112–25; Peuckert and Lauffer, 1951, 181–82). It merely reflects folklorists' interest in traditional genres with fixed forms, such as international folktales, migratory legends, ballads, and proverbs. The life and social dimensions of tradition are studied primarily from the perspective of storytelling situation, narrative technique, and the narrator's personality and repertoire (see Tillhagen, 1962). For the investigation of folk beliefs, however, this type of study is not promising.

Von Sydow never tested his ideas about memorates, legends, and source criticism of belief material in a broader, applied study. This became the task of other scholars, primarily of Finns and Swedes. In 1935 Gunnar Granberg published an exemplary study of the Scandinavian forest spirit tradition and a short methodological examination of memorate and legend concepts (1935a, 120–27). Albert Eskeröd significantly furthered the study of folk beliefs with his article "Interessedominanz and Volksüberlieferung" (Dominant Interest in Folk Tradition, Nilsson, 1936) and with his dissertation "Årets äring" (Annual Feast Days, 1947). In Finland, Martti Haavio published a comprehensive work about Finnish household spirits (1942). Unfortunately, these scholars did not influence international research, for only short abstracts of Granberg's and Eskeröd's dissertations were translated, and Haavio's study was published only in Finnish. When I began a dissertation about Ingrian spirit beliefs (Honko, 1962), I appreciated the work of this Swedish-Finnish school. Their results provided a good methodological starting point. Many problems were already solved, but it was apparent that analysis could be deepened in the direction of social psychology and sociology.

As noted above, the purpose of genre analysis is to define concepts and identify categories used in source criticism. What, for example, is a *folk belief*? This term has been applied to different traditional items. For the term to have practical value, it should be defined according to some formal criterion. This criterion is found in the fact that a belief is normally expressed as a direct and general statement (text A above). "The barn spirit does not let you sleep in the barn; he drives you away" is a belief. Such a generalization cannot be accepted until its validity has been tested by frequency analysis. One must ask: Do Ingrians generally believe that the barn spirit drives out people sleeping in the barn? On the basis of broad evidence, it can be demonstrated that this is the case; that is, the belief belongs to the "collective" tradition (see Eskeröd, 1947, 74–79; Honko, 1962, 125–29). But quite often the belief is a creation of the collector. He or she heard a memorate, but recorded the information in a generalized form. There are also investigators who would rather treat material as "beliefs" than as exact memorate-quotations. Works in primitive religion are filled with statements that begin, "The Voguls believe . . ." as though the belief were embraced by the entire society (see Lienhardt, 1961; Malinowski, 1916, 237–54). The differences between individual and collective traditions are generally ignored.

According to von Sydow, memorates are "first-person narratives about personal experiences" (1948, 60; contrast with Jolles, 1929, 200–17). Through them we grasp living folk beliefs, people's supernatural experiences. Belief in spirits is not founded on speculation but on concrete personal experiences, reinforced by sensory perceptions. In this respect spirits are empirical beings. (On the basis of whether they can be seen or not, supernatural beings can be regarded as empirical—spirits and the dead, for example—or etiological, like giants and mythical heroes. Some beings, such as the devil, can appear in both groups.) Although the investigator is unable to see the spirits, he or she must admit that the informant really saw them. In general, informants react critically to supernatural experiences. They consider true only what they themselves, or some acquaintance, experienced. If, for example, the collector asks, "Are there any spirits in the barn?" the informant normally avoids a generalized description of what a spirit looks like and what it does. Instead, he or she begins, "Last fall when I went to put more wood in the barn's stove, then [such and such happened]." In other words, the informant reports a memorate. The overwhelming majority of my material, gathered by careful collectors, consists of memorates.

Memorates are a valuable source for the study of folk religion primarily because they reveal situations in which supernatural tradition was actualized and influenced behavior. On the basis of memorates we can reconstruct the social context of beliefs, which is fundamental to the functionalist approach. We can learn who had the experience, in what circumstances (time, place, situation, and so on), how it was interpreted, and how it influenced behavior. From case to case we can draw conclusions about functional prerequisites and the consequences of the actualization of a belief. Because memorates live in narrative tradition, we must consider how this might have caused secondary changes in the memorates. The investigator must determine how accurately a memorate reflects supranormal experience. The problem of deciding whether the kind of experience the memorate relates is possible or probable is primarily one of perception psychology. The investigator has to consider the modality of experience: Are we concerned with visual, auditory, or tactile perception, or a combination of all three? Was the experience perhaps a dream, a hallucination, an illusion, an eidetic perception, or a hypnagogic image? What was the duration of the experience? Was the spirit's appearance lifelike or vague? What were the perceptual conditions? (For example, was it dark, was it possible to test the perception?) What was the psychophysical condition of the person who had the experience? (Was he sick, tired, drunk, or under the power of some strong expectation, desire, or fear?) Perceptual features that are psychologically improbable are often secondary, added in narration. There are memorates that contain individual, unique, or "unnecessary" details. Others are poorer and more schematic in content. Others, along with authentic experiences, contain motifs learned, for example, from legends. For the analysis of supernatural experiences, the first group is most valuable. But from the point of view of folk belief, those containing secondary alterations are also valuable, for memorates told many times tend to become codified and approach collective tradition, particularly if that tradition includes parallels and patterns. Such memorates depict supernatural experience not as it actually was, but as it should have been, according to the bearers of tradition.

C. W. von Sydow and Gunnar Granberg stressed individual, unique elements as the principal characteristics of memorates (von Sydow, 1948, 73; Granberg, 1935a, 121). Martti Haavio came to a different conclusion: "Those memorates in which the individual element is dominant are noticeably rarer than those in which the motifs are connected with general folk tradition" (1942, 9). This is borne out by the fact that newly learned supernatural tradition provides models that form the basis for new experiences. Also the degree to which different memorate features are traditional can and must be determined by frequency analysis. For instance, in text "B" the notion that a spirit drives a sleeping person from a place belonging to the building's supernatural owner is traditional. On the other hand, the feature that the owner is a deceased person is rare in Ingria; however, parallels can be found in Finland (Honko, 1962, 344–45).

In general, it is not difficult to differentiate between memorates with individual features and stereotyped international legends. However, between these genres there is room for a number of transitional forms, partly because a memorate can in time develop into a legend. When an exciting description of a supernatural experience spreads from one district to another, it becomes schematic (unnecessary details are dropped and new motifs added), and the spirits' activities, for example, become concrete and graphic. Although this product is no longer close to the original experience, it may remain in harmony with memorate and belief tradition in a locality. It can be called a belief legend *(Glaubenssage);* its value as a reflector of folk belief is considerable. Generally speaking, however, legends alone cannot be used as evidence for belief in some spirit. In an area where the fire spirit is not found in memorate tradition, a legend about conversing fire spirits can nevertheless exist (for example, a spirit complains that he is treated poorly in his house, people spit into the fire, and so on, whereupon another urges that he burn the house in revenge). It would be a mistake to suppose that the fire spirit belongs to the locality's supernatural beings. The text in question is a migratory legend whose purpose is not to testify that the fire spirit exists, but that fire is sacred and must be handled properly. Other legends are preserved because of their vivid fantasy motifs and their narrative interest. These are sometimes called fabulates, sometimes entertainment legends *(Unterhaltungssagen).* In source criticism, it is important to prune from the materials fabulates, entertainment legends and international migratory legends not based in a region's actual folk beliefs. However, one must remember that the same legend can function in one area as a fabulate and in another as a belief legend.

That tales cannot be used as primary material for the study of folk beliefs needs no further demonstration. But two other traditional forms, ficts and metaphors, have sometimes caused misconceptions. C. W. von Sydow readily demonstrated how the "corn mother" and other Mannhardtian "fertility demons" were nothing more than pedagogical ficts used to keep children from trampling down the grain fields (1944, 15–16; 1948, 79–84, 89–105, 170–75; Honko, 1962, 136–37). The Ingrian well spirit is a typical fict; it is not connected to memorate tradition. Adults frightened children with the well spirit so that they would not fall into the well. Although fict-beings belong only to children's culture, they have the same sociopsychological function as other belief traditions: they maintain social norms. In Ingrian prayers and charms a "maiden of the wind" or "old woman of the wind" is sometimes mentioned. However, one must not conclude on the basis of poetic expressions that Ingrians believed in a special wind spirit. These are metaphors personifying the wind. Taking a metaphor literally leads to the kind of religious fancy Max Müller called "a disease of language."

In an investigation of empirical, supernatural beings, memorates must be considered primary sources. The central problem is to learn when, where, and why supernatural experiences originated, and how people act in encounters with them. What follows are some ideas about how to proceed in an analysis.

First, one must establish who the tradition bearers are. I oppose the notion that beliefs are primarily the possession of "gifted narrators." Actually, tradition is not maintained by individuals but by social roles. The tradition of a fisherman is different from that of a cattle breeder; in learning a profession or role, people also learn the supernatural tradition connected with it. The same individual can occupy several social positions and roles, but only one is active at a time while others remain latent. Similarly a person can know various kinds of supernatural traditions, but the tradition that comes to mind in a situation is determined by his or her active role at the moment. Role behavior can best be depicted in terms of social value and norm, and spirit images can be brought into correlation with social roles, values, and norms. It is primarily individuals functioning as master or mistress of a house who maintain the tradition of the house spirit. The value governing behavior can be called the "fortune of the house"; it includes the protection of the house from mishap, the orderly conduct of the family living there, the family's well-being, prosperity, and protection from destructive outside influences. In-group attitudes dominate the value; expected behavior is expressed as norms. The house spirit appears when a norm has been broken (disorderliness, quarreling, drunkenness) or when misfortune threatens the house or family (fire, death, leaving home). The house spirit is also actualized in connection with major changes, such as the building of a new home and moving rites. Similarly, it can be shown that cattle breeders maintain the belief in the stable spirit; that barn warmers maintain the barn spirit tradition; and that women who bathe last on Saturday evening believe in the bathhouse spirit (Honko, 1962, 243–48).

Space limitations permit only one diagrammatic example of analysis. The following is a common supernatural experience. One evening a man goes to heat the barn. He is rather tired; the heating has continued for two days without interruption. The responsibility for drying the grain is his alone: he must supervise the placement of the sheaves, keep the temperature at the correct level, take care of the ventilation. The stove must not get too hot; the danger of fire is obvious. Children and thieves must be kept out of the grain. As he sits by the fire, he decides to stretch out for a moment. Against his will he dozes off. Suddenly he hears the barn door squeak and looks up: an old man with a gray beard and white suit is looking at him disapprovingly. In an instant the being disappears. The man goes to the door; there are no tracks in the snow. The man looks into the stove; the fire is about to go out. He puts in more wood, goes to the house and tells others about his experience. They conclude that the barn spirit came to wake the barn warmer because the fire was about to go out.

It is easy to discern the factors that create a frame of reference and lead to the vision (fig. 1). The value governing the role of the barn warmer ("the success of the grain drying") had been endangered by the violation of a norm ("you must not sleep"). The norm and the barn warmer's need for sleep created a conflict; the man's sleep was disturbed by stress and guilt.

These factors were "primary" stimuli actualizing a frame of reference. The door's creaking was the "releasing" stimulus, a noise to which the man ordinarily would have paid no attention, but which now awakened him. The man feared the spirit would punish him, for in tradition the norm is strengthened by sanction. Given the poor perceptual circumstances (half-dark, unclear outlines) the tired man's "creative eye" began to act; he "saw" a pale figure in the doorway. Perhaps he had heard that the barn spirit has a gray beard; and so

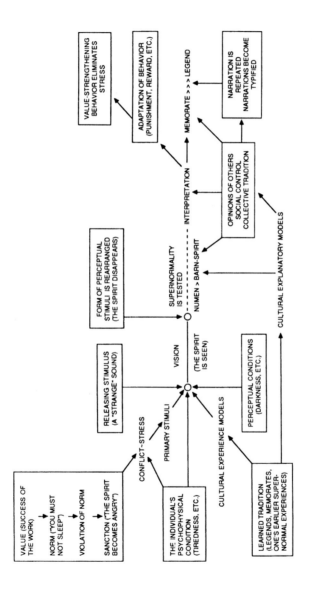

Figure 1

this feature became part of the hypnagogic image born between sleep and wakefulness.

When he looked at the door a second time, the perceptual material was structured differently; the being had disappeared. His rapid disappearance and the absence of tracks in the snow were supranormal criteria precluding the possibility that the being had been a human. It must be noted that during the experience itself a person often does not recognize the creature he sees. He might already be convinced of the supranormal nature of the vision, but the interpretation does not yet occur. This kind of supernatural being, which as yet conforms to no exact image, can be called a *numen*, defined by Otto as "supernatural being without concrete manifestation" (1936, 29–30). The term is necessary because in many instances tradition provides no explanatory model, and these experiences remain at the numen stage (see Simonsuuri, 1961, 45–48). Interpretation is frequently a result of later deliberation. A person's memories can accumulate supernatural experiences whose meanings become evident only after weeks or even months. In this way omen memorates are formed; an unexplainable event is interpreted retrospectively as an omen of a later catastrophe. A person who has experienced a supernatural event is by no means always alone in making the interpretation; the social group often participates. There may be spirit belief specialists whose opinion is decisive. The readiness to have experiences and the ability to interpret are not always equally developed: one may be prone to experiencing the supernatural, while another is able to explain it. The group controls the experiences of its members, and if a figure of authority in the group happens to be a skeptic, the supranormal character of the experience may be rejected.

The above model applies to experiences that begin with a norm violation, experiences characterized by the supernatural world's actualizing itself unexpectedly. Subconscious expectations are negative; contact with the spirit is not sought, but the spirit appears. The person is fearful; the spirit is the subject of the action, the moralist, while the person—the object—is punished. Sudden appearances of a spirit are generally graphic events in which the spirit is seen clearly and its activity experienced as concrete fact. But there are other types of experiences. In ritual behavior the situation is different: contact with the spirit is actively sought; the person is the subject of the action, the spirit the object. The expectations toward the spirit are positive; it is hoped he will help and reward. In contrast to behavior violating the norm and endangering social values, the behavior in ritual strengthens social values and conforms to the norm. Graphic, clear appearances of a spirit do not usually occur in ritual. The spirit's "answer" is read from trifling signs, and from the success of those endeavors for which the ritual was organized (Honko, 1962, 110–13).

The purpose of this survey has been to call attention to a neglected traditional genre, the memorate, and its central position in functional analysis of folk belief. The following suggestions might be worth consideration:

1. It is necessary to recognize and define different traditional genres because their source value varies.

2. Every generalization needs the support of frequency analysis. Individual and collective tradition must be distinguished.

3. The degree of probability and authenticity of supernatural experiences must be appraised by means of perception psychology.

4. When studying the supernatural in narrative tradition, it is important to note the interaction of memorates and legends, and particularly of social control directed toward the tradition and modifying it.

5. Before we can say anything about the function of folk beliefs, it is necessary to relate supernatural tradition to social roles, values, and norms.

CONCEPTS OF THE SOUL IN NORWEGIAN TRADITION

Bente G. Alver

Growing up as I did in a village in Jylland, I constantly witnessed the exodus from the country to the city, with its greater pleasures and hardships. People found the road between the local store and the filling station too monotonous, and few discovered that there were other roads that crossed it. As an adult engaged in folklore research, I have encountered on the part of scholars the same urge to escape from the local duckpond. In our libraries, shelf after shelf is filled with literature about the beliefs of other cultures, but our own beliefs are shrouded in silence. Archived material about our traditions is not improved by lying dormant, nor is there much opportunity for collecting new material. Thus, concepts about the soul are almost unexplored territory in Norwegian research, despite the fact that the greater part of our tradition is imbued with them.

Thanks to modern studies in comparative religion, it is no longer necessary to raise the question of whether people believe they consist of more than what is reflected in smooth surfaces. At every stage of their personal development—and in their relationships with each other and with life itself—people have generally asserted that behind the walls of the body dwells the unaccountable presence we call the soul, best symbolized, perhaps, as a bird.

The Ego-Soul

If, on the basis of Norwegian tradition, we attempt to articulate popular concepts of the soul, their essence would be what is called the *hug*, which corresponds to Åke Hultkranz's definition of the ego-soul (1953). The word *sjel*

Original title: "Conceptions of the Living Human Soul in the Norwegian Tradition." Published in *Temenos*, 1971.

(soul) first entered our language with the arrival of Christianity. The Old Norse *sál* or *sála* occurs only in the later texts, and then always as a reference to the Christian definition of the soul (Fritzner, 1883–96). The concept we today designate as the psyche—but not nearly as complex—is defined by the term hug (Old Norse *hugr*). Hug represented qualities which are now called *thought, wish, desire,* or *temperament.*

Normally, every person had a hug. The hug could free itself for long or short periods of time and live its own life outside the body. If a person were deprived of the hug, he or she was said to have been *hugstjålet* (hug-stolen), a popular designation for abnormal behavior apparently used to explain various degrees of psychic disorder. According to tradition, a supernatural being was to blame if a person had been hugstjålet. It was also believed that people's hug could be turned towards or away from each other, causing them to become friends or enemies. Such a *hugvending* (hug-turning) could be performed by most people with the help of magic. These beliefs are very old, and many rites used to "turn" the hug have been collected:

> *To make everyone love you:* Take the right foot of a hen, carry it with you; then all your enemies will be your friends again. (Bang, 1901–2, 517)
> *To make a woman love you:* Take the heart of a snake and make her eat it without her knowledge. Then she will desire you. (Bang, 475)
> *When one is bewitched and loves someone against one's will:* If, against your will, you must love and run after someone, put on a pair of new shoes and walk rapidly in them for a mile, causing your feet to sweat. Take off your right shoe, pour in beer or wine and drink it. Within the hour you will hate the one you loved. (Bang, 378)

From the descriptions of these rites for hugvending, it appears that the hug can be apprehended concretely, coerced the way one coerces a headstrong child. For example, if you wished to turn someone's hug toward you, you were supposed to stick the hooked end of a frog bone in the person's clothing and give a gentle tug. If you were tired of this *hugsøkning* (hug-seeking), you could push it away with the forked end of the bone (Reichborn-Kjennerud, 1928, 183).

There is a widespread belief that a hug can be so strong that it can assume a *ham* (shape). Although this is not considered an everyday occurrence, the hug has often been encountered in a ham. According to tradition, a hug in a ham is known as a *hugham.* As a rule the hugham is visible, and usually assumes one of the following shapes:

1. The shape of the person.
2. The shape of an animal that has some relationship to the person's character, as the character is interpreted by the milieu.
3. A more abstract shape such as fog, light, vapor, fire.

There are strong ties between the hug and the person. Injuries to the hug

while it is outside the body are suffered by the person. If the hug is killed while
it is in concrete form, the person is killed, too.

According to tradition, a person whose hug is in a ham is sometimes said to
be *hamgalen* (ham-mad). This corresponds to the Old Norse *hamramr*. A similar
word, probably invented by scholars since it does not appear in traditional
material, is *hamløber* (shape-runner). This term refers to several different
concepts, but the general reference is to a person who, more or less intention-
ally, allows the hug to go about in a ham in order to accomplish something.
Thus the witch can be described as a hamløber when she sends her hug out on
assignment. The term also applies to women whose hug rides astride people
and animals in a *mareridt* (nightmare), and to the *mannbjørn* (man-bear) and
the *varulv* (werewolf), despite the fact that these last two are metamorphoses
and neither bears any relationship to the hug. The difference between a person
who has sent out the hug and one who has changed shape, or been changed
(metamorphosis), is that the former can be observed in two places: in his or
her own shape and in the hugham.

There seems to have been a widespread belief that a person's hug can affect
nearby animate or inanimate objects. It makes no difference whether the hug
is weak or strong, friendly or malicious, aimless or on an errand. Descriptions
of the hug can be divided into the following categories, in which the first word
refers to the hug's shape, the second to the person's relationship to the hug:
(1) invisible/unconscious; (2) visible/unconscious; (3) invisible/conscious;
(4) visible/conscious.

The Invisible/Unconscious Hug

The term *hugsing* refers to the invisible/unconscious hug. The verb *at hugse*
refers to the Old Norse *hugsa*, which means to take notice of; to think, to think
about. "To hugse a person" means to harm them through unconscious desire.
Traditionally, hugsing is often connected with a meal. According to popular
belief, envy affected the eater, causing him or her to choke on the food or
become nauseated and lose appetite. These beliefs gave rise to the custom of
inviting strangers to have a bite to eat if they came by at mealtime, in order to
avoid any form of hugsing. Even today people say, "Well, I don't grudge you
your food!" if someone chokes on something. The phrase has lost its roots, but
people still say it to ward off suspicion of having caused the unpleasantness. It
was believed that if a person *hugset* someone inadvertently, they could make
amends by admitting it.

One can, according to tradition, hugse oneself; this seems surprising, but
there is a simple explanation. You can have such an uncontrollable desire for
something—for a certain kind of food, perhaps, or a certain experience—that
at the moment the wish is fulfilled, you feel psychically exhausted, overwhelmed
by nausea. To most people, whose sensitivity has not been destroyed by self-con-

trol, this is a well-known phenomenon. This indisposition has been interpreted as a person's own desire turned inward.

In ancient times, an ordinary reflex movement manifested as a tingling sensation in nose or ear or fingers was interpreted as the effect of a stranger's hug, as a sign that someone was thinking or talking about you, or that a stranger would soon be coming to the farm. You could figure out whose hug it might be according to where the sensation was. The right side of the body meant a man's hug, the left side a woman's. This notion was less a widespread belief than an entertaining guessing game to figure out who might be thinking about you:

> Whenever a burning or twitching sensation was felt somewhere in the body, people would say, "I have your hug now." They were able to tell if it was the person they were with, according to where it was felt in the body. A tickling sensation in the little toe was a sign of irresponsibility. (NFS Nils Lid I, 57)

Hiccupping, sneezing, or yawning were also regarded as the result of a stranger's hug. When people were afraid that they were being *hugsøkt* by the thoughts of an evil person, they would mumble Jesus' name or make the sign of the cross.

The terms used to describe various manifestations of the hug indicate its concreteness. The expression *hugbit* (hug-bite), a term referring to belching and other symptoms of cardialgia, indicates that it was regarded as a biting spirit. A similar notion is reflected in the term *reham*, or *rehug*, which is the name of an illness. The prefix *re-* comes from the verb *ride*: the hug is visualized as riding, thereby causing the illness. The same sickness is called *flog* or *ålaup*, which refer to the hug's having flown into a person. The most common magic against injuries inflicted by the hug is stroking or touching the sick person, indicating that one knows one is to blame for the illness, and is trying to control the effects of one's hug. If someone is unaware that they have caused harm, but are suspected by the milieu, then a third person can touch them and then touch the afflicted person, thereby neutralizing the damage:

> There was a boy in Østlandet who had a terrible stomach ailment.
> "They're *floging* him to death!" said the father, and swore and was furious. Then a stranger came to the farm, and the man went out to greet him. When the stranger touched the boy, it was as if he stroked the illness out of him. (Skar, 1961, 492)

People tried to counteract the effects of this unstable hug-being by not allowing it to wander, by thinking good thoughts in order to keep from harming someone inadvertently. It was obvious that certain people had a hug that was stronger and more unstable than others, and people were nervous about them. Certain people's hug were so strong that they could cause beer barrels and milk pails to leak if they desired the contents:

They talked so much about a *flogham*, but I didn't believe it til I saw it. We had a tub of milk in the loft. Suddenly it started to leak. The milk trickled between the staves and ran along the floor. Then someone came in who hadn't had any milk, and was thirsty at the moment. He was given something to drink. The tub immediately became watertight, and has never leaked since. (Skar, 1961, 492)

The word *ovund,* or *avund,* refers to envy. The term often occurs in reference to magic, where it indicates an envious thought intended to cause harm. But ovund was also dangerous because most people are capable of envy, and those who are easily envious could cause harm inadvertently. People were afraid of the ovund; it could cause sickness or death, and was endowed with an almost corrosive power. Ovund was said to be so strong, it could crumble a stone to dust:

There were two neighbors out walking; their names were Olav and Uv. Now Uv was prosperous, but Olav was badly off, and became so envious of Uv that he nearly wasted away. They were together, as I said, and Uv knew very well what was bothering Olav, and wanted to test him. He picked up a stone, but concealed it; Olav thought he had found something special, and asked, "What did you find now?" "Oh," said Uv, "I'm not telling a soul. What I found can't be bought for money." Then Olav was so envious he was quite beside himself. They came to a shack. Uv decided that he didn't want to carry the stone any longer, so he hid it under a log in the corner when Olav wasn't looking. Olav went about year in and year out, as they say, and was envious of what Uv had found. Uv realized this, and it happened that he came by the same shack again. He didn't forget to look for the stone, but all that was left of it was dust. So you see that envy can corrode a stone. (NFS Moltke Moe 54, 45)

Whenever people had a fine herd of cattle, they were afraid that others would begrudge them this, and be envious of them. They called it *agonn* (avund), and believed that it would affect the cattle. Avund was worse than magic, they said. (Moe, 1924, 122)

It is not difficult to understand that people's negative emotions could cause sickness or unpleasantness; it is harder to imagine that an emotion as beautiful as longing could harm the person one is longing for. Our experience is that one can become sick with longing, not that one becomes sick from being longed for. In tradition, however, often the longing of young people for each other manifests itself as sickness in the beloved. After a long separation, a man longs for a woman in such a way that his hug is about to destroy her. Only when he goes to the farm, and actually sees her wretched condition, does he realize that he is harming her. He touches her and strokes the sickness out of her. In an older society with a long working day, it is possible that farmers could not afford to have young people incapacitated because of a bleeding heart, and that these notions were used as disciplinary, cautionary norms which kept young people focused on their work, just as sailors at sea had rigid tabus to eliminate everything that reminded them of home and loved ones.

A longing imposed from the outside was called an *elsk;* the symptoms were the same as those caused by longing. An elsk could be imposed by a supernatural being who desired a mortal as a partner, or by a dead person. In the latter instance, it was usually a mother in the Kingdom of the Dead who longed so much for her living child that the child would become sick and fail to thrive.

These beliefs in the power of longing find expression in ballads about the grieving lover who drags his beloved back across the threshold of death. It is only for a moment, but long enough to discover that the longing of the bereaved makes life in the grave unbearable:

> Each time you cry for me and are sad,
> My coffin is filled with dried blood.
> But when you sing and are glad
> Then my grave is festooned with roses. (DFG 90, 17–19)

Here the dead person speaks for society; people are not allowed to abandon themselves to sorrow and longing. As a part of the great machinery of life, they must continue to function, and longing causes pain to those one loves best.

The idea that longing is dangerous to the loved one is also reflected in tradition about the *mare,* in which one's hug could ride someone in a nightmare. The mare is often perceived as the desire of an unmarried woman for a man. These mare—perhaps they could be called "erotic mare"—are thought to be invisible, but palpable, hug. The person is ridden as an act of vengeance, and, in much of the tradition, the mare has developed into a separate supranormal being with a variety of shapes, all of which leave the impression of being tremendously heavy and suffocating.

The Visible/Invisible Unconscious Hug

The hug played an important role in communication, particularly when a family member was absent from home. At such times, a person's hug might appear unexpectedly and very briefly, usually in a familiar attitude: sitting for a moment in a favorite chair, walking across the yard, standing by a bedpost. They would be in their own shape, and you might believe for a moment that they had actually come home. But the shape would vanish, and then you would know that it had been a hugham. Such visits were not popular. They were assumed to be a warning, and usually preceded a message that the loved one had died or been in danger. Sometimes the hug is barely perceptible: an unpleasant premonition, a sigh through the house, a knock or cry which sounds like the absent person's voice. Tradition explains that, in a difficult situation or at the moment of death, a person's hug goes home, or tries to send a message—called a *hugbod*.

It is possible to collect a considerable amount of such material today:

> Gunleik Heggtveit, in Brunkeberg (born 1725), was a rich man, and had many children. One of his sons was called Sveinung. He was staying at Hestskodike during the last summer his father was alive.
>
> One night, late in summer, Sveinung was sleeping alone in the barn at Hestskodike. Around midnight he woke up and saw his father standing on the barn floor. And he leaned over the railing, stared down at him and said:
>
> "Sveinung, Sveinung my son, get up and follow me!" Sveinung thought it was strange for his father to be there at night. But all the same, he put on his clothes and followed him outside.
>
> Gunleik slowly headed west along the road to Brunkeberg Church, and Sveinung followed. He talked to Sveinung about one thing and another, and told him how to arrange his life and take care of himself. There was a girl—her name was Aaste—and Sveinung had proposed to her. But he mustn't marry her, or else he would have nothing but sorrow and pain, said his father, and then he mentioned another girl Sveinung ought to marry.
>
> They walked and chatted like this for a long time, but when they came to Sothoug, Gunleik vanished, and Sveinung was standing alone in the road. Only then did it occur to him that something was wrong. So he went straight to Heggtveit, where he learned that his father had died three hours before—at the very moment when he had come to him in the barn at Hestskodike. (Flatin, 1930, 144)

> If a person appears who isn't really there, then he is soon going to die:
>
> A couple of days before grandmother died, my mother came to me and said, "Your grandmother is going to die now. I was in the *stabbur*, and looked up through the window," she said, "and then I distinctly saw your grandmother walking along the path to the meadow. I thought this was strange, because I didn't think she was well enough to walk so far, and I didn't know of any errand she could have there. But when I came back down in the entryway, your grandmother was standing there washing some cups."
>
> That evening grandmother got sick, and two days later she was dead. (Grimstad, 1953, 33)

A belief that is closely related to the notion of hugsøkning is designated by the term *vardøger (vardywle, vardøwle, vardiwle, vardyr)*. The prefix is *vor(d)*, derived from the Old Norse *vordr*, which means "keeper, custodian." In Norwegian dialects, it recurs in words like *gardvor(d)* and *tunvor(d)*, names for supranormal beings that watch over the farm and the farmyard (Solheim, 1951, 143ff.). Vor(d) also refers to a concept of the soul. The suffix *-øger (iwle, ywle, øwle)* is not etymologically traceable (Torp, 1919), but in context it refers to the hug, where thought and person are dogging each other's footsteps. The vardøger goes ahead of the person and warns of his or her approach. In Norwegian dialects, this concept is also called a *gangferd, fyriferd,* or *føregangar*.

The vardøger is most often experienced by those closest to the person, who best know his or her patterns of behavior, and often when they are waiting for this person. Traditionally, the vardøger is an aural experience:

> Granny Opgar'n, yes, everybody called her that because she had lots of grandchildren and lived at Opgar'n Nabset. One evening she was up at the Opgard cabin at Blikkeberg *seter*, waiting for her son Arne. He was supposed to come and help bring the cattle home in the fall. So she sat up to wait for him that evening, but when it had grown too late for him to come, she went to bed. After she had been lying there awhile, she heard the hoofbeats of a horse outside. She heard it stop, the horse snorted, Arne took the pack baskets and carried them into the shed. Then he went out again, opened the gate, led the horse into the pen and closed the gate again. Then everything was quiet. She lay there waiting for him to come, but no one came. Then she got up and went outside, but no one was there. She called out, but received no answer. Then she went back inside and put the hook on the door before she went back to bed. Then, after a little while, someone came and took hold of the door, but nothing else happened. Arne didn't come until the following day, but then it sounded exactly the way it had the night before. When she told about this, they asked her if she hadn't been afraid. "No, I wasn't afraid. But when I went to bed, I said to myself, 'The one God will spare need not beware!' And if I hadn't put the hook on the door, then they wouldn't have taken hold of it! (Nergaard, 1925, 156)

The vardøger experience has its origins in ordinary psychic phenomena dictated by the attitude of a person waiting to hear a familiar pattern of sounds. In earlier times, this experience was explained supranormally: a person was longing to come home, or thinking about a goal, and this caused the hug to go off on its own. Originally, a vardøger was manifested as an aural experience, but has gradually merged with the tradition of sighting the image of a person before he or she arrives. The visible vardøger has often merged or been confused with the hugham, and the two concepts are very similar:

> One day, while Ivar Naalsyn was engaged to Ane, he was out in the forest. His sweetheart usually brought him his food. When it was almost dinnertime, he caught sight of his sweetheart coming with the food. He was glad, and ran to meet her. But then she stopped. This surprised him very much. Finally she disappeared behind a mound. But she was dressed exactly like Ane, his sweetheart. After a little while Ane came with the food. (NFS Langset V, 302)

Because of the similarities in the two traditions, their names are often confused: they are given the same name, or one tradition is given a variety of names. However, there is a discernible difference between the two concepts: you encountered a vardøger when you were expecting a specific person; an experience with a hugham, on the other hand, was unexpected.

According to tradition, the appearance of a hugham or a vardøger could be a warning of death, and attempts were made to circumvent the warning. If you saw a person's hugham and did not tell him or her, then the omen might not come true. This notion is common today, as well: "What you don't know won't hurt you." If a person arrived immediately following the vardøger, he or she was going to die. If some time elapsed, the person would live a long life:

> Mother was a dairy-maid up at the home seter at Rødalen. I was a little girl at the time. One day she saw an old woman from Øye, called Ingebjorg Øye. Mother saw her coming by a hay barn below the seter. She thought she was on her way to pay her a visit, and so she put on the coffee pot. But an hour elapsed before the woman came to the seter—even though the spot where she had been seen was only a short distance away. When Ingebjorg was leaving, she said, "Thank you. I'll never come back again!" And she never did, because she died in the fall. People maintained that if they saw somebody's *drøygen* (vardøger) before lunch, he would have a long life. But if they saw the drøygn after lunch, he would be "shortlived" as they call it. (NFS Hermundstad III, 80)

The Invisible/Conscious Hug

Woven into our extensive traditions about magic are many notions about the hug, its instability and power. Although it was believed that everyone had a hug, interest was greatest in the strong hug. In magic traditions, there are visible and invisible hug, but the most important quality is that the hug is conscious and has a goal.

It seems obvious that all magic has an intense willpower at its core: one craves, wishes for, desires something, and the ritual is built on this. In the past, there was a strong belief in the power of thought and desire, and the hug has an important place in this.

Throughout Scandinavia there is a wealth of material about witchcraft. Most often it describes the transformation of people and animals. Someone wanting to do harm could strengthen the hug through a pact with the devil and cause death and destruction with thoughts alone. The power to do evil could manifest itself in different parts of the body, so we have the terms *evil eye, evil hand, spiteful tongue, evil foot,* which reflect the belief that evil, or the evil thought, was transmitted through the eye, the hand, the tongue, or the foot (Lid, 1935a, 18ff.).

Frequently described in the tradition is the ability to attract things through the power of thought. From ancient times the belief prevailed throughout Europe that witches always have enough butter. One of their methods was to drag it out of people's churns while the churning was in process: as a precaution, people might conceal their churning time from strangers. Often it is the witch's hug that does the work. If a churning was unsuccessful, one could take a red-hot scythe and slash it to and fro in the heavy cream; then the witch had to release her hold. Glowing steel is an ancient precaution against evil in general. That the hug was involved in butter-dragging is evidenced by the reports that end many accounts of the discovery that such-and-such a woman had been badly slashed at the same time. People visualized the witch's hug in the cream and imagined that the injuries caused to the hug by the scythe had transferred to the witch's body:

> Once they were churning at Våland, but they didn't get any butter. Someone must have bewitched the churn. So they heated the scythe until it was red hot, and thrust it down in the churn. On the following day they went to church, and there they met people from Møgedal. They exchanged greetings, and the man from Våland asked how they were getting along at Møgedal. "Oh, not very well," said the Møgedal man. "My wife cut three fingers off one hand."
> "Well, it served her right, she was in our churn. We churned the whole day without getting any butter," replied the man from Våland. (NFS Tore Bergstøl IV, 7)

Butter obtained by the witch through *hugdragning* (hug-dragging) was closely linked to the witch's hug, and it was possible to tell if butter was "witch-butter" or "honest butter." A special knife was used. There are a number of rites that tell how, and of what material, such a "butter knife" could be forged; a knife that had been used to kill something could also be used. If the butter was "witch butter," drops of blood would run along the incision.

In the complex of traditions about the witch's relationship to things she obtains for herself at the expense of others, there are strong beliefs about the witch, her hug, and her victim:

> On a farm at Sørfold, there was a woman who wronged her neighbors so they were unable to profit from their cattle. She did her churning in an out-of-the-way spot, and her trough was full of butter no matter how little she churned. But her neighbors were unable to get any butter. Then the woman became sick and had to stay in bed. In the meantime, a man came to the farm and asked if he could borrow a little butter. The woman had a serving-girl in the house. She went to the mistress and asked if she could lend him the butter. Yes, the man was to be helped, said the woman. "But I shall tell you how to go about it: You mustn't slice the butter out of the tub, you're to scrape it out with the blade of a knife." But the girl disobeyed her mistress. She just stuck the knife into the butter and scooped out a piece. As she did so, blood started trickling out of the butter where the knife had been. She slammed on the lid and ran inside. There she found her mistress lying dead in the bed. (Mo, 1952, 101)

The Visible/Conscious Hug

The witch's ability to drag butter from a churn might involve her hug in a ham. If the churning failed to produce butter, one should look in the cream or under the churn: if an animal were found, it had to be picked up with fire tongs and burned in the fireplace. It was believed that the animal was the witch's hugham, and when it was burned, or when the spoiled cream was poured on the fire, the witch would be seized by a terrible thirst, and sometimes a suspected member of a community would be found suffering from severe burns.

The witch's hugham was usually in the shape of a cat, a hare, a toad, or a big black bird, the same animals she was thought to become when she transformed herself. The designation of certain animals as "evil" is due to the fact that these animals were associated with witches, and popular belief usually assigned one of these shapes to the witch's hugham. (Because she can appear in two places in connection with the churning, we are dealing with a hugham and not a transformation.)

There was a belief throughout Scandinavia that the witch had a special helper, usually called a "troll cat." In Norwegian dialects it is also called *truss, skratt, smørkat, trollnøste, trollnøa.* The last two names indicate the most common shape of this creature: a ball of yarn. As a rule, the troll cat is described as a little gray or brown ball of yarn that rolls from cow to cow and sucks milk, only to roll home to the witch and spit it out in her milk pails.

The troll cat is also described as having the shape of a cat, but its function is the same: to steal milk for the witch. There is some confusion, however, between a troll cat in the shape of a cat, and a witch's hug in cat shape. Tradition tells us that if a troll cat in a cat shape is injured, the witch suffers the injury too; if a troll cat in the shape of a ball is destroyed, nothing happens to the witch except that she loses the ball.

In their fear of the troll cat, people have actually attacked innocent real cats as well as troll cat balls, behavior which is related to the fact that a real phenomenon, the so-called aegagropilae, has been associated with the troll cat. Aegagropilae are balls of undigested matter formed in the cow's stomach which are expelled with excrement. When dry, they can roll along the ground. People have believed that they were seeing a troll cat in broad daylight, and most often tried to beat it to death.

Beliefs about the witch's hug in the shape of a cat are stronger than those about the witch's hug in the shape of a ball. This is probably due to the fact that tradition describes the witch's preparation of such a ball. It was generally believed that she had to sell her soul to the Devil so that he could breathe life into this being, because the witch was unable to bestow life herself. Perhaps it was difficult to reconcile these perceptions with the concept of the hug. Even so, both types of troll cats have been closely related to the witch. It was believed that she had to take it with her to the grave; otherwise she would have to return from her grave to get it.

Judging from tradition, the troll cat was a very greedy creature. Sometimes it had sucked up more milk on its expeditions than it could hold. The waste, which was attributed to the troll cat, was often called troll-cat vomit or *tusse-dung,* which actually might have been quick-growing mushrooms, various types of algae, or secretions from insects. When this was burned, the witch felt as if she were burning, too.

Other Concepts of the Soul: Vor(d) and Fylgje

In addition to beliefs about the hug, there are other concepts of the soul, such as the *vor(d)* and the *fylgje*. In tradition, the concept of the hugham often merges with that of the fylgje and the vor(d). The most important difference between these concepts is their function in relation to human beings and the world at large. Although the hugham and the fylgje often have the same appearance, the hug and hugham lead very unstable lives between the individual and the surroundings and can be consciously controlled, while the fylgje and the vor(d) are passive, and people have very little control over them. With vigilance it is possible to retain them (which is desirable), but it is not possible to direct them.

The vor(d) represents the alter-ego. It is sometimes described as an "accompanying or protecting spirit," although it is not clear what its protective function is. The vord can be synonymous with hug, but it seems to be a more complex concept of the soul than hug, which is merely a part of it.

People could not get along without either the hug or the vor(d). In Norway, as in other Scandinavian countries, it was customary to accompany guests to the door and hold the door open, saying, "I'd better let your vor(d) out behind you." People must have believed that more of a guest was present than could be seen, and it had to have time to get out. If you prevented the vor(d) from joining its owner, you were guilty of causing the person to be *vor(d)stjålet* (vor(d)-stolen), which was parallel to hugstjålet. The concept of the vardøger has merged with the concept of letting out the vor(d), despite the differences between the two. Perhaps people concluded that, since the vardøger came ahead of the person, it must be present somewhere, and had to be let out when the guest left. In tradition we often find that the visitor is accompanied to the door in order to "let out the vardøger."

The concept of the vor(d) is probably the most widespread notion of the soul in our tradition. From a witchcraft trial in 1660, there is a description of the vor(d) that depicts it as a kind of unattached soul. The accused woman, who was from Mandal, told the court:

> There is a vord in people's breasts, which goes out at night when they are asleep. And if an evil spirit comes and prevents it from coming back again, that person will lose his mind unless it returns in a day or two. (Østberg, 1925, 84)

In Norwegian tradition, the vor(d) appears in various shapes: as the person, as different animals, as a light, mist, and such like. It is often invisible, but perceptible. The word vor(d) can designate that which leaves a person at the moment of death. It was a widespread custom to leave the door ajar when someone died, to let the vor(d) out. This description from Telemark dates from the end of the eighteenth century:

The *Vor* is the spirit of the dead person, which often reveals itself at the moment it leaves the body as a thick, narrow, long, whitish cloud, at times extinguishing candles, at times entering animals which become enraged thereafter, and wish to accompany the body, uncontrollable until they hear the lid being nailed to the coffin. (Wille, 1786, 253)

The whereabouts of a departed vor(d) is a matter of conjecture. There are a number of illnesses whose names contain the prefix vor(d), such as "vord pinch" and "vord scratch." These described unexplainable marks on the body, which were believed to have been made by the dead.

The concept of fylgje is described as an accompanying spirit. In ancient times, the fylgje was credited with a protective function, revealed when the person was in a critical situation. This criterion has been lost in Norwegian oral tradition, unless the idea of accompanying can be interpreted as a protective function. The fylgje is described as appearing in the shape of the person or of an animal that had some relationship to the person's character as it was perceived by the milieu: a coward's fylgje would take the shape of a hare; a sly person's a fox; a ladies' man's a cock; and so forth.

People had to be clairvoyant in order to see the fylgje. It was generally supposed that cattle could see more than people, and if cattle were restless when a stranger entered the barn, pulling at their tethers, looking around, and mooing, then the stranger's fylgje was a beast of prey. In the following text from the nineteenth century, it is apparent that we are dealing with the concept of the fylgje, here called a *valdøvvel:*

The cow can see the person's "valdøvvel"; that's why it sometimes glowers or rolls its eyes and bellows when someone goes by. The person the cattle are mooing at has a beast of prey as it's "valdøvvel." If you carry in an armful of wood, you mustn't drop it with a crash so as to frighten away the "valdøvvel," since it is dangerous to lose it. (NFS Moe 106, V7)

An old woman from Markabygda here in Leksvik said that as a child she had heard the following account from an old woman: in her youth she was on her way to a dance to which she had been invited. It was late in the summer. She didn't really want to go to this dance, she said, but she went all the same, after she had finished the evening chores at home. When she was almost at the house, she went a little to one side before going in. It was late in the evening. She went behind a big tree which stood by the house. She stood there for a moment, and wondered if she shouldn't turn around and go back home, because deep down inside she didn't want to go to this dance. But it's funny, when you've been invited by someone you would like to know better. Then it suddenly occurred to her to peep in the windows. The dancing had begun, but there weren't many couples on the floor, only five or six. Just inside the window, a lanky bumpkin was swinging his partner in the dance. He was known to her as one who never gave his horses enough fodder in winter. In the poorly lighted room, she caught a glimpse of something following him: his fylgje—a horse that was nothing more than skin and bones, swaying from side to side, too starved to stay on its feet. The next man leading his partner was a fat glutton from a big farm further down in the parish. His fylgje was a fat pig, humping along on all fours. In the third couple was a man nicknamed "Rosvold the Fox" because he tried to hoodwink everyone he talked to. Behind him a fox came slinking. Next came a fellow with a sprightly girl in his arms. He was called "The Lady Killer," because he ran after all the girls in the district, and behind him was a cock. The girl was ready to faint on the spot, when she saw all the evil fylgje in animal ham who were mingling with the dancers. She went home, and never went to dances again. (NFS Kruken VIII, 46)

The Dream-Soul

Today there is a tendency to use material from the sagas to illustrate the concepts of dream-life in ancient times. These texts contain a wealth of exciting material about the dreams of our forebears; however, these dreams are used to catalyze the action in the texts, and therefore cannot be used as reliable information about people's relationship to dreams, not even during the time of the sagas. The sagas are literature. They contain beliefs, but are no more sources for popular beliefs of the past than contemporary historical novels are for the present. In recent tradition, there is very little that can shed light on dream-concepts. But in ancient times, the dividing line between dream and reality was not as strong as it is now. It was believed that part of the alter-ego—we can call it the dream-soul—left the sleeper and experienced life outside. From personal experience, people regarded dreams as experiences of the soul. Since there was no threshold between worlds, the soul could pass through the realms of the living and the dead. As we know from our own experience, a dream can seem so real that we can reach out for someone long lost, and remain in a half-waking state, wistful because no one was there. People have believed in dreams as omens; therefore, you were not supposed to recount an unpleasant dream, lest it come true. On the other hand, there were rites by which one could make dreams come true, and usually they contain an element of newness: one slept in a new bed, in a new room, in a new house, wearing new clothes, for example. Even today there are people who count the windowpanes before going to sleep in a new room, because their dreams will then come true. Material about dreams has been collected at random. The fact that there is little material does not mean that there were no concepts attached to dreams, but rather that the theme was too self-evident for informants and collectors to deal with. Today, the notion of the soul's leaving the body is rare, but the notion of dreams coming true is quite common. It is difficult to verify this kind of information because the memory of the dream may be colored by experience.

In Norwegian tradition there is one legend about the dream-soul. Since it is a migratory legend, it has limited value to Norwegian concepts of the dream-soul (Christiansen, 1958, type 4000). It is called "The Guntram Legend," because the oldest variant, recorded by Paulus Diaconus, a historian who died in 797, is associated with Guntram, king of the Burgundians (Liestøl, 1963, 208ff.). There are two main characters: a dreamer and an observer of the dreamer's soul, which, as a tiny animal, leaves the sleeper and goes on a journey of its own. After the dream-soul has returned, the sleeper awakens and tells what he dreamed. The one who observed the journey of the dream-soul describes what he has seen. "The Guntram Legend" is really a legend about buried treasure, but in Norwegian tradition the treasure motif has been lost, and it has developed into a legend about mortals who have a dream-soul. The following variant comes from Gudbrandsdal:

> There is an ancient belief that the soul is somewhere else when one is dreaming. Thus, in Lessø, it is believed that every person is accompanied by a tiny animal called a *vord*. Now it happened that two reindeer hunters were out hunting. As it was getting late in the evening, they lay down to sleep and wait for the reindeer—because in earlier times, when there were plenty of reindeer, no one bothered to go a long way to look for them, but waited until they came. After they had been sleeping for a while, one of the men awoke, and he wanted to wake the other. But he couldn't get him awake, even though he fired a shot over his body. Finally he caught sight of a tiny mouse that was scurrying back and forth by a brook as if it couldn't get across. Well, it finally came up to them and ran over to the sleeper's head. There it vanished, and, at the same moment, the man woke up. He said he had dreamed that he was struggling to get across a river. (NFS Asbjørnsen VIII, 70)

From the tradition of the Same (Lapps) comes this variant which has retained the original treasure motif:

> Three men set out to find the North Pole, but were stopped by the ice. When the wind started to blow, the ice was scattered and they came to open sea, and by the time they realized where they were, they were off the coast of Russia. So they set out for home again. As they traveled, they lay down to sleep, and one of the men dreamed about some money hidden nearby. Another man was awake, and saw something resembling a bumble bee crawl out of the sleeper's nose and fly over to a bush. He watched closely. The bee stayed by the bush for a while, then came back and entered the sleeper's nostril.
> They got up in the morning, and the man told his companions: "I dreamed there were a lot of silver coins by a bush!" The other man said nothing. The time came for them to set out again. Then the man who had watched the bumble bee said, "I'm not leaving here. You can go on, but I don't want to go today."
> When the others had gone, he went over to the bush and began to dig at the spot where he had seen the bee. He found a lot of silver coins and objects of silver, so there was quite a load. He walked the whole day. Then he lay down to sleep. He dreamed that a man came to him and said, "You have done wrong not to tell this to the man from whose nostril you saw the bee come. You must give him a share of the money. If you don't, you will fare badly." He got up, and

thought, "I can't bring myself to give him any of the money." Again he walked for a long time, and when it was dark he lay down and went to sleep. Again the man came in his dream and said, "You shall give your companion half, because what you saw was that man's 'fortune'!" When he came back home, he told the man what he had seen and why he had stayed behind, and gave him half the treasure. He went to sleep again that night, and dreamed that an old woman came to him and said, "If you hadn't given him half of the treasure, you would have been turned into an idiot and ruined your life." (Qvigstad, 1929, 333ff.)

In Norway, the notion that the soul assumes the shape of a tiny animal and leaves the body during a dream does not occur in the memorate tradition and, in all likelihood, was not part of collective tradition. On the other hand, the belief that the soul went on its own journey while the person slept still exists, and appears in the way people treat a sleeping person. There are tabus against touching sleepers, especially babies. A change of position might confuse the soul so that it could not enter the person again. The superstition that one must not wake a sleep-walker has its roots in this idea. The contemporary reason given is that the sleepwalker may go crazy from the abrupt awakening; but we need not go back very far to discover the idea that this rude awakening could prevent the soul from returning to the person, thus causing the loss of the alter-ego.

The Free-Soul

In popular tradition, the most specialized form of the unstable soul is the one on which shamanism is based. This is a metaphysical concept that a soul was not only directed by the individual, but could assume any ham appropriate to the situation. These concepts were associated with specialists—people versed in the art of magic. The activities of shaman among the Same (Lapps) must have added weight to beliefs that certain people could obtain useful information by the transmigration of the soul. But in tradition, the soul's domain was limited to the perceivable world, while the shaman's soul travels everywhere.

There is a migratory legend that exists throughout Norway called "The Finn's Journey" (Christiansen 1958, type 3080), based on these concepts of the soul. The main character is a Same who offers (or is asked) to obtain information about how things are in a certain place. This he does by falling into a trance and sending out his soul. To prove that he is telling the truth after he comes out of the trance, he produces an object (usually silver) which he has brought with him. Despite the fact that "The Finn's Journey" is a migratory legend and should therefore not be used as a source of Norwegian concepts, it was popularly believed that the Same were skilled in magic, and it might well have been believed that they were capable of sending their souls on journeys. Nevertheless, the legend shows a vacillating attitude toward the Same's ability to send out his soul:

Nirid Sønnstveiten, old Anne Golid's brother, was a skipper. Once his ship was all the way down by the coast of China. With him was a Lapp boy, who knew a bit more than others. One day Nirid said, "Well, Lord knows how my folks are doing back home now. I've been away nearly a year, and when I left, my wife was going to have a baby. I haven't heard anything from home since I left, so I don't know if she's alive or dead."

"If you'll give me five quarts of brandy, then I'll go home and visit your family in two hours," said the Lapp boy.

"Ha, ha!" said Nirid. "You could never find my home, as far away as it is now. But you know I'd gladly give you five, even ten quarts of brandy if you could do it."

"Well," said the boy, "just tell me about one thing that you'd recognize, so I can bring it back with me."

Nirid told him about a silver spoon which the *tussefolk* (fairies) had left behind, and which had been handed down on the farm for hundreds of years, from generation to generation—and which each owner had marked with his initials. This was what the boy was supposed to bring back with him.

Then the Lapp boy drew a circle on the deck, seated himself on a chair in the middle; no one was supposed to come inside the circle for two hours. After a while the boy fell asleep, and then a black bird flew up and perched on his shoulder, and started picking and picking at some froth in the corner of the boy's mouth. It did this for a while, then flew away. Two hours later it came back with something in its beak. Then the boy woke up. He was holding an old silver spoon in his hands. He gave it to Nirid and asked if he recognized it. Nirid was quite beside himself, for he recognized his silver spoon at once.

"Well, now I can tell you how your folks are getting along at home," said the boy. "Your wife has a handsome, strapping boy, and they're both well. I saw your father down on his knees by the chopping block, cutting wood. Your mother was sitting outside a little house, spinning yarn on a spindle or a peg. She seemed to be frail and fretting."

Nirid made a note of that day. When he came home after a long time, he asked if they had noticed anything on that day. Yes, there had been a terrible banging and roaring. They thought the house was going to fall down that night. And the strangest thing was that the old *tussespoon* had vanished completely. No one had seen it since. Then Nirid took the spoon out of his pocket, and told them what had happened. (Flatin, 1930, 116)

During journeys of the free-soul and the dream-soul, the body remains passive, and the person does not revive until the soul is back in place. To some extent, this tradition has merged with the tradition of the witch. It was occasionally reported that witches sent their hugham to the Sabbath, and they slept restlessly in their beds during the ceremonies. In accounts of the witchcraft trials in Finnmark, there are often reports about witches attending the Sabbath in animal shapes. In my opinion, this is a carryover from the idea of the shaman's hugham. It does not usually appear in accounts from Norwegian witchcraft trials.

Conclusion

In earlier times, it was generally believed that the hug was an active factor in human life, and beliefs about it appear in much of our tradition. In recent years this popular belief has gotten a new lease on life through widespread interest in parapsychology, clairvoyance and witchcraft.

Concepts of a *skyggesjel* (shadow-soul) have existed in many cultures. Even though there are items in Norwegian tradition that suggest a very close relationship between people and their shadows, I have been unable to draw any conclusions about belief in a shadow-soul. Most likely the shadow has been regarded as an organic part of the person.

Despite the scanty material on the dream-soul, it is my opinion that people believed in it. Our sporadic collecting and inadequate registration are partly responsible for the lack of materials. Here is an opportunity for new collecting. Concepts about the soul's leaving the body in animal shape while the person is sleeping, and the belief that the person can be injured if the soul is hurt, have disappeared. But the belief still prevails that through dreams one can affect the surroundings, and send and receive messages.

Belief in the free-soul following the body as a kind of accompanying spirit or leaving the body on errands, was widespread in earlier times, but no longer exists in Norway. On the other hand, belief in the soul's tangible departure from the body at the time of death still exists. In tradition the soul is not necessarily described as visible at the moment of death, but as perceptible—as something light and happy, or dark and threatening, depending on the kind of life the person lived. The stories told about the circumstances surrounding a person's death often seem to be a tapestry of popular and ecclesiastical ideas about the soul and its journey.

The following accounts were recorded in the nineteenth century, but I have heard many people in our time tell similar experiences:

> More than fifty years have passed since an old, unmarried woman died in Leiret. Throughout her life, she had been a good person, and she was content when she saw that her time was drawing near. It was in the summer, and the window was open. At the very moment she departed this life, they saw a white shape part from the body and rush out the window, so that a handkerchief lying on the windowsill was carried along in the gust of air and fell down in the garden. The old folks said it was her soul that had left the body. (Nergaard, 1925, 98)

> Haldor, from Øyegard at Lone, was said to have died in such a fine way. When he breathed his last, a ray of white light left him and went up to Heaven. I dare say he was saved when he died, old Haldor. It was such a fine death. Haldor had been an unusually good man while he lived. He always read his Bible, and prayed and held vespers in his house. God have mercy on his memory! (Hermundstad, 1955, 220)

THE DEAD WITHOUT STATUS

Juha Pentikäinen

In that it contains the sociological term *status,* the concept of "dead without status" is a reference to social position; it indicates that the problem before us may be considered social as well as religious. The dead without status are those whose admission to the community of the departed has, for one reason or another, been denied. Such dead persons, lacking position or status either in the communities of the living or those of the dead, remain in a permanent transition phase that may be compared to the Catholic concept of Purgatory. Finnish belief tradition embraces a similar concept, *sijattomat sielut* (placeless souls), which refers to those among the departed who are restless. In German tradition they are called *arme Seelen* (poor souls). For example:

> A man died. He was buried with a silver cross around his neck. When silver is placed with the dead (or around the neck) they have no place "in the earth." They become placeless. The earth does not accept the silver. Those who as a result of the silver have become placeless are not *manalaiset* (underground dwellers). They are just placeless and have no place in the earth or in heaven. They must always be floating and walking until the silver is removed. (SKS Paulaharju, 14456, 1930)

This record comes from a Greek Orthodox district, where there exists a norm tradition supported by a sect called "Old Believers." Putting silver in a grave was considered a sin, because it resulted in the dead person's restlessness. The following belief is found all over Finland: "If you die a bad death, you will haunt" (e.g., Heinjoki. S. G. Taponen KRK 139:12; Karstula. K. Krohn 220, 1884). The basis for this concept is found in a Swedish-Finnish church law which, even into the twentieth century, classified the departed and their funeral ceremonies in four categories, according to the manner of death: "public," "quiet," "shameful," and "depraved." "Public" funerals were the norm. "Quiet" funerals were for stillborn children, the unbaptized, people who had committed suicide in a

Originally published in *Temenos,* 1969.

fit of temper, alcoholics, and those who had given their bodies for anatomical research. The priest was present, but was allowed to read only the committal. "Depraved" burials were for victims of duels, for anyone who had been killed in anger, died in prison, or lived an ungodly life, for murdered children, and for unknowns found dead. Their graves were situated in the "worst corner" of the graveyard, still seen in many churchyards today. The priest was not present and there was no Christian ceremony. "Shameful" burials were for deliberate suicides (who were excommunicated) and for the executed. Their bodies were buried in the forest (Bælter, 1793; Lehtonen, 1931).

There is an evident link between ecclesiastical custom and folk tradition. People who died in ways categorized as problematical by the legal tradition of the church appear in folk belief as "placeless souls" not even allowed the respectable name of "departed" (SKS Rautiainen, 2086, 1949). We must remember here that there are different theological positions espoused by various churches and religious groups, most of which are also manifested in folk belief. Among these we find the question of the position of the unbaptized child after death (Pentikäinen, 1968a, 61–62, 217–21).

Religious historians have advanced different theories about death and the departed. In the nineteenth and early twentieth centuries, theorists such as Lévy-Bruhl (1922) stressed the difference between natural and supernatural death. By "natural" Lévy-Bruhl meant "rational," and by "supernatural" he meant "speculative" or "irrational." This distinction would have been more useful if the starting point had been not a scholarly theory but ideas embraced by the community itself. As a functionalist, Malinowski calls death "the supreme and final crisis of life," an exceptional, unexpected event, creating problems for and demanding measures from the community (Malinowski, 1954, 47, 149). For the individual, death means one's destiny in the afterlife, while for the community it is a factor that shakes cohesion and organization. Every death changes the communal structure, and the quality of the change is determined by the status accorded the person in life. During the ceremonies surrounding death, others must take over the duties of the departed. An excellent example is provided by the English cultural anthropologist Daryll Forde in his description of burial customs among the Yakü people in eastern Nigeria: the problems caused by the death of a distinguished person—the problem of a successor, intrigues, and financial arrangements—are all resolved in the course of the burial ceremonies (Forde, 1962).

Many theories about death mistakenly regard events involving the individual and those involving the group as independent of each other. Malinowski's theory is contradictory in that he acknowledges no connection between the welfare of the deceased's spirit *(baloma)* in the afterlife and the rites directed to him or her. Malinowski's own material shows that burial rites are necessary in order to prepare the departed for transition to the other world: the body is dressed and decorated for the journey (Malinowski, 1954, 156–57). The preparation is necessary despite the fact that an individual's position in the afterlife is determined solely by the manner of death. According to the Kiriwina concept, the abode of the dead is divided into three sections. The war dead, suicides, and the drowned go to the best part; the poisoned go to the second part; anyone killed by witchcraft goes to the third. People who die of sickness or old age are also accorded the last position and therefore die in the least desirable way (Malinowski, 1954, 149ff.). The order of precedence is exactly the reverse of that in Swedish-Finnish church law.

Another dimension missing from Malinowski's theory concerns *rites de passage* (van Gennep, 1909, trans. 1960). According to van Gennep, death and the afterlife are new states of existence into which people move in the same way they move into phases of earthly life: birth, childhood, puberty, engagement, marriage, pregnancy, fatherhood, profession, or group membership. In both ancient and modern societies these passages are made public and sacred by means of rites that follow similar patterns everywhere. There is first the detaching from the previous position (separation), then an intermediary phase between two positions (marge). The third and final phase is the taking up of the new position (agregation). Van Gennep divides his "rites of passage" into three groups: rites of separation, rites of transition, rites of incorporation. Lauri Honko has defined these rites sociologically as "traditional rituals, organized by society, whereby the individual is moved from one social status to another" (Honko, 1964a, 121). Burial customs have not, so far, been analyzed as rites of passage. However, on the basis of Finnish material, it is clear that rites of transition and incorporation are more important in burial ceremonies than are rites of separation. The central problems concern how the deceased are moved into the community of the dead and how the remaining society reorganizes itself.

The intimate relationship between the family and its dead may be envisioned as a circle, one half of which is under the ground, the other half above. In the Finnish province Karelia, for example, dependence is so complete that the rights of the dead are like a form of taxation. The family organizes the funeral as well as periodic commemorative ceremonies, and provides for the dead by granting them part of the annual harvest (Waronen, 1895, 108–12; Honko, 1965, 275–80; cf. Pentikäinen, 1968a, 47, 54ff.). The dead direct threats against the family in the form of warnings against neglecting rites and against improper behavior. As Uno Harva observed, "In every phase of individual or family life, the dead are . . . the guardians of morals, customs and social organization. In this respect, not even the god of the upper airs can compete with the dead in the other world" (1948, 511).

Many important relationships between the family and the dead are actualized in the rites of annual festivals. The appearance of the dead at these occasions is seen as positive in spite of the fact that their behavior may be threatening. If they appear at the right time and place, they have a constructive social function. A considerable number of events meaningful to a family occur immediately following a death. In Karelia the critical period ends when certain ceremonies are performed six weeks after a death. Supranormal experiences happen to family members responsible for equipping the departed, choosing the burial site, and generally observing the norms of mourning that determine the position of the departed in the afterlife. Even though the dead person is a relative or acquaintance, an encounter is usually frightening and surprising. This fear is evident, for example, in laments that never ask for a quick return of the dead (Honko, 1963, 114–15). On the contrary, he or she is forbidden to wander at home as a frightening ghost, but is asked instead to return as a soul bird after an appropriate lapse of time.

Only the dead who have been properly equipped by the family may become objects of a cult. In Finnish beliefs about the dead, the most ancient division is between *family dead* and *other dead*. It would be interesting to explore the connection between this division and the widespread tradition of the so-called walking dead. The pertinent material is varied, consisting of stereotyped international legends and memorates. In the Nordic material (cf. Pentikäinen, 1968a, 365), the "walking dead" can be divided into two groups: the "guilty" and the "innocent." The former includes dead who "walk" because of a crime committed while alive: child murderers, people who committed perjury or moved boundary stones, witches or anyone who stole community wafers or asked the devil's help, gluttons, drunkards, card players, and generally anyone who had led an ungodly life. The second group of "walking dead" includes those whose haunting is not explained as punishment for crimes committed while alive. The "innocent dead" may be further divided according to role: (1) "solicitous dead" (mothers who died in childbirth, jealous husbands, persons engaged to be married, those with social or economic responsibilities, those who had hidden their money or had left a task or a promise unfulfilled); (2) "unsatisfied dead" (someone dressed negligently for burial, left unburied, or not buried as wished, someone grieved for too much or not mourned at all, someone buried in a wet place or feeling lonely in the cemetery); (3) "avenging dead" (anyone who had been badly treated, bewitched, or murdered, especially murdered children); (4) "disturbing dead" or *Poltergeists* (Simonsuri, 1961, No. C 401–500; Wessman, 1931, No. 22–29). The most recent stratum in the tradition of the "walking dead" is represented by an abundance of legends about the "guilty dead." Often there are Christian explanations for this restlessness: the "walking dead" is a sinner who has broken a Christian norm. On the other hand, the problems of the "innocent dead" reflect the intimate relationship between living and dead members of a family in regard to some unsatisfied need. The same is suggested by legends and memorates in which the dead person appears in a solicitous role to caution or express sympathy with the living. By contrast, the "avenging" and "disturbing dead" are mostly from outside the family.

In his article "A Running Stream They Dare Not Cross," Martti Haavio has written about the beliefs attached to the dead who have not been equipped for their journey to the land of death. There are both "souls which find rest and souls which find none" (1959, 129). Among the latter are the murdered, unburied, unbaptized, or otherwise unequipped, expressing their placelessness in one way or another. Haavio shows that the problem is supranormal and communal: people who have died a natural death and are properly provided for by their relatives reach the land of the dead. The opposite is true for the dead who have not been properly equipped. They are "without status." Elsewhere I have shown that the exceptional character of these dead appears in many cultures in at least three different ways: (1) Burial ceremonies differ from the norm: if they died a "bad death" (see Sell, 1955), they are buried with special rites—without coffin or ceremony, apart from others—or are left unburied. (2) No one feels obliged to equip these dead or to be concerned about what will happen to them in the afterlife; they are like strangers no one provides for. (3) It is believed that an individual who has died a bad death will not reach the community of the dead; he or she will haunt the living in one way or another (Pentikäinen, 1968a, 49).

Dead children provide a typical example of the dead without status. The problem with abandoned, murdered, unbaptized, aborted, or stillborn children is that they have died before the proper status-conferring rites could be performed. Their position is problematical in that they have never belonged to the community of the living and therefore cannot belong to the community of the dead. Burial ceremonies are either performed in a special way or are left unperformed. It is evident that the child is considered an outsider: he or she has at no point been a member of the family or been accepted in the community of the dead, which is the object of the cult.

In terms of religious phenomenology, *naming* was the most important symbol of social acceptance of a child. Name-giving rites transfer not only the name of a living or dead relative but also his or her personal "qualities" (Ploss, 1911, 408–56), thus signifying the child's official membership in the family. The condition for social acceptance was normally that the child be shown to have a father and a mother—in many cultures, an illegitimate child was rejected, abandoned, or killed. In Viena Karelia a newborn child was taken from the sauna (the usual birthing place) to the house and there wrapped in the father's shirt to confirm the latter's acceptance (Paulaharju, 1924, 28ff.). The mother's acceptance of the child was demonstrated by a ritual feeding.

In Nordic tradition, naming is an older rite than Christian baptism. In the Icelandic sagas a father demonstrated his approval by receiving the child that was brought to him, pouring water on it, and giving it a name (Reichborn-Kjennerud, 1933, 83). The question of keeping or abandoning the child was settled at the moment of name-giving. A child that for one reason or another was not accepted and not given a name was exposed (Gunnlaugs saga, 1938, 55–56; Hardar saga, 1945, 11–14). In both the sagas and the provincial laws, the exposing of a baptized child was considered murder. The pre-Christian *Hardar saga ok Holmverja* (ca. A.D. 950) states laconically: "Murder was this, that children were killed after water had been poured over them" (1945, 11–14). Norwegian and Swedish provincial laws called the exposing of an unbaptized child "murder of a pagan" and prescribed exceptionally severe punishments for it (Pentikäinen, 1968a, 78). Thus, according to both saga and legal tradition, naming is the most important criterion of social acceptance. Similarly, a child which had been placed at its mother's breast could not be abandoned. This rite, central to the public demonstration of the mother's acceptance, is also ancient. According to an eighth-century Frisian saint's legend, a child had to be drowned if it was to be abandoned "prisquam lac sugeret matris"—before it had sucked its mother's breast (Reichborn-Kjennerud, 1933, 84). The fact that naming is a real symbol of status is supported by the Scandinavian provincial inheritance laws, in which name-giving and the first maternal feeding are criteria for inheritance rights (Møller, 1940, 316–17, 417).

The Nordic dead-child tradition is an especially rich field for the scholar. The geographic region is inhabited by different linguistic and cultural groups that coexist and overlap: Scandinavians, Finns, and Lapps. From a historical perspective, we may also include the Greenland Eskimos, who apparently adopted most of their dead-child beliefs from the Norwegian Vikings who lived on the island for five hundred years between A.D. 986 and 1450 (Pentikäinen, 1968a, 352–53). The geographical and historical comparison is interesting in that one can observe the same phenomenon at several different periods. The subject of child abandonment arises in the Icelandic sagas from the eleventh to the thirteenth centuries, in Norwegian and Swedish provincial laws between the twelfth and fourteenth centuries, and in Finnish and Lappish material from the eighteenth to the twentieth centuries. Among the Eskimos child abandonment was still part of the social system in the twentieth century. The Eskimologist Knud Rasmussen discovered in 1923 that women in Malerualik—a village belonging to the Netsilik Eskimos—killed thirty-four percent of their offspring, sixty-four percent of whom were girls (Rasmussen, 1931, 139–42).

Child abandonment seems to have been an approved custom in the Nordic countries before the advent of Christianity. The tradition follows the old Roman and Germanic practice according to which the head of the family, usually the father, had the right to decide whether a child born into the family was to be provided for or exposed. Abandonment of children was made a criminal offense in Iceland in 1018, in Norway between the eleventh and twelfth centuries, in Denmark and southern Sweden somewhat earlier (Pentikäinen, 1968a, 68ff.). The first important phase in the Nordic dead-child tradition coincides with the advent of Christianity and in the centuries immediately following. The second important phase was in the seventeenth and eighteenth centuries, when child-murder in Sweden and Finland was the crime most commonly punished by death (Boström, 1929, 174, 180–81). In the first phase the belief tradition concerning dead-child beings became established; later legends arose in which the central element was the discovery of the child-murderer by supranormal means. These two strata are evident in Finnish and Lappish material, and they are clearly borrowed from Scandinavian tradition

(Pentikäinen, 1968a, 288–91, 325–34). The question of cultural borrowing is an interesting subject. In Lapland, for example, plentiful survivals from different periods can be found, periods whose traces have elsewhere either become rare or disappeared.

In Nordic tradition there is an interesting geographic division concerning the criteria for supranormality of the dead child. In the west—Iceland, the Færoes, Norway, western Sweden, and western Lappish districts—the dead child "walks" because it is unbaptized. In the east—eastern Sweden, Finland, and eastern Lappish areas—it does so because it has been buried in unconsecrated ground. We are dealing with two theological problems stemming from different periods. One stresses the lack of a name, the other the lack of burial. Common to both is the fact that the dead child is without status. This distinction reflects the history of the early church: historically speaking, the problem of baptism preceeded the problem of burial. A similar geographical division is found in rites for "laying" dead-child beings. In the west dead-child beings are pacified by baptismal rites, in the east by burial rites. The *in extremis* baptismal rites in Norwegian and Lappish tradition can be traced back to ancient Norwegian law (Pentikäinen, 1968a, 217–21, 320–22). In Sweden and Finland, on the other hand, we find the tradition of the "quiet burial." In either case, what is common to these baptismal and burial rites is that the restless dead are provided with the status that has been lacking.

History and Legend

HISTORICAL LEGENDS AND HISTORICAL TRUTH

Brynjulf Alver

On a field trip to Setesdal in May 1961, Arne Berg, Olav Bø, and I met an old silversmith. He was a fascinating man, intelligent and articulate. Like everybody else in Setesdal, he was interested in history and tradition, and whenever he related a tradition he insisted that what he told was "true." In Setesdal there is no getting around one subject when you talk to anyone with historical interests: Johannes Skar and *Gamalt or Sætesdal* (Old Traditions from Setesdal). That's exactly what happened in the case of the silversmith, and he wasn't altogether happy about Johannes Skar's books.

"He doesn't write the truth," he said.

"How's that?" we asked.

"Well, he tells about the shield maiden who shot an arrow at St. Olaf in Heddi. That's not true, you know; St. Olaf never came to Setesdal!"

The silversmith was right, of course. Johannes Skar wrote down a legend he had heard, but the legend was not based on historical truth. St. Olaf never came to Setesdal.

The silversmith's skeptical rationalism leads us straight to a controversial topic: What measure of truth is there in oral tradition? The narrative traditions most relevant to this question are historical legends, so called because they describe historical persons and events. But that doesn't mean these legends always tell about real events or are factually accurate. In many cases we might call them quasi-historical village tales. Often these stories contain supranormal motifs, but usually there is an allegedly historical person or event at the center of the narrative.

We can conveniently divide historical legends into two groups: those legends whose historicity we can check against written documentation, and those we

Original title: "Historiske segner—historisk sanning." Published in *Norveg*, 1962.

cannot. The archaeologist Karl Rygh has provided an example of the first group:

> In 1876 I heard a legend in Strinden about an armored knight and his horse lying under a huge rock on a certain slope. He had been crushed by an avalanche as he went riding by. I dug around and under that rock as far as possible, and sure enough, there were the bones of a man and a horse as well as a "steel" (for striking sparks from flint) and two spear points from the Viking period. There had not been any grave at that place.

In this instance the legend had preserved precise information about an event that occurred a thousand year ago. There are many similar examples, as in the following story from Sweden:

> On Husby Farm in the parish of Vendel, Uppland, there is a big grave mound people call Ottar's Hill. The mound is about 40 meters in diameter, 8 meters in height. Archaeologists excavated the mound in 1914–16. In a hollow below a heap of stones they found a wooden bucket with gilded bronze fixtures. The bucket contained cremated bones, pieces from a board game, and fragments of a bone comb. The grave can be dated by the find of an Eastern Roman coin bearing the image of Emperor Basilikus (476–477). The coin had been used as a pendant in a necklace and, since it was somewhat worn, the archaeologists hypothesized that the grave might be from the first decade of the sixth century, which is when the king of the Ynglings, Ottar Vendelkråka, is supposed to have died. They concluded that Ottar's Hill must be the king's grave. (Lindquist, 1936)

In this instance the name of the gravesite was enough to preserve the memory of a historical event over a period of 1,400 years. In oral tradition, however, this name was not connected explicitly with the historical king named in the sagas: that connection was first suggested by scholars. A third example of a verifiable legend takes us to Denmark:

> People in the township of Bølling used to tell about a wagon filled with gold lying in a bog by Dejberg's Vicarage. And what happened when they excavated the bog in 1881–83? They found the remains of two wagons. To be sure, there was no gold. That was something that had been added in oral tradition. The two Dejberg wagons have been dated from the pre-Roman Iron Age. (Pedersen, 1888)

The find at Dejberg leaves the folklorist speechless with awe. Here is an example of oral tradition preserving the essential "truth" over a period of some 2,000 years! Outside Scandinavia there are analogous examples reaching 3,000 and 4,000 years back in time. Of course, not all legends are as reliable. On the contrary, at times an event occurring only a few years ago is so distorted in oral tradition that we hardly recognize it at all. There is, for example, the story about the murderer "Strong Såve" from Telemark. The legend (discussed in detail by Halvor Nordbø, 1928, 53–61) exists in several variants, which fall into two groups. The following version, recorded by Johannes Skar (1911, 107–10), represents the first group:

Såve Nyland [Strong-Såve]

There were some men competing in lifting a stone on Hadde-Moor, but none of them could even budge the stone. Then Strong Såve came along:

"You're lifting like a bunch of weaklings."

"You try it, that fellow is hefty," they said.

Såve lifted it up on the roof of the shed; but the roof broke and the stone filled the whole shed. So then Såve had to drag it out again.

Såve did something incredible in Hardanger. Six men were trying to pull a cow out of Lunse-Bog; but they had to give up.

"Aren't there any men left in Hardanger you can get together to pull the cow out?" Såve sneered.

"Well, come on, big mouth from Telemark, let's see the kind of man you are," answered one of them.

"Move over!" said Såve, taking him by the shoulder and flinging him far out into the bog. Then he grabbed the cow by the horns and flipped her out like a newborn kid.

Såve killed a man; it happened at a wedding in Øverland. Gunnar Uppistog was sitting on a bench by the table and Såve on a stool across from him. That Gunnar was such a big mouth, he carried on and called him names. Såve took it in stride for a long time, but suddenly it seemed that the devil got the better of him.

"I'm going to nail you!" he said, and stuck his knife right through Gunnar and into the wall. Then he realized what he had done and ran away.

Såve was sentenced to outlawry. He stayed in the hills or wherever he could. His family brought him food and whatever else he needed.

"Ståli the Thief" ruled ruthlessly in the villages. People didn't know what to do; no one dared touch him. Then the minister at Vinje came to Såve: if he could bring Ståli tied hand and foot to Vinje, Såve would be a free man. He got Olav Nordgarden to join him and took off as fast as he could. Hearing that Ståli was in Rauland near the coast, they followed the road to the west and cornered him in Hardanger, in the smithy. Såve had such a reputation for being big and stout that Ståli knew him immediately and met him at the door with a sledgehammer. But Såve grabbed him by the wrists, and they fought so hard the anvil flew through the door. Såve won and tied Ståli up and led him to Vinje like a wild animal.

But Såve didn't get his freedom for all that, and he stayed in the woods. One day the minister was out riding when he met him on the road.

"I've wanted to thank you for your loyalty and for keeping your word," said Såve.

And the minister shook his hand — he wasn't on his guard. Then Såve squeezed and crushed every bone in his hand. It was of no use to the minister for the rest of his life.

Såve froze to death. They found him frozen stiff high up in the mountains between Vinje and Setesdal. They raised a pile of stones over him and it is there still. It's called "Såve's Cairn."

As an example of the second group of traditions about "Strong Såve" we will examine a variant collected by H. Tvedten (1895):

> Once Såve was invited to a feast in Etland. At the feast there was a man known for his strength who had heard rumors about Såve and wanted to fight him. Såve was a quiet sort and he tried to keep away from the man, but it was no use. The fighter kept egging him on. Then they say that Såve went to a rock-strewn slope and began lifting stones while talking to himself:
>
> "If I can throw a stone this size, I should be able to take the Etland man."
>
> When Såve came back to the farm where the wedding was held, the man from Etland started to egg him on even more. Finally Såve got angry. He took the kerchief from his neck, removed the silver buttons from his collar, and took off his jacket. It was quite a fight, but finally the Etland man had to give in. Såve pummeled his opponent with his bare fists until he drew blood and then he said:
>
> "If you beg me, I'll let you go." But the other man answered: "Hell, no, I won't beg as long there's life left in me."
>
> Finally Såve got so enraged that he took his knife and stuck it into the chest of the Etland man and he died there on the floor. After the killing a woman from Etland said:
>
> "I knew there was going to be a crime, because the night before the feast I saw the Wild Hunt unsaddle their horses here."

What are the facts behind the Såve stories? From Halvor Nordbø's study we learn that Såve was a real person from Nordgarden Grunge in Grungedal. On the evening of the third day of Christmas in 1712 he killed Ole Åmundsson at a Christmas party held at Øverland. According to court records, both the killer and the victim were quite drunk. A number of witnesses had also "tied one on" and were not able to give a full account of what happened. According to court records, Guttorm Salomonsson testified:

> On the evening of the third day of Christmas he and others were invited guests at a Christmas party at Øverland, and the accused, Såve Jensson, and the man who was killed, Ole Åmundsson, were also there. The witness didn't arrive at Øverland until evening. There he heard that Jensson and Åmundsson had quarreled earlier that night, and now they were sitting together and drinking when another man, Halvor Torbjørnsson, walked up to Ole Åmundsson and asked him whether he had called him a dirty dog. The latter answered no; but then Jensson said something, and when Åmundsson heard what he said, he answered: "Go to hell" and other unseemly words. Then the accused stuck him in the throat with a knife, and he died almost immediately. He did not put up any resistance or have any weapon or knife. But the accused ran away instantly and disappeared, and the witness left the farm right then.

Margit Pålsdaughter testified:

> At the Christmas party at Øverland, Ole Åmundsson abused Såve Jensson, calling him a Nordgård scoundrel and saying that he was going to get his before Christmas was done. Såve didn't say anything, but a little later they started

fighting and then Såve, afraid of his threats, stuck a knife into Ole Åmundsson's throat and he died right after that.

The court's sentence contains the following striking characterization of the accused and the victim:

> As documented, the accused, Såve Jensson, appears to be an uneducated, unintelligent, and timid man who previously never as much as upset a child, let alone with words or deeds harm any man. Nevertheless, as several witnesses have proven beyond any doubt, on the night of the third day of Christmas he did kill the old man Ole Åmundsson, not in blind rage, nor accidentally, or in self-defense, inasmuch as the victim did not carry any weapon, knife or other arms, but, when fighting with the accused, had merely made some insults, as set out and explained in the documents to this case.

And then the sentence:

> Considering the events described, this humble court feels constrained by law and by its conscience to find Såve Jensson, who long since has fled and made his escape, guilty as accused, and sentences him to pay with his life for the life he has taken, and to lose his head by the sword, and declares him an outlaw wherever he can be found, and his possessions forfeited to the crown.

Table 1

	Oral Tradition	Contemporary Documents
The murderer	Såve Nyland Såve	Såve Jensson (Nordgarden Grunge)
The murdered	Torjus Kvasterud Gunnar Uppistog The Etland Man Olav Vinjer A fighter	Ole Åmundsson Old man
Time and place of the murder	Wedding at Øverland Party at Etland	Christmas party at Øverland
Method of killing	Stuck in the chest /with a knife	Stuck in the throat
Motivation	Victim insulted S. Fighter goaded S.	Victim insulted S. /threatened to beat and shoot S. before Christmas was out
Characterization	Strong, Brave Famous for feats At times abnormal reactions	Ignorant, Clumsy Cowardly
Sentence	Outlawed	Outlawed

Table 1 is a systematic comparison of the oral traditions about the murder with contemporary written sources. This comparison reveals that all variants of the legend refer to the murderer by his real name. But in only one variant is the place of the murder given correctly. In all variants the killing occurred at a wedding instead of a Christmas party, perhaps because violence tended to be more common at weddings. Some of the variants describe the circumstances of the killing in detail. In every instance it says that Såve used a knife, but none of the variants mentions that he cut Ole Åmundsson's throat. The motivation for the killing is authentic in most of the variants, as is the sentence. However, none of the legends gives the historical name of the victim, and the characterization of Såve that constitutes the very focus of the entire legend cycle is as unhistorical as it can possibly be. This fact is all the more noteworthy inasmuch as the court took special care in detailing the personalities involved in the tragedy.

How, then, do we decide whether the legend tradition about Såve, dating back no more than 150 years, is historically true or untrue? The answer to this question depends on what we mean by historical truth. Speaking from the perspective of the folklorist with a passion for history, Knut Liestøl would no doubt find that the legend cycle about Såve preserved a gratifying amount of verifiable fact. In reference to so-called family histories—that is, groupings of stories told about a given family—Liestøl had this to say (1922, 154):

> We usually find that the skeleton of the story is historical. The men and women described did live; none of them are fictional. The names, even of less important individuals, are usually correct. The family relationship between given persons is most often the right one, and so is the order of generations. The same applies to many descriptive details, often minor pieces of information one would not expect to survive in oral tradition for any length of time. . . . Many of the tradition bearers must have had a scholarly turn of mind. They must have been trying to differentiate clearly between the past and the present.

A historian, on the other hand, focusing on data rather than intentionality, would find historical legends woefully inaccurate. Halvor Nordbø, a historian with a strong interest in legend traditions, dismisses them as mere lies and fictions (366–68):

> The first thing we notice is how unreliable even the skeletons of these family histories are. . . . We have seen that they contain many migratory legends, which is not surprising in itself. . . . What is surprising, however, is that the migratory elements for which there are no historical bases at all, should have invaded the very core of family histories to the degree that they replace the skeleton of underlying historical facts. And the matter becomes downright incomprehensible when we consider that large portions of these family histories were shaped while the grandchildren of the main characters were still alive, and that the stories were written down no more than one generation after the events took place. This is the problem in a nutshell: how could family histories become so

unreliable in such a short time right under the nose of the family itself? How could these people tell such things?"

But we need not despair. Despite the apparent opposition of these two scholars, they are essentially in the same camp. Thinking and writing from a historian's rather than a folklorist's perspective, they are looking for data accuracy in historical legends, that is, for a kind of truth that is largely irrelevant to folk tradition. The "truth" they isolate is found more easily and reliably in tax, census, and court records, official letters, diplomas, inheritance and church registers, and so on. When we look at the "official" record concerning Såve Jensson and his crime, we find that the historical murderer was a coward and a weakling; but within fifty years after the event he emerged in oral tradition as "Strong Såve," an enormously powerful, brutal bully. Why?

Looking at the killing more closely, we notice how unmotivated it was. The victim did call Såve a scoundrel and threatened to beat him up. But he was drunk when he said this and Såve could have easily walked away. The victim was an old man, and Såve had never hesitated to run away from difficulties and threats before. According to contemporary sources, the killing was perpetrated in a state of intoxication and desperation by a man who throughout his life must have been ridiculed as a weakling and a coward. In one senseless moment the weakling gathered all the courage he didn't know he had and cut the throat of his tormentor.

Såve fled; he was never captured but lived as an outlaw until he froze to death. His tragic death, combined with the irrational aspect of the murder, caused the event to be commemorated in oral tradition. The legends' focus on the personality of Såve can be construed as an attempt to explain how he "became a killer." But there are other reasons why Såve was recast as a courageous, good-natured hero who was supernormally strong. In oral tradition it is not possible to depict a murderer as a coward, lest he appear as the negative counterpart to the victim. He can be brutal or he can be kindhearted, but he cannot be cowardly: no one would bother to tell his story, nor would anyone care to hear about him. There were too many stories about great fighters and masters of hair-pulling and head-butting for the young men to waste their time hearing about a coward who stuck someone with a knife when he was drunk. Significantly, both from the legends and from the court testimony, it is clear that people tended to take Såve's side. The victim was by no means innocent of what happened, and it was probably because of the villagers' sympathy for Såve that he was never caught. Therefore the narrative version of Såve and his tragic fate expresses the common man's view of what "really" happened. The inconsistencies between the court documents and the oral narratives are appropriate to their different functions: legend tradition cannot remain viable and at the same time retain a precise record of factual details. Thus the legends about Såve's crime do not relate objectively what did take place in this instance, but rather convey a generalized view of the events and a popular evaluation of the circumstances leading to the murder. Even though most people felt sympathy for Såve, the villagers could not find any logical reason why the tragedy should have happened. The legends explain it by saying that Såve was abnormal: sometimes something came over him and then he was no longer in full control of himself. According to some variants, there was even some magical power in his knife. Johannes Skar recorded the following story:

> He had moods sometimes when he was barely himself. Once he came to Straum's Farm. He was standing by the door and seemed subdued and depressed. "Won't you sit down?" said the woman. So he sat down. She had a little boy; he came over and wanted to sit in Såve's lap.
> "Take the child!" said Såve. But she didn't respond.
> "Take the child, I tell you!" said Såve and pushed it away; but she just went about her business.
> "Take him, quick! Otherwise, I'm afraid I'll hit him!" shouted Såve. She grabbed the child like lightning.
> His knife—there was something awful about it; Såve couldn't get rid of it. He threw it away, but before he knew it, it was back in the sheath—whatever he did, it always came back. Finally he tossed it into Troll Valley Pond—then it disappeared.

As we have seen, the legend tradition about "Strong Såve" relates another kind of "truth" than historical sources can provide, although we would probably not find this quality in every legend cycle: there is no question that certain legends give an entirely historical description of events in the past, without embellishment or fictionalizing. But in those instances the events themselves are such that they can survive in oral tradition. No doubt life often obeys the same stylistic laws as folk literature.

If we now turn to the second major classification—legend cycles whose historical content we are in no position to test—we need not doubt that they, too, may contain historically precise descriptions of events and circumstances. But that in no way constitutes the most important content of these legends. For example, let us examine a selection of legends about the Black Death, perhaps the widest ranging oral tradition we have, while written sources are limited. This is not surprising because, although the Black Death was without doubt the greatest disaster ever to befall the Norwegian people in historical time, the epidemic effectively put a stop to practically all writing in the country.

It is not known how many people died during the Black Death. Some legends suggest that only one-third of the population survived; the same is asserted by Icelandic annals. Historians' estimates vary between ten and eighty percent, neither of which can possibly be correct. Other historical sources illustrate the impact of the disaster; for instance, as late as 200 years after the epidemic had subsided, the government issued regulations governing the use of farms abandoned during the Black Death.

The epidemic started in China in 1343 and moved west along trade routes.

By late summer of 1349 it reached Bergen, probably by means of an English ship. From here it spread along the coast north and south and inland to Voss, Sogn, and Valdres. By September or October the epidemic had laid waste much of western Norway, Trøndelag, Hålogaland, and Østland, north of Oslo. In the late fall it reached Vestfold; by November it had devastated Tunsberg; by the New Year it came to Telemark.

There are many stories about how the epidemic spread through the country. In oral tradition, it was personified as a man or a woman or a couple, sometimes as a child:

> When the Black Death came to Nordfjord, the people saw him in the shape of a man or a woman. The man carried a rake, the woman a broom. On the farms where the man used his rake, some of the people survived. Where the woman swept with the broom, they all died. (Borchgrevink, 1956, 131)

People imagined that the man and the woman had to have help as they made their way through the country. A number of legends tell how they were exhausted and had trouble walking after the long journey, how they tried to get a lift on a wagon or asked to be carried over the mountains, how they came to a river and needed to be ferried across. "When they came to rivers, they had to have someone carry them over; they couldn't make it across fjords and lakes on their own," tells Olav Sande from Sogn (Segner II, 99). A very common legend describes it like this (Strompdal, 1929, 170ff.):

> When the Black Death was raging, a man came to a farm in Upper Vefsn—some people say it was Laksfors—asking to be ferried across the river. The farmer understood what kind of man he was, and said that he would be glad to ferry him over, if only he escaped the Black Death. The stranger opened a big book he carried, and after turning a few pages, said that unfortunately he could not promise him that, but that he would promise him an easy death. The farmer then ferried him across. When he came home, he felt tired and went to bed. He fell asleep and never woke up again.

The legend types represented by these excerpts obviously do not convey historical fact. The plague was not a couple carrying a rake and broom, and the book containing the names of the people who were to die never existed. These are strictly fictional motifs. Nevertheless we must acknowledge that even without forcing the material we find in these legends important kernels of historical truth. Even though people did not have precise medical knowledge of infectious disease, they grasped that the epidemic moved along the routes of travel. They also understood that the disease did not easily cross over mountains or bodies of water, precisely the insight the legends preserve. And we find impressively precise descriptions of the symptoms of the illness: the exhausted sleep of the man after ferrying the plague—a very common motif in Norwegian legends of the Black Death—corresponds to the coma-like sleep followed by death consistently identified with the epidemic throughout the Middle Ages.

But let us go further in looking for the factual background in legend motifs. For instance, in Hjelmeland, Rogaland, the following is told: In Vormedalen, not far from Funningsland, there was a mountain farm called Torstølen. When the plague came to the village, a man by the name of Tor fled to the mountains and lived there all winter. Next year toward spring he was up on a hill looking down to Vormedalen when he saw smoke from a single chimney at Laugeland. On all the other farms the epidemic had killed everybody. This is a legend motif we find most frequently in Agder and Rogaland where the disease raged at its worst. We must not attach too much importance to the personal or place names—they are certainly not historical. But we may be sure that the legend quite realistically depicts the fear gripping people when they observed person after person collapse, and terrified people fleeing to the woods and mountains to escape the awful threat.

Other legends tell of people turning the sick out of their homes, or trying to suppress the epidemic by burning or drowning the "Pest," or trying to escape by making special vows to God. We must be cautious not to accept these legends as historical documentation of what actually happened. But they do convey the sense of helplessness of people struggling to escape a catastrophe the causes of which they did not understand.

It is told in legend that people carried their dead to cemeteries for burial as long as there were people to do the carrying. But when the last person on a farm died, the corpse had to remain lying where it was. Sometimes the dead were buried in mass graves, and it wasn't always certain that those buried were really dead. From Rogaland we have a story that the people on Frøyland Farm in Time buried twelve bodies in one day. Icelandic annals report that in Bergen eighty corpses were buried in a single cemetery in one day. There were several cemeteries there, and Bergen was a small town at the time, so the loss of life must have been dismally great. The same annals reveal that in the district of Agder seven parishes were completely depopulated within a short period of time. Here we see an instance of the few existing historical sources corroborating oral tradition. We can be sure that the legends do not give us precise figures, but taken as a whole the legends give us a reasonably realistic picture of the scope of the disaster in the hardest-hit villages. While in occasional instances it is possible to prove that a legend reliably describes a specific event, it is important to emphasize that the value of the legend tradition as a historical source rests elsewhere—in the overall picture that body of tradition gives us of the catastrophe and of the mark it left on the imagination of the people. The most moving descriptions from the period are perhaps the Telemark legends about the horse carrying the dead on Møstrand:

> There is a tune called "Førnes Brown." During the Black Death so few people were left on Mjøstrond that they didn't have anyone to lead the horse carrying

the dead, but someone was constantly digging at the church—it was the Rauland Church—so they tied the corpses on a sled and put snowshoes on the horse, and it plodded off by itself. Then they turned it around by the church and sent it back home. But one time one of the snowshoes came off in the mountains, and then the horse didn't fare too well; it started limping, it was quite awful. You can hear it clearly in the tune, how the horse is limping. Oh, yes, that brown horse was never forgotten. (Moe, 1924, 74)

This legend is mostly fiction. For a number of reasons we must assume that the tune "Førnes Brown" is much younger than the period of the Black Death, and it doesn't serve any purpose to ask whether they really let a horse freight the dead across the mountains to the church in Møstrand by itself. The only kernel of historical truth in the legend is that people remembered the Black Death coming to Telemark during the winter.

The traditions about the Black Death have much to say about conditions in the villages after the epidemic was over. According to one migratory legend, there were only two people left in a village, a boy and a girl who eventually discovered each other, married and gave rise to a new generation. This legend is common throughout northern Europe, personal and place names changing from variant to variant. There is most likely nothing factual about the story except that it illustrates how few people survived the plague. We can illustrate this further with a variant recorded on Stryn in the 1950s:

In Stryn the epidemic wiped out the whole village. The only survivor was a girl at Stauri called Siri (the name has been traditional at the Stauri-Farm since then). In Horningdalen there was also only one survivor, a boy by the name of Jon. He thought it was awful to live there all by himself in Horningdalen. One day he left to see whether he couldn't find any people in the neighboring villages. When he got to Gullkoppen Mountain, from where he could see all the way down to Stryn, he saw smoke rising from a chimney at Stauri. It didn't take him long to get down there. But when he got to the farm, he couldn't figure out who had started the fire; there wasn't a living soul anywhere. It took some time before he discovered a girl hiding below a brewing vat. It was Siri. She had become afraid of people because she had been alone for so long. But eventually they made friends and got along well. And the legend tells that the people in Stryn are descended from these two—Siri and Jon at Stauri. (Borchegrevink, 1956, 133)

After the epidemic was over, certain economic consequences became manifest. Land values fell and with them the tax base. Many properties changed hands because owners couldn't pay their mortgages. Often it was nearly impossible to get labor, and farmers had difficulties bringing in their harvest. People who bought farms often suffered great losses because property prices kept dropping. Many farms were abandoned and fell to the crown because the deeds were lost and the rightful owners were unknown. Good plowland reverted to pasture or woods. Many cattle died or ran into the woods.

The legends describe a period of lawlessness after the plague. Many people acquired land illegally; cotters and leaseholders moved onto manor farms. Times were good for people who were greedy for land. "Later people on some farms owned a great deal of land," Torkell Mauland wrote. "That was due to the Black Death, people say" (1931, 42). None of the individuals named in these legends can be traced. Perhaps some of them were in fact historical, but it doesn't really matter. It is not the specific event which is important in this tradition but the overall picture given of the period after the Black Death.

The same applies to traditions which are demonstrably unhistorical, such as the many etiological legends explaining place names people believe to be connected to the Black Death. The Bjelland Farm in Holt, Agder, is supposed to have derived its name from a bell found after the Black Death. Øksendal in Bakke supposedly received its name in an even more fantastic manner. Once during the epidemic a man found a magnificent house in the middle of a dark woods. He thought that the "invisible folk" lived there and sank his ax into the threshold to keep it from disappearing. Therefore the farm got the name Øksendal (Ax Valley). In Høgsfjord there is a village called Kålabygd. Here the pest is said to have come in the shape of an ugly old woman who went around in the village with a broom and swept in every house. Wherever she went, everyone died. But when she came to Kålabygd, there was a strapping woman who grabbed the broom from the old woman and chased her away with a firebrand. That was the end of her power, and that is why no village around there escaped the Black Death as easily as the one named after the firebrand (kolsna). In Mandalen (Man-Valley) supposedly only one man survived the pest, in Kvinesdal (Woman-Valley) or Kvinnherad (Woman Township) only one woman, and in Time only ten men (ti menn) survived. In Sokndal—often pronounced Soggendal—the people had only a single sow (sogge) left to eat. There are hundreds of similar etymologies, but none of them have any historically demonstrable connection to the Black Death.

In conclusion, we must ask why historical legends survive. It is clear that there must have been some competition between the various legends to remain viable. Life in the villages changed constantly, there were new crop failures and new epidemics, new strongmen and new stories of tragic love. There was so much to tell about that not every story could live on. An oral tradition survives only if it conforms to the laws of all storytelling. The story must be stylized and shaped in such a way that storytellers want to tell it and audiences want to hear it. Most importantly, a story must be *memorable:* and the most important qualification of a storyteller is a reliable memory. It is possible that the ability to remember was more developed in former times than now, but it is reasonable to assume that a storyteller had heard a narrative many times before making it part of his or her own repertoire.

Based on general laws governing memory and forgetting, we know that storytellers would transmit a story precisely as they had heard it time and again. We also know that the stylization of plots and motifs in these legends is not determined entirely by epic tradition, but also by the desire for the story to live on. It aided the storyteller's memory if the narrative fit similar stories. This is one of the reasons why idiosyncratic details tend to drop away. The core of the legend is often historical, based on real events, and now and then various details are more or less authentic. Nevertheless that is not what is most important. Legends are fictions designed to recreate an occurrence through imagery. The historical details lose their specific importance while the overall impression of the events unfolds as epic drama.

The "truth" of historical legends is not identical with the "truth" of legal documents and history books, and official documents themselves are not necessarily "objective" reports. In many instances we should consider them the representation of one view of an event. Legend tradition constitutes another view. In epic form, historical legends reveal the reactions and reflections of the common folk, their impressions, experiences, and their explanation and evaluation of events that are important to them.

TRADITION, MILIEU, AND CULTURAL VALUES

Birgit Hertzberg Johnsen

The basis for the present study is a legend tradition in the area of Leksvik in Northern Trøndelag concerning a soldier by the name of Anders Solli who was killed by wolves on his way to church on Christmas Eve, 1612. The study of this tradition involved fieldwork in Leksvik, including interviews and the registration of various artifacts connected with the legend. The goals of the project were (1) to investigate the contemporary viability of a local historical legend tradition in a rural milieu, and (2) to shed light on the process of transmission of legends. Since older archive materials typically contain little information about the context surrounding folklore and rarely give any data concerning the process of transmission, neither diachronic nor synchronic dimensions of transmission have been discussed in regard to historical legends.

It is not enough to differentiate storyteller and audience. The form in which the legend is passed on is equally important in understanding the process of transmission. Earlier it was assumed that legends are usually transmitted in the form of extended epic narratives. Not surprisingly, this is the form in which we find legend materials recorded in the archives. Nevertheless, it is probable that a great deal of legend tradition survives in non-epic forms.

One important question in studying so viable a folk genre as historical legends is why certain events are singled out to be passed on from generation to generation, while analogous events—rather than becoming part of the oral tradition of the region as a whole—are preserved only by a limited number of persons within an area. Only the tradition bearers themselves can answer such questions; we need to ask how they use their own tradition and what value they find in the traditions they elect to preserve and pass on. Ultimately, we need to be able to map out the viability of legend tradition in contemporary society.

Original title: "Her Ulve Mand har revet Aar Seksten Hundred Tolv. Tradisjon, miljø og verdirelatering—en sagnstudie." Printed in *Norveg*, 1980.

Material Documentation

On a wall in Leksvik Church, side by side with a memorial to the dead from the Second World War, there hangs the sword with which Anders Solli allegedly defended himself when he was attacked by the wolves. In the sacristy of the church there is a stained glass window bearing the likeness of Lieutenant Ellef Tetlie, who, according to tradition, bears responsibility for Anders Solli's death, inasmuch as it was on his orders that the soldier headed for the church. The most important memorial, however, stands in the hills between Dalbygda and Markabygda. Here, in 1929, on a moor called Korsmyra (or simply "Korsen"), local people erected a monument where the wolves, according to legend, killed Anders Solli. Until then the place had been marked only by a wooden cross and, later, a stone.

Oral Tradition

To this very day, more than 350 years after the event, people in Leksvik tell the story about Anders Solli. The legend is usually told as a brief narrative that conforms to a fixed pattern. The main elements are these: Anders Solli lived in Markabygda; because he was a soldier, he was to go to the church one night during the Christmas holidays to take part in a procession; on the way he was attacked by a pack of wolves and killed; the next morning passers-by found only the sword and his right hand; this happened in 1612. Even if these fixed elements are always included, the legend has not stagnated to a stereotyped narrative during the 350 years it has survived. Rather, it remains flexible and displays all the characteristics of a viable oral tradition, as shown in the following variant told by a seventy-seven-year-old man from Leksvik:

> He was on his way to the church. It was Christmas Day. He set out in the evening, going south through the woods. Then there came a pack of wolves. And as I heard it, well, you could see there had been a struggle; he killed one of them and the others ate that one. And then they came back, but then his sword had frozen fast to the sheath. And they say, that's when the wolves tore him to pieces. The only thing they found was one of his hands. That's what I've heard. (Informant 11)

Anders was supposedly killed by the wolves because the sword got wet with blood when he killed the first one and froze to the sheath, so that he couldn't defend himself later. Some people tell about the fight with great imagination:

> But he killed one of the wolves or two. It happened just north of the memorial on the hill over there, Carpenter Hill. That's where he killed a couple of them. And the rest of them fell on them and devoured them. And then they went after

him once again, you know. But then his sword had gotten bloody and it froze to
the sheath. And when they came back, you know, he couldn't pull it out.
(Informant No. 5)

People in Leksvik sing a song about Anders Solli, the "Wolf Song" or "Solli
Song." There has been some discussion in the area about who wrote the song.
Most likely it was composed by a sexton named Lars Grande, probably a little
before 1850. Others maintain that the author was a man by the name of B.
Moholdt. In content, the song substantiates the legend.

Besides the information in the song, people in the area offer additional
details. Some say that Anders killed the first wolf at a place called Carpenter
Hill, about one kilometer north of Korsen. Others think that it happened at
Korsbua, which is no more than a few hundred meters north of the memorial.

The time of the event has been much discussed in the area. The song says
that Anders was killed on Christmas Eve, but on the memorial stone it says that
it was Christmas Day. Therefore many people claim that the inscription must
be wrong. They maintain that Anders left the evening before Christmas. It is
not plausible that he went directly to the service on Christmas Day, because this
does not correlate with the time it takes to ski to Midtbygda. So people conclude
that he must have intended to stay overnight at Dalbygda and then go to the
service and the procession from there. The tradition varies as to which farm
Anders spent the night on. Individuals who include this detail tend to make
reference to both versions: one in which Anders skied to Midtbygda at night,
the other in which he left early the next morning. The song says that Anders
had only half a mile to go when the wolves attacked him. Even if we calculate
the distance in "old" miles (11.3 km per mile), however, this figure is not
plausible; it is in fact much farther to Leksvik Church in Midtbygda. The
tradition that Anders stayed overnight at a farm in Dalbygda is not generally
known in the area. Therefore some have speculated that perhaps he was going
to a church in Dalbygda and not to the main church in Midtbygda; this would
correlate more accurately with the distance given in the song. There is no
church in Dalbygda now, but according to legend there was a church on
Tetli-Farm, because there is a field called "Church-Meadow." The local legend
about the church on Tetli has thus been connected to the legend about Anders
Solli.

Another important detail is that Anders traveled in moonlight. "Through the
frozen window / the moon shines pale," the song says, and many people have
heard from their parents that there was moonlight when Anders was killed by
the wolves. The question of the historicity of Anders Solli's death is so important
to the local milieu that at the time the memorial was raised, special efforts were
made to investigate this detail. An astronomer by the name of Sigurd Einbu was
contacted, and he calculated that there was no moonlight on Christmas Eve,
1612 (Grande 1931, 59). People therefore tend to reject this detail and consider
it an invention by the author of the song. Nevertheless, there can be little doubt

that the legend has included this detail in the past, even if few versions do so today. It appears that the moon was an important element in explaining why the wolves killed Anders. In the old days people believed that wolves were especially greedy when the moon was shining. When they saw their own shadows, they thought that there were more of them and attacked more readily.

The debate about the moonlight continued. In 1979, in a letter to the editor of *Trønderavisa*, Hans Georg Killingbergtrø, who used to live at Leksvik, wrote that there was moonlight at Christmas in 1612. The astronomer who had calculated the phases of moon to prove that oral tradition was in error had overlooked the fact that the calendar used in Norway at the time was the Julian (not the Gregorian) calendar. Killingbergtrø's revised calculations show that there was a full moon late at night on the third day of Christmas, 1612. In other words, as recently as a decade ago, the general concern that the tradition somehow might not be historically accurate led to a renewed investigation. And once again the viability of the tradition strengthened its claim to historicity. People once more tell the legend without feeling the need for apologetic commentaries concerning the all-important detail of the moonlight.

The song says that the churchgoers found Anders's right hand. This tradition is widespread today and some people appear to believe it firmly. The motif of the right hand's being left behind has its basis in the ancient notion that wolves are not able to eat that part of the human anatomy.

Another part of the tradition involves Anders's fiancée, Sigrid, but it is not as widespread or fixed. As a rule, it is said that Sigrid took the tragic fate of her lover so much to heart that she died shortly thereafter. Most people think that Sigrid lived at Rota-Farm and that Anders stopped there before he passed through the forest. But there is also a tradition that Sigrid came from Sollia, just like Anders. Almost everybody says that Sigrid died shortly after Anders was killed by the wolves, but the manner of her death varies. Some say that she went insane, some that she froze to death on a Christmas night, at the very spot where Anders was killed.

Genre

While both the song and the legend have important positions in the tradition, it is not impossible that some of the details of the legend derive from the song. Many informants employ words and expressions from the song when they tell the legend. But it is impossible to say today what the relationship between legend and song was originally. If the originator was Lars Grande, then it is not unlikely that he treated certain parts of the legend material with artistic freedom. Two other songs he based on legend traditions from Leksvik, "The Gunnhild's Stone" and "The Giant Graves on Leksvik Promontory" (Grande 1932, 65–68), are clearly fictitious. The legends upon which the two songs are based are little known in Leksvik today, and the songs are not widely sung.

The reason people do sing the "Wolf Song" is probably that the poem is based on and faithful to a living tradition, in contrast to the other two songs. Nevertheless, whenever people hear details in the legend that differ from those in the song, they do not hesitate to point to the legend tradition as the primary and correct version. In spite of the importance of the song, it is accepted only insofar as it agrees with the legend tradition which people have learned from their parents or older people who have authority in these matters.

The oral tradition about Anders Solli splits into several branches differentiated in form, content, and distribution. The most widespread is the short epic version describing the events themselves. This legend is very stable, both in form and in content, and is common in the oral tradition of the area. The song, as transmitted in oral tradition, is well supported by printed texts. Neither the form nor content of the texts varies, but the melodies do. Even if the song is less widely known, it must be considered a general oral tradition in Leksvik, comparable to the short version of the legend.

Side by side with those two stable traditions about Anders Solli there are others which are noticeably different in form and content. In part, these are legends or loosely structured legend materials; in part, they are details in non-narrative form. Besides being unstructured and variable, this part of the tradition enjoys only limited distribution and is tied to specific localities within the general area.

Transmission

The most important questions about transmission are these: Which persons are conversant with various aspects of the tradition, to whom do they transmit the tradition, and what are the performance situations in which the tradition is passed on? The oral tradition about Anders Solli consists of narrative material that varies in form, content and distribution. To clarify the viability of this many-faceted tradition in the milieu, it is necessary to ask whether the process of transmission changes in keeping with the lore itself. There are a number of people in Leksvik who command almost the entire tradition, but most individuals are familiar with only certain parts of it. In analyzing the process of transmission, diachronically as well as synchronically, one of the chief questions is whether the transmission of different elements of the lore follows the same pattern, or whether there is variation.

The Main Legend Tradition

When people in the area come together, they do not usually tell a long, coherent narrative about Anders Solli. The reason for this is simply that the story of his death is so well known that an epic presentation is of little interest.

Typically an informant, when asked whether he has told the story to anyone, answers: "No, everybody knows it already" (Informant No. 12). When people in the area talk about the story, they tend to discuss specific details. But when an outsider comes to the area, the legend is told in its entirety. It appears that many individuals are able to tell the legend, but few of them actually do. Most people have heard the whole legend at least once, usually the first time they heard about Anders. Most often this happened when, as children, they passed by Korsen and saw the area where the event took place. Nobody recited the song on this occasion, but they always told the legend. Most often it was boys accompanying their fathers on some errand in the woods who were taken to the place where Anders was killed and were told the legend:

> I wasn't quite ten years old, when we went to the place where my father told about it. . . . We had been to the woods. . . . . We came to a rock slab over there. . . . Yes, my father told about what happened then. He said it was Anders Solli. But I remember how sad it was. (Informant No. 12)

People traveling to their summer farms heard about Anders on their way across Korsen: "You know, we got it with our mother's milk. Our way up to the summer farm went right past Korsen for several generations" (Informant No. 8).

Several individuals say that they prompted to hear the story when they saw the rock out on the moor and asked about the memorial: "It was when I came past there. You know, you get curious and ask what it is all about. . . . Then I found out that the stone is there because a man had been killed by wolves there" (Informant No. 5).

The school, too, transmitted the legend tradition. There probably wasn't much discussion of the event in the classroom, and no one remembers having learned the song in school by heart. But the teacher would take the pupils on field trips to Korsen, and there tell the story: "The teacher would take us on a trip at the end of the school year. I remember we were at Korsen. And then he told about what had happened there" (Informant No. 4).

One informant came to Midtbygda when he was six, when his father bought a farm there. The informant had never heard the legend at Hindrem, where the family was from originally, and he doubts that his parents knew the story. The farm in Midtbygda to which they moved used to be a coach stop, and one of the workers there was a good storyteller. He told the informant about the killing.

Most people say that they first heard the legend from their fathers as they passed the place where the event occurred. One had heard it from his maternal grandfather, some from their teacher, and several had heard it at home and from older men in the area. The women informants report the same thing. None remembers having heard the story from her mother or any other woman. The transmission of the legend can thus be traced back through several intermediaries, and invariably the sources are men. The interest in the wolf legend has been most pronounced among men.

The Song

Earlier on, the "Wolf Song" was sung both by men and women. Especially in homes where there was much singing and playing of musical instruments, it was common to teach children the song about Anders. If it was the mother who sang the song, she probably got it from her own mother or grandmother: "I learned it from Mother; she hummed and sang like a fiddle . . . we didn't write it down, but I believe Mother learned it from her grandmother" (Informant No. 8).

The song was not generally known in the area until it was sung by a small male chorus at the unveiling of the memorial stone in 1929. To be sure, somebody had recorded the song before, and other people knew it by heart. But many heard the song for the first time in 1929, when a stenciled text was distributed—which was to become very important for the dissemination of the song. In spite of the fact that the song is not frequently sung in the general area now, most people know that it exists, and many know a verse or two. Those who know the song learned it at home.

Local Tradition

In addition to the common tradition of the legend and the song which most people have learned from their parents, there are other elements which are not very widespread. Parts of the legend cycle have clearly been tied to Dalbygda or to Markabygda. Nevertheless many individuals in the Leksvik area are familiar with the tradition from Midtbygda, having heard it from people who learned it at home near where the local tradition existed, or whose family moved from there.

The legend about Sigrid, the girl who was engaged to Anders Solli, appears to have been told by people connected with Markabygda and the farms around there. Any traditions about Sigrid told outside this area could always be traced back to Markabygda. People in other places within the general area always derived the tradition from there, either directly or through an intermediary. One of the informants from Midtbygda had heard the usual short narrative about Anders in his home. Later he heard the legend about Sigrid from an old man who in turn said that he had learned it from his father. But that gentleman hailed from Sollia, the place where Anders and, many believe, Sigrid came from. Another informant in Midtbygda had never heard that Sigrid went insane until he heard that detail from another man from Markabygda.

The tradition that Anders stayed overnight at a farm in Dalbygda is not generally known either. The tradition comes from Dalbygda, and it appears that some people in Markabygda do not believe it. The same is true of the story that Anders was going to a church in Dalbygda. This is not generally accepted, and people interested in history claim that there never was a church at Tetli. The tradition about Anders Solli and Lieutenant Ellef Tetlie also comes from Dalbygda. The traditions about Sigrid, Lieutenant Tetlie, and about Anders's staying at a farm in Dalbygda were originally tied locally to Dalbygda and Markabygda and not known elsewhere. But when the memorial was raised in 1929 there was naturally a lot of talk about the event. People began discussing details and the local tradition spread to some degree. Most informants had been to the place before and had heard the legend, but no one doubts the importance of the raising of the memorial to the viability of the tradition: "And people talked about it especially when the memorial was put up. And then they also talked about Ellef Tetlie" (Informant No. 10).

Form and Transmission

The study of transmission shows that the tradition about Anders Solli follows definite patterns that in part can be traced back through several generations. Diachronically speaking, the usual pattern was that especially parents—sometimes grandparents—passed the tradition on to their children or grandchildren in the form of the generally accepted legend. The first time someone from Leksvik heard the legend, it was in the form of a coherent, but not very detailed, narrative known to most people in the area. The situation precipitating the telling of the story was consistent: the legend was told when people passed by the place where the event occurred. The wooden cross, the stone, later the memorial, actualized the legend. The visible memorial out on the moor signaled that something unusual had taken place. The uninitiated asked questions which the older generation responded to by passing on the legend tradition.

On the other hand, synchronically speaking, transmission of the legend complex takes the form of non-narrative conversations about the alleged events. The narrative situation is different: synchronic transmission occurs when adults come together and talk about various subjects. Such conversations develop at home in the evening, and children can learn about the tradition by listening to the adults conversing. One important exception to this pattern occurs when legend material is transmitted to people who come from outside the area. Strangers are not familiar with the story, and thus belong in the same category as children. This appears to be the only instance where the complete legend is transmitted between individuals belonging to the same generation.

Oral Tradition—Written Stereotyping

The story about Anders Solli has often been presented in print, and people in Leksvik read written versions of the legend with great interest. It has become an especially popular Christmas story, often reprinted by local newspapers, most recently in the Christmas edition of *Trønder-Avisa,* 1978. An entire page, complete with illustrations, was devoted to the legend. The first time the story appeared in print was in the form of the song reproduced in a Christmas magazine in 1901, illustrated by the well-known artist Andreas Bloch (Holst, 1901).

When people read the story about Anders in magazines or newspapers, they check to see whether the story is "right." If the printed version does not correspond with their own, they usually insist that theirs is the correct one. This is quite natural, considering the general attitude among the people of Leksvik toward their oral tradition. They often discuss details of oral tradition, without always coming to an agreement. The same attitude manifests itself when they come across traditional materials in journals and local newspapers. Even though the legend is presented in a fixed, stereotyped form, there is little to indicate that people in general are influenced by it. The influence of printed sources has not been strong enough to alter tradition or to make tradition solidify and stop being productive.

The Legend as Historical Source

Today the legend is well known in Leksvik largely because it is considered historically accurate. If its content had not been considered "true" all along, the legend would not have survived. Therefore it is no surprise that what most interests people in Leksvik in connection with the legend is the question of its historicity, particularly the accuracy of specific details.

People are aware of some of the variations in oral tradition and can account for these in terms of specific localities and personalities. But informants have more or less the same basic attitude toward the legend, believing that it tells about a historical event, but that oral transmission may have caused some minor changes: "You know it passes from person to person. Something might get added and something taken away. It's hard to say" (Informant No. 5).

These days one notices people showing some insecurity concerning the legend's historicity. Research in connection with local history has revealed certain facts that cast doubt on the reliability of the tradition. The sources show that in 1612 nobody lived on Rota-Farm, which, according to one part of the tradition, was Sigrid's home. However, the farm is mentioned on the tax rolls of 1647. The suggestion has therefore been made that the death occurred considerably later than the legend says. The year 1612 is a categorical element of the tradition, but several informants have noted that there was no organized army in Norway at that time and that therefore the date cannot be right, if Anders Solli was in fact a soldier. No one doubts that something did happen on Korsen and that a man named Anders Solli was killed by wolves there. But the circumstances of his death, and the year it happened, are subject to debate. Therefore we shall take a closer look at certain details, in part by referring to sources other than oral tradition.

Seen from a zoological perspective, it is not impossible that a pack of wolves would attack a man, but it is not very probable either. Norwegian scientists generally reject the legend as pure fiction, according to J. A. Pedersen of the Zoological Museum in Oslo. If Anders Solli really was killed by wolves, as the legend claims, a reasonable explanation might be that he first got injured some other way and thereby became easy prey for the animals. But zoologists doubt that he fought the wolves as the legend describes.

All informants agree that the victim's name was Anders Solli and that the tragedy occurred in 1612, though there are no historical sources to document these assertions. However, on the tax lists from 1626 we find several families identified with the Solli Farms.

It is not unreasonable to assume that Anders Solli was a member of the rural militia and therefore carried a weapon. Late sixteenth-century law permitted such a person's being equipped with a *tessak* (a curved sword). But the Norwegian Museum of Defense has stated that the weapon displayed in Leksvik Church as that of Anders Solli is a Swedish *kommisvärja* (a military sword made after the pattern of 1685), most likely left by the Swedish army, which was in Trøndelag in 1718. This dating precludes any possible historical connection between the weapon in Leksvik Church and a person living in the Leksvik area in the early 1600s. A closer investigation of this aspect of the tradition, furthermore, shows that it differs from the rest of the tradition about Anders Solli. All informants can recall where they heard the other parts of the story, either from their fathers or some other known individual in the area. But no one was able to identify an oral tradition connecting the weapon to Anders Solli prior to 1929, when it was borrowed from Inderøy Rural Museum and used to cut the ribbon for the unveiling of the memorial. The traditions regarding the weapon begin at the year 1929, and statements about it are vague and imprecise.

The Need for Historical Legitimacy

In spite of the fact that it is not possible to say for sure whether the event took place, there is no doubt that it is the historical background that today gives value to the legend in the milieu. In the desire to legitimize the legend people have gone as far as securing a weapon as proof of the legend's historical truth. But even if the people of Leksvik value the legend almost exclusively as a historical source, it is important to place the tradition in a larger perspective.

A legend of this type would not survive in oral tradition if it did not have a more important function than merely throwing light on a historical event.

The Viability of Tradition

What is it that makes this particular legend so special? Why was it transmitted for generations, and why do people continue to tell it today? To account for the viability of a given tradition we must look for the external conditions that keep it alive, and relate it to specific social and cultural values within the traditional milieu of the area.

One of the reasons the legend about Anders Solli is so well known in Leksvik today is that people simply don't get a chance to forget it. The sword, as well as the stained glass window in the church, reminds people of the event. The tangible memorials on the moors are most important in this connection. Seeing the wooden cross, the stone, and later the monument actualizes the legend for anyone passing by the place. One of the main reasons the legend has been so well preserved and has become a generally accepted tradition in the district is that the visible reminders of the event are strategically placed along the road between Dalbygda and Markabygda. People from Markabygda walked by them on their way to the village, and anyone who had a job in the outlying areas had to pass them. It is reasonable to assume that, if Korsen had not been situated so close to the road, the legend would not have become generally known in the district.

It is illustrative of this point that Andreas Grande, the individual who took the initiative to raise the memorial, would almost certainly not have done so if he had not seen the memorial on the moors. He rarely came to that part of the district, but once he was in Markabygda marking trees for cutting when he noticed the stone and became fascinated by the story about Anders Solli. Subsequently he started a communal effort to raise a permanent memorial to Anders.

The road between Markabygda and Dalbygda was rerouted in 1964, and people rarely pass the memorial now. But still there is little chance for anyone to forget the tradition, because the story appears at regular intervals in local papers and journals as stereotyped legend. Both the repeated written descriptions of the event and the visible reminders consolidate the tradition. The more often the story appears in print, the more believable it becomes. By the same token the artifacts on the moors are cited as solid evidence for the historicity of the tradition: "The memorial proves that it is true, that this thing about Anders is a fact" (Informant No. 2).

The Anders Solli legend was widely disseminated and its relation to other traditions in Leksvik firmly established long before the memorial was raised in 1929. Today it can be traced back to persons born in the first half of the nineteenth century. To gain a historical perspective on the function of the legend, it is important to see it in context of older traditions in the area. Many legends from older times, especially those about predatory animals, continue to live in oral tradition. The legend about Anders Solli thus belongs to a larger complex of traditions about wolves and other beasts of prey. In neighboring districts similar stories have been told about people in the past killed by wolves. What makes the legend about Anders different from similar legends is that this tradition is so vigorous and productive. The explanation cannot simply be that it tells about an unusual event, since other legends concerning people killed by wolves are equally widespread in rural tradition today. Rather, the prominent position of the tradition about Anders Solli must find its explanation in the value the milieu assigns to the legend.

The significance of the legend is not only that a man was killed by wolves; it is equally important that Anders was a soldier. There are traditions in Leksvik about the war with Sweden: among other things, people say that the Swedes once occupied half the district, and to this day that area is called "Old Sweden." The Anders Solli legend belongs in the context of that war tradition. Anders is seen as a hero; he fell for the fatherland and, more importantly, for his home district. The people who eulogized him at the unveiling of the memorial emphasized the fact that Anders had been a soldier. This tendency to connect the tradition about Solli's death with patriotic values is further accentuated by the placement of the sword next to the memorial for Leksvik's dead from the Second World War; it shows that he is considered a heroic son of the district, not because he was killed by wolves, but because he died as a soldier.

One must conclude that the legend has been and continues to be productive because the milieu assigns enduring values—such as local patriotism and national pride—to the tradition: Anders Solli is cast as a soldier whose task it was to defend the district and the country. This aspect is emphasized by the tradition bearers themselves. Analytically, it provides the only satisfactory explanation of why this particular legend is so much more productive than other traditions about predatory animals and killings by wolves.

The Tradition Process

The viability of the legend is revealed indirectly by certain characteristics of the tradition process. The legend is never transmitted in epic form among individuals belonging to the same generation because it is assumed that everyone in the area is already familiar with the basic outline of the story. This outline takes the form of a firmly structured legend that is transmitted diachronically from the older to the younger generation. Diachronic transmission occurs relatively rarely, namely when an individual is initiated into the tradition. Synchronic transmission is limited to non-epic and less firmly structured tradition material that is localized in certain areas of the district. Synchronic transmission between adults usually takes the form of discussions regarding the reliability of given details of the tradition. Only when a stranger is introduced to the milieu is the legend told in its complete epic form. This insight is an important contribution to the history of legend research, permitting us to draw the following general conclusion: the epic form of a legend exists latently in a given milieu and is activated each time a new individual is initiated into the tradition—be it a child in the community, a visitor from a neighboring district, or a folklorist from the capital. Thus there is a fundamental distinction between the diachronic and synchronic processes of transmission, not only in respect to time, but also in regard to the content, structure, and social function of a tradition.

Tradition as Dynamic Factor in the Cultural Milieu

The overall conclusion of this analysis of a localized legend complex is that oral tradition is an active force in popular culture, a fact that lends to the concept of "productive tradition" a more comprehensive and dynamic significance than that something is told and retold. The considerable material effort involved in raising the memorial to Anders Solli illuminates the role of tradition as an action-promoting factor in popular culture. To be sure, the motivations for the project are partly individual, but it could not have been carried out without the general cultural base of the milieu. The example shows further how the "productivity" of tradition in fact involves continuous self-reinforcement not only by repeated oral retellings but also by transmission through other media (Hasslöf et al., 1970; Bringéus, 1976). The raising of the memorial, the placing of the weapon in the church, and the repeated illustrated printings provide constant visual reminders of the legend. All of these non-oral manifestations demonstrate that the oral tradition is "productive," and that this productivity has its source in the value system of the traditional milieu.

Folk Song and Folk Singing

FOLK BALLAD AND FOLK SONG

Reimund Kvideland

Ever since the Grimm Brothers, philological-literary considerations have dominated folklore studies, including the study of folk ballads. Research has focused on the question of origins and original form, on time and place of the ballad's origin, distribution, adaptation, and development. An important factor in this research tradition "has been the more or less conscious assumption that one cannot understand anything without first understanding its origin" (Holbek, 1981, 130). Another important premise has been the idea that folk ballads represent a form of "natural" or "universal poetry."

But if we are to understand the theoretical base for our concept of the folk ballad as phenomenon and thus of ballad scholarship, we have to reach back to the debate concerning nominalism vs. realism, or essentialism, as Karl R. Popper has called it (1969, 26–32). The adherents of nominalism maintain that universals differ from proper names by being identified with a group or class of things rather than with individual things. Popper uses the example of the concept "white." The nominalists consider "white" to be a label attached to a variety of different things. For them, concepts are no more than useful terms of description. The adherents of realism or essentialism, on the other hand, maintain that we do not first collect a group of individual things which we then call "white." We identify a thing as white because of a certain indwelling quality it shares with other things, namely the quality of whiteness:

> This property, denoted by the universal term, is regarded as an object which deserves investigation just as much as the individual things themselves. (The name "realism" derives from the assertion that universal objects, for instance, whiteness, "really" exist, over and above single things and sets or groups of single things.) Thus universal terms denote universal objects, just as singular terms denote individual things. These universal objects (called by Plato "Forms" or

Original title: "Frå visetekst til sangaktivitet." Published in *Sumlen. Årsbok för vis- och folkmusikforskning*, 1982.

"Ideas") which are designated by universal terms were also called "essences."
(Popper, 1969, 28)

The essentialists therefore maintain that we must penetrate to the essence of
things to be able to explain them. They ask: What is power? What is justice?
Through this type of question they seek to reveal the essential meaning of
concepts and thus of the nature of the thing named by the concept.

How does this apply to folklore studies? When we operate with terms such as
"the folktale" or "the ballad," we give expression to essentialist thinking. Some
scholars today understand that there is no such thing as the ballad. Max
Kommerell, for example, maintained as early as the 1930s that "the folksong is
first of all a concept, and as a concept it is an invention. . . . Skeptics would say,
Herder has not only invented the concept, he also invented folksong" (Kommerell, 1933, here quoted after Klusen 1969, 7). Ernst Klusen opens his book,
Volkslied. Fund und Erfindung (1969) by quoting Kommerell. But, by and
large, ballad research has been and still is dominated by methodological
essentialism rather than nominalism. Walter Heimann has pointed to the
importance of essentialism for ballad research in Germany (1977). The same
can be said of Nordic research. Even the term folkevise has been derived from
the German Volkslied, which in turn is Herder's erroneous translation of
Percy's term popular song.

One of the consequences of concentrating on the folk ballad as idea or
concept has been the limitation to one specific genre. From the multitude of
folk songs, researchers have picked out those that live or lived in tradition and,
among those, only the ones that meet certain formal criteria. In Scandinavian
research, folk song has thus been identified with the medieval, epic ballad. In
the survey published in Danske studier in 1974, for example, Iørn Piø, Gustav
Henningsen, and Birgitte Rørbye maintain that until the end of the 1950s
"Danish folk song research concerned itself with the medieval ballad" (1974,
120). Or, checking under folkevise in the standard handbook Kulturhistorisk
leksikon for nordisk middelalder (Cultural-historical lexicon for the Nordic
Middle Ages), we are referred to balladediktning. There Bengt R. Jonsson
defines the ballad "as an epic song which in the Nordic countries most often is
called folkevisa. It is stanzaic in form, has end rhyme and one or two lyrical
refrains (1956, column 316). In the same work, the articles concerned with
other song categories—such as work songs, elegies, political songs, or cradle
songs—do not mention the term folkvise at all. In other words, the term is not
considered relevant there.

This is a debatable approach, of course, but it mirrors the mainstream of
folksong research. Erik Dal, for example, defines folkevise as follows: "By
folkevise we mean anonymous songs originating in the Middle Ages and first
recorded by the nobility, but later preserved in oral tradition. Usually epic in
character, the folkevise consists of stanzas with two to four irregular lines,
usually with four stresses per line . . . and rhyming aa or aya. It is also equipped

with a refrain, sometimes internal refrain with partial repetition of the stanza" (in "Nordisk folkeviseforskning siden 1800" [Scandinavian Ballad Research since 1800] [1956], 18). Dal maintains that the folkevise is to be distinguished from "non-musical, epic, Latin poetry as well as from religious and troubadour-like lyrical poetry which derives from different sources (1956, 19). He adds, "By nature and function, the folkevise is a song and dance genre." We can find numerous examples of this genre fixation, which limits the definition of folk song to a specific genre. At times it is expressed explicitly, but most often it remains an unspoken assumption.

The Danish literary historican Oluf Friis, for example, says that "during the Middle Ages the ballad became the dominant art form" (1948; quoted after Piø, 1977, 10). In keeping with National Romantic thinking, the ballad was tied to the concept of the "folk," another imaginary category. This "folk" is not thought of primarily as the basic social layer, but rather as the essence of being human. It contains the best of human qualities and characteristics. We can imagine it realized: (1) in an egalitarian culture, where "all the folk sing as one man," to borrow a much-used phrase from Geijer, (2) in a sociocultural upper class like, for example, the Danish nobility, (3) as a culturally and artistically developed peasant milieu. Because the existing, preserved ballads usually did not measure up to the ideal, it became necessary to postulate an older and superior cultural phase, "a society in which the esthetic sensibility was highly developed" (Liestøl, 1915, 245). By the same token, because it was assumed that the genuine ballad represented a highly developed cultural element (Jonsson, 1967, 6), it became important to reconstruct the original form. Steenstrup emphasizes the importance of "bringing to light the genuinely oldest form" and separating new elements from the original ones (1891, 2). This, more than the esthetic sensibility and historical passion of literary interpreters, has made reconstruction such an important factor in ballad research, both as a stated goal and as a means of popularization.

Another consequence of the hypothesis of ballad origins was that research came to focus on the folkevise as medieval poetry, as fornvise (ancient poem). Its subsequent development was looked upon as a phase of decline and therefore as less interesting. We see this clearly in the titles of ballad editions, which are often programmatic: "Danmarks Gamle Folkeviser" (Denmark's Ancient Folk Ballads); Steenstrup, "Vore folkeviser fra middelalderen" (Our Folk Ballads from the Middle Ages) (1891); von der Recke, "Danmarks fornviser" (Denmark's Ancient Ballads) (1927–29); Liestøl and Moltke Moe, "Norske folkeviser fra middelalderen" (Norwegian Ballads from the Middle Ages) (1912); Geijer and Afzelius, "Svenska folk-visor från forntiden" (Swedish Folk Ballads from Ancient Times) (1814–16); and Arwidsson, "Svenska fornsanger" (Ancient Poems of Sweden) (1834–42). This selection should suffice to make the point.

The hypothesis of a negative development or decline is also reflected in the systematization of ballads by subject matter and type. Both in scholarly and popular editions it is usual to begin with mythical ballads and end with jocular ballads. The catalog of types of the medieval ballad in Scandinavia has the following revealing disposition: A. Ballads of the Supernatural, B. Legendary Ballads, C. Historical Ballads, D. Ballads of Chivalry, E. Heroic Ballads, F. Jocular Ballads. The following sequence is typical for Norwegian literary histories: Supernatural Ballads, Heroic Ballads, Chivalric Ballads, Historical Ballads, Legendary Ballads, Animal and Jocular Ballads. A contemporary Marxist critic, Georg Johannesen, reads this sequence not as a logical system, but as an historical hypothesis: "The sketch of a synopsis for the years 500 to 1500 . . . ideologically based on the concept Middle Ages" (1980, 43). In other words, in this paradigm folk song is defined in terms of a single genre which in turn is assumed to represent certain important cultural and esthetic values. But the model implies yet other qualities, one of which can be expressed by the following well-known saying: "Wo man singt, da lass dich ruhig nieder, böse Menschen haben keine Lieder" (Where people sing, you may rest secure. Evil folk have no songs.) (Büchmann, 1937, 209). The normative perspective implied by this quotation is that both singing and the songs themselves contain ethical, as well as esthetic, qualities. The ethical and the esthetic are two aspects of the same thing. Moral goodness is defined as an essential element in the ballad. "Real" singing and "good" action are perceived as derivatives of the same axiomatic definition of being (Heimann, 1977, 185).

Yet another quality is the "natural." This quality is closely connected with the concept of the folk. All these qualities corroborate each other and become necessary elements in the definition of the "true" ballad. The ballad is defined as universal, which in turn is associated with the natural. The natural is beautiful, true and good. This normative view of the ballad is, of course, a static concept. The ballad neither changes nor develops. It cannot develop because that would mean changing its essence. But it is affected by the general decay of civilization. New ballad forms are therefore but an echo; at best they "have the appearance of the ballad" (Liestøl, 1934, 35).

Methodological essentialism and its normative theory have provided the foundation for the philological-literary analysis of texts which has dominated ballad research for such a long time. But another factor enters here. There is a direct connection between the development of folkloristics and the growth of the bourgeoisie. The bourgeoisie based its ideology in part on the glorification of the past and the "folk." Bengt Holbek formulates this ideology as follows: "The so-called folk (were) designated the guardians of the ancient national treasures. To be sure, they were no longer able to make use of them themselves, but they had faithfully passed them on from generation to generation" (1979, 218). Of course, not all traditional songs could be raised to national status, but in the "best" of folk songs the bourgeoisie could find an ideal portrait of itself (cf. Johannesen, 1980, 41).

The first little Norwegian folksong collection appeared in 1840 under the title "Samling af sange, folkeviser og stev i norse almuedialekter" (Collection of songs, ballads and verse in Norwegian dialects). Among the forty-six texts in that collection, only two or three would be classified as ballads today. Later scholars felt the need to excuse Jørgen Moe and the publisher, P. T. Malling, for their choice of subject matter: "They just didn't know any better." Later the term folkevise came to be used exclusively in reference to the medieval ballad, and other categories of folk song were given other labels. Once more we can see this clearly reflected in the titles of subsequent collections of folk songs. We need only point to such representative works as Grüner-Nielsen's "Danske viser" (Danish Songs) and "Danske skæmteviser" (Danish Jocular Songs). The same tendency can still be seen in the recent series of "Folkliga visor" (Popular Songs) published by the Swedish Folksong Archives. The first volume, edited by Monica Lantz, appeared a year ago under the title "Sjömansvisor" (Seaman's Songs).

When it comes to the methodologies used in studying folk songs other than the ballad, we find a direct extension of the same principles applied in ballad research. In regard to jocular songs, for example, Grüner-Nielsen is concerned about the "place of origin, history of development and area of distribution" (1927–28, VIII). Also Iørn Piø has pointed out that the "research which followed in the wake of Danske viser (Danish Songs) has largely focused on love songs, especially on those which, seen from a purely literary-esthetic perspective, are the most beautiful" (1979, 375). As examples, Piø points to the work of Hans Brix (1935, 1938) and Ernst Frandsen (1929, 1954).

And yet there are clear indications of a new orientation in folksong research. I would like to characterize these tendencies as follows:

1. The concept of folk song itself is being expanded. No folklorist in Scandinavia today would use the term folkevise as synonymous with the medieval ballad, notwithstanding the fact that the ballad still enjoys greater prestige than other folksong categories. How far one should expand the genre canon is not being discussed at present. There is widespread agreement, however, that all traditional and anonymous songs should be included. But the question of whether these two criteria by themselves are decisive, is being raised more and more loudly (Bausinger, 1968). With reference to the work of the German scholar Jan M. Rahmelov, I suggested that "all songs except those sung by professional singers in their role as professional performers," should be considered part of popular song tradition (Kvideland, 1973a, 102). The social anthropologist Frode Nyvold has applied the proposed definition in an analysis of "Kulturaktivism i Oksitania" (Cultural Activism in Oksitania) (1979). But it is probably too optimistic to believe that the expanded concept will become generally accepted. Perhaps a principle discussion to clarify the scope of the folksong genre would be called for at this time.

2. Text-oriented research has taken on new dimensions. It is no longer merely philological in orientation. More differentiated interpretations of the text are being tried. Aspects such as use, function, and intention play a larger role in research than before. This permits a more intensive study of songs in context,

as exemplified by Mattson's studies of drinking songs and Espeland's studies of cradle songs (Mattson, 1974; Espeland, 1979).

The question of intention may prove particularly fruitful. We have seen examples in Karl-Ivar Hildeman's analysis of political songs from the late Middle Ages in Sweden (1950). The question of intention is especially important in studying propagandistic songs, such as, for example, emigrant songs (Kvideland, 1975; Thomsen, 1980) and strike songs (Strejk! 1972) as well as the analysis of the publication and commercial dissemination of songs. Piø's studies of the broadside producer Julius Strandberg provide an example of the latter (1976).

3. Another expansion has developed through the study of repertory. The songs are interesting not only as isolated texts, but as part of the singer's repertory. However, much (if not most) of the repertory studies so far have been limited to the comparison of variants in the traditional sense. Rarely is repertory studied, for example, from individual and sociopsychological or socio- and cultural-historical perspectives. One of the possible reasons, as Piø, Rørbye, and Henningsen have pointed out, is that research in this area has not developed from an articulated theoretical base, but rather from the observation that people today are still singing (Piø, 1974, 120). In other words, we witness new empirical applications, but the theoretical foundation remains more or less the same. Nevertheless, we can glimpse some signals of a new theoretical departure in the work of Thorkild Knudsen, Svend Nielsen, and Karsten Biering.

4. Piø has challenged various wings of folksong research by asserting that "we have never studied the ballads as folk songs, but that is precisely what they are and always have been" (1977). I can only agree with him when he says that we have to rid ourselves of our infatuation with the text (Piø, 1977, 12).

Here we have arrived at the core of the problem. As a literary genre, the folk song is and remains a text, while as tradition it is a musical objectification which can manifest itself only in performance. Folklorists have tried to solve this dilemma in a number of ways. A song consists of both text and melody, people argue, calling for melodies to accompany printed editions of songs. But I still do not see any place that text and melody have been combined in analysis. Each has been studied separately, rather than being considered an integral unit in tradition.

Our scholarly point of departure should not be song considered as ideal type or category, but rather the observable phenomenon that people sing. The object of study must be primarily the fact of singing, considered as cultural expression. That means that the primary material for study does not consist of songs qua text or musical objectification, but rather of the functional context in which the songs are found. This means in turn that we should focus our analysis on the cultural activity or, if you will, on social behavior. But we must also look behind the activity to reveal the underlying presuppositions, the needs precipitating the activity. This leads to the problem of the relationship between song activity, norms, and the perception of values. What is the role of the song in respect to norms and values? Does it strengthen and sustain them, or does it promote their dismemberment? How do norms and values determine the activity of singing? Who provides the subject matter of songs, who controls the subject matter—the government, the entertainment industry, the mass media, parents, teachers, or organizations? How do these interact with or counteract each other?

Another question concerns the context in which songs are used. Here we must consider all types of activities, from the introverted song an individual sings to him- or herself, to various forms of spontaneous social song, to organized group singing at public occasions.

At this point I can only hint at some aspects of the larger problem. In most areas we lack a fundamental theoretical and methodological analysis. We also lack an empirical base, but the latter can be found in today's society.

Some of the most stimulating new ideas and research have come from the milieu around Ernst Klusen at the Institut für musikalische Volkskunde (Institute for Ethnomusicology) in Neuss. His epoch-making contributions are being carried on by scholars such as Günter Noll, Wilhelm Schepping, and Walter Heimann. But in the Nordic countries we are not totally asleep either. In May of 1981, the Norwegian musicologist Jon-Roar Bjørkvold received a doctorate for his dissertation on "Den spontane barnesangen—vårt musikalske morsmål" (Spontaneous Children's Song—Our Musical Mother Tongue). At three kindergartens in Oslo, Bjørkvold for an entire year observed all forms of song activites, from formulaic song to improvised singing to readymade songs. Respecting the children's own forms of cultural expression, he analyzed how they used song as a socially determined language. I make bold to characterize Bjørkvold's dissertation as a milestone in Norwegian and Nordic scholarship. It is a good example of the kind of new insights this type of research can give us (Bjørkvold, 1979, 1985; see also Suojanen 1984 and the present volume).

In an article about problems, methods, and aims in European ethnomusicology, Arthur Simon has isolated a series of concepts which are useful to our understanding of new trends in ballad research (Simon, 1978). Both disciplines demonstrate development

from evolutionism to culturalism,
from historical study to cultural anthropology,
from formalism to the study of sociocultural context,
from text analysis to the analysis of process,
from the comparison of variants to the analysis of repertoire,
from focusing on a single genre to an expanded concept of folk song,
from esthetic analysis to functional analysis,
from literary to folkloristic analysis.

These changes do not indicate evolutionary progression from one level to another, but rather a cumulative process. New research methods are added, but none of the previous ones is relinquished entirely. When I plead for folksong research which focuses on the activity of singing, I do so in order to place folk song in a cultural context. I am looking for cultural research which can give us new insights into social behavior and social mechanisms.

THE DYNAMICS OF RELIGIOUS GROUP SINGING

Päivikki Suojanen

The present essay is an ethnomusicological survey of hymn singing in the Beseecher movement in Western Finland. My methodological aim is to map out the empirical study of musical activities in a microculture. The material consists of three hundred hours of taped singing which I recorded as an in-group observer during prayer meetings between 1968 and 1979. Altogether the material represents 688 song units from the repertoire of the oldest Finnish revivalist movement, the Beseechers, located in the area of Rauma and Pori in Western Finland.

Hymn singing constitutes the most characteristic aspect of musical behavior among members of various religious movements in Finland. In the older revival movements of the Church of Finland, singing is a creative musical as well as a social phenomenon. Nor must we overlook the fact that singing has been and continues to be a form of personal devotion. Singing here refers to face-to-face group singing in religious meetings. Every Finn understands roughly that there are audible differences between the singing of Laestadians, the Awakened, and Beseechers, but the differences have not yet been the subject of systematic investigation. Are they related to the use of the voice, rhythm, tone, or melody? Does each of the revivalist movements have its own singing style? Strictly speaking, what do we mean by "singing style"? Revivalist movements in Finland and other countries have engendered numerous hymn collections independent of church-authorized hymnals and used by people in prayer meetings and home devotions, usually without accompaniment. Hymns were also sung during work—when carding wool, weaving, cooking, and even milking. Singing was also common on birthdays and name days, and at weddings and funerals.

In an article published as early as 1938, Ilmari Krohn (1867–1960) referred

---

Original title: "Zur Methodologie der Volksliedforschung (Gesangsforschung). Bericht über Forschung zum religiösen Volksgesang." Published in *Jahrbuch für Volksliedforschung*, 1985.

to one of the most interesting aspects of religious folk singing in Finland, namely individual variation of melodies:

> In Pori I met an elderly woman who did not wish to show her ignorance and made up melodies on the spot, one after the other. I did notice, however, that they were all variants of the same chorale, skillfully altered to fit the meter of each hymn. For lack of better judgment I disregarded these melodies because I didn't think that they were very important to the hymn tradition of the people. I later regretted this omission, for these melodies were vital proof of the techniques by which melodies are adapted by ordinary people to hymns with different meters, if the proper melody does not happen to be known. (Krohn, 1938, 64–65)

Similar melodies are still sung today, which means that the field of folk hymn singing remains wide open to research, although in a different form than during the time of Krohn. As I see it, religious folk-singing expresses three modes of human behavior. First, it is religious behavior expressing a concept of the sacred shared by individual and group. Second, it is a form of ritual behavior: it is normed, periodical, communal, and holistic. Third, it is musical behavior representing communal values and world view through the medium of song. Each chorale has its own notation, but the melody is embellished in various individual styles in spite of the fact that it is sung communally. The point that characterizes folk tradition and is central to scholarship is the question of creativity. The singer presents more than text and melody. His or her creative personality is reflected in the choice of songs and in the variation of certain elements. In my view creativity in singing is a function of: (1) the interpretation and variation of melody and text, (2) the performance style, (3) the choice of songs to be performed, and (4) the choice of new songs to be learned.

The religious, ritual, and musical modes identified here are integral parts of the same behavioral phenomenon, but their separation illustrates the multidisciplinary nature of our field. The study of this type of folk music combines linguistics, folkloristics, ethnomusicology, anthropology, social psychology, music history, history of religion, and cultural history. Religious singing is a form of communication within a given group, and its effect is based on the same principles as a speech or sermon. As communication, the most important distinction between preaching and communal singing is that the latter is produced by the entire audience. The sermon, by contrast, is produced by one person who is accorded performance status for the purpose of that task. For the duration of the singing event, the relation speaker-listener, leader-follower, shepherd-sheep, ceases to exist. Each participant is given an equal role as singer.

The *singing act* is defined as the smallest unit sung by a prayer (cf. Dell Hymes's "speech act"). The *singing event* (cf. "speech event") is a chorale or religious hymn larger than any singing act in a given situation. In studying singing acts and events in a religious community, we focus on the underlying norms: How does the singer relate to the microgroup and situation through song selection?

How do listeners and participants respond to him or her? In any holistic analysis (cf. Pentikäinen 1978, 25) of singing as a form of communication, the focus is less on text and melody than on the relationship between group and individual. The metastructure of sung communication can be considered on six levels:

1. From a sociocultural perspective, the specific environment in which a person lives plays a central role in singing. The singing community shapes the singer and not the other way around: singers move away or die, the singing tradition survives. Groups maintain the singing culture and tradition. Primary groups—family, relatives, and village community—influence the transmission of the song tradition the most. After the primary groups, religious groups play the most significant role in the transmission of tradition. Every prayer meeting represents a range of acceptable behaviors on a scale of social norms. These norms influence the role of the singer and effect social control of the singing event. For example, musical accompaniment and arrangements for several voices are regarded positively or negatively by different religious communities in Finland. Individual status corresponds to a person's social position. The singing community consists of social positions in a context of individuals striving for a common goal. Within the status that naturally falls to an individual (ascribed status) gender-specific behavior is determined by, for example, a female singer's not being the equal of male singers in the devotional meetings of the Beseechers. Only on the basis of age can a female singer improve her position, and, with the help of a good musical ear and a thorough knowledge of tradition, achieve enhanced performance status as a singing initiator.

2. I owe to perception-psychologist Orlo Strunk (1962) the division of personal psychology into cognitive, affective, and conative aspects of religion, which I apply here to the various experiences of an individual. *Cognition* is the ideological knowledge received through religious songs and chorales which the singer assimilates to a firm order of precedence in his or her own mind. A chorale confronts an individual on the personal level (sung by him- or herself), the group level (identifying, unifying the group), and the supranormal level (transcendental communication). *Affection* refers to the feelings of an individual arising from the singing event. Through extensive field work and depth analysis of the Beseecher movement in Western Finland, I have developed the following model of the emotional structure of singing and/or relations in the group (Figure 1).

Conative aspect refers to the intention of the singer and the goal-oriented qualities of hymn singing. Note the sociogram illustrating the hierarchy of power in Beseecher hymn singing in Western Finland (Figure 2).

3. In the metastructure of tradition, language itself (texture) accentuates the norms of the singing community. For example, members of the Beseecher movement in Western Finland to this day sing in the language of the old Finnish Bible (1540–1820). In analyzing the singing style of the Beseechers I have isolated pauses, tempo, intensity, quality, and use of the voice, as well as individual variation in group singing. These are factors by which the singing

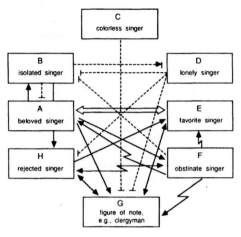

Figure 1

style of, for example, the Finnish Lutheran Church can be differentiated from that of other religious communities. The characteristic singing style of the Beseechers in their home prayer meetings is robust, intense; the use of the voice is simple; women's voices sound shrill, even harsh, because of the tubular, compressive use of the voice; older singers tend to avoid pauses. Some of the singers like to sing a melisma or pre-note between verses. In content and structure Beseecher hymns accentuate areas of traditional emphasis in the community and, especially in regard to structure, reveal transformations in the world view of the community. Therefore, through text analysis of Beseecher

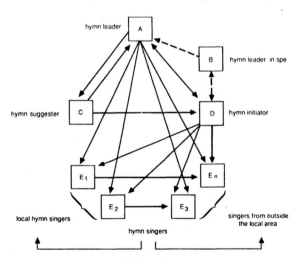

Figure 2
Power Relations in the Hymn-Singing Group

hymns sung in prayer meetings during the 1960s and 1970s, I have been able to document changes in the movement during that period.

The melodies must be considered in relation to the texts which, among the Beseechers, represent a written tradition. It is my experience that the Beseechers primarily select hymns on the basis of the text and then find an appropriate tune. During the fifteen years I lived in the community I cannot recall a single instance when a hymn was not sung because no suitable melody could be agreed upon. Once a text has been chosen a melody is constructed. Occasionally, after a shaky introduction and perhaps several simultaneous attempts, the melody starts faltering. It even happens that during the entire hymn no common tune is ever found. However, the average length of Beseecher hymns is fourteen verses, and there is usually time to achieve homogeneity as the singing goes on. A melody becomes more uniform with repetition.

If two good singers simultaneously introduce different variants of the same tune, two factors determine which will be chosen: of these the most important is familiarity of the tune to the majority of local singers; secondarily, the stronger voice will prevail. There are some Beseecher melodies of great complexity, but on the whole they tend to be transparent in structure, and their variants differ little from each other (for example, HSHL 106; HSHL 8, 9, 155). Perhaps the unconscious reason for choosing simple and plain melodies at the meetings is that it allows participants to achieve maximum unity in singing. Ornamentation of the basic melody is a characteristic of Beseecher singing: unaccompanied communal singing tends to avoid extended notes but does develop individually varied melisma. Even when melismatic variation is collective, however, there are some who will not join in singing the melisma. The same is true of individual emphases, crescendos, and diminuendos. Glissandos at times precede important notes. Occasionally one can hear several variants simultaneously: the basic melody is the same but individual interpretations differ. Compare the following variants of a verse in HSHL 9, "Eurajoen nuottipainos" (1963) (Figure 3).

Because *melodies* are transmitted orally, they differ locally within a given tradition area: a melody may be sung in a major key in the northern part of the area, and in a minor key in the south. There may even be significant differences between neighboring villages in the same parish. During the 1960s and 1970s, hymns at the Beseecher meetings were sung mostly in minor keys. Notably, chorales interspersed with kneeling prayers were decidedly minor in character. Established keys of Lutheran hymns were adapted daringly. This trait perhaps reflects a period of crisis in the Movement. The relation between melody and text in Beseecher hymns fluctuates; notably the number of syllables or repetitive elements in each verse varies, so that the count of syllables per note can be two-or threefold, or the other way around. This proves a severe test for outsiders joining a meeting for the first time, but for members of the group it is a precious sign of shared identity.

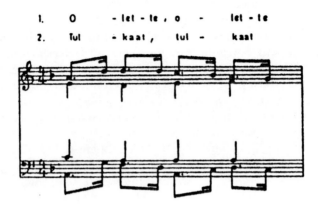

(1. You are, you are)
(2. Come here, come here)
Individual variants

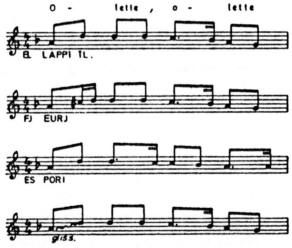

Figure 3

The hymn "Jeesuksen veri se lasinen meri" (HSHL 127: 1–11), sung as frequently at recent meetings led by ministers as it was at lay meetings earlier, is a concrete example of how singers insert notes or leave them out, extend words through apocope and for rhythmic reasons add new ones. "Mutt siinä sitten toivossa" is sung "Mutta siinä sitten toivossa" (4th verse); "Ett' Karitsan emäntä jo valmis on" becomes "Että Karitsan emäntä jo valmis on" (8th verse); "Siell' hupaista on olla kanss' enkelein" is sung as "siellä hupaista on olla kanssa enkelein" (9th verse); "Siellä pyhäin paris" is sung "Siellä pyhäin parissa" (10th verse); "Se autuunden tie" becomes "se on autuuden tie" or "Hän on autuuden tie" (11th verse). An accompanist discovers that beginning with the second verse the notes on paper no longer correspond to the notes sung by the participants. This is illustrated by the examples in Figure 4.

(1. Upon whom the parish is founded)
(4. That sometime we will land in the heavenly port)
(6. She lives with her bridegroom forever)
(8. That the bride of the lamb is prepared)
(9. There we find rest together with the angels)

Figure 4

1. From the perspective of individual and social psychology the various *behavioral roles* are of interest. Figure 5 illustrates two roles played at Beseecher meetings:

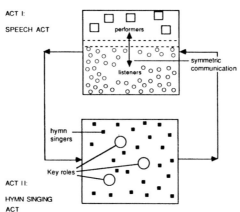

Figure 5. The *participants* are preacher, beseechers, accompanist, host, and/or hostess. When a preacher gives a sermon or someone else speaks, the roles are divided between performers and listeners (act I). However, when there is singing after the sermon (act II) entirely different roles emerge. Key roles in hymn singing are the hymn suggester, hymn initiator, hymn leader, persons aspiring to lead (hymn leader in spe), as well as local hymn singers and singers from outside the local area. The participant singers find their proper place in a hierarchy of power according to their respective roles. At the top of the hierarchy stands the hymn leader, at the bottom singers from outside the local area.

Hymn Leader   (4b)
Hymn Leader in spe (4a)
Hymn Initiator   (3)
Hymn Suggester   (2)
Local Hymn Singer - (1)
Singer from Outside (0)

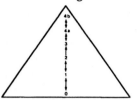

Figure 6. Hierarchy of Power Roles in Singing

The methods of visual anthropology, particularly proxemic and kinesic observation, constitute an important basis for the study of singing and roles. Tape recordings and transcriptions are not sufficient in assembling the needed data. *The referential system* finally determines what happens at the prayer meetings, what is sung and how. Primary stimuli—subjectively remembered and imagined conceptions of the meeting room and participants—and above all releasing stimuli (objective stimuli from the outside) such as an outside speaker, finally shape the dynamics in situ at the meetings. *Social* control functions in religious communities in Finland in various ways. The most radical public means of control is perhaps the method of interruptive singing practiced by the Awakened and Beseechers. An unpopular speaker or an unwelcome address is interrupted by means of collectively initiated singing.

5. In studying social context, basic research into how singing functions to create a sense of community is very important. Context is gradually becoming the basis for understanding what singing means to adherents of a given tradition, as well as to how all singing finally functions. *Meaning* can be analyzed through interviewing singers about the value that religious folk hymns, chorales, and singing have for them. The *function* of singing is discovered by studying its use and meaning.

6. In the transmission process, *collective tradition* includes the body of material that is generally known and accepted by the community and that forms the basis of social control. It can be described by means of frequency and repertoire analysis, which is the method I have used in studying the Beseecher movement. The collective tradition during the 1960s and 1970s has turned out to be rather limited and stereotyped in choice and application. Individual tradition, on the other hand, is transmitted from generation to generation by individual tradition bearers, but is not widespread. With the exception of a few hymns, the collection *Siionin virret* (1790) represents this tradition in the Beseecher movement today. In studying communication through singing it is important to discover the cultural-historical means by which singing is transmitted and learned. At first the child assimilates hymns by imitation at home and in meetings. In school he or she learns texts from hymn books, while the meetings teach the creative singing model. From the perspective of analysis, contact- and key-persons at the meetings are important because they illuminate mutual influences between the parish and the larger tradition area. They know the singing tradition beyond the borders of the parish and can tell which is the "correct" variant to choose at a prayer meeting. Another important basis for

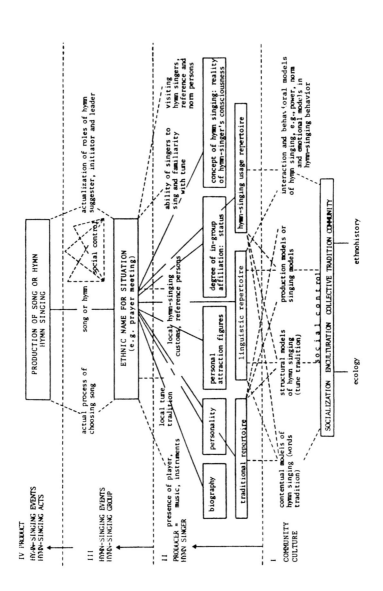

Figure 7. The Ideal Structure of Hymn-Singing Production

the study of the singing tradition is local microanalysis, for example, geographically speaking, of a given village or, socially, of a singing community.

The metastructure of singing in the tradition of the Beseechers of Western Finland can finally be summarized schematically as a process developing from its basis in sociocultural norms to the actual product of collective tradition, the religious hymn or chorale. This is illustrated in Figure 7.

SPONTANEOUS SINGING AMONG CHILDREN

Jon-Roar Bjørkvold

The study of singing as a sociomusical process, especially among children, is a relatively new field in Scandinavia, first explored by musicologists and folklorists in the 1970s. The following paper presents certain aspects of an earlier study of spontaneous singing among preschoolers at three different kindergartens in the Oslo area. The methodology is a combination of musicological and folkloristic approaches, which allows us to study the forms and functions of children's singing from a perspective not available to either discipline by itself.

Children's impromptu singing occurs as a spontaneous element in a larger context, as part of some activity the child is involved in—alone or together with other children. The unified sequence of events combining singing and other external activities can be characterized as a sociomusical process. If we focus on the song and its musical structure or text in isolation, we lose sight of the sociocultural framework which makes the song meaningful to the children at a given moment. Therefore it is important to consider both musical and social elements (form and application) in order to understand the nature of spontaneous singing among children.

In contrast to musicologists, folklorists and anthropologists have been preoccupied with the concept of culture. Culture is defined as "ideas, values, rules and norms which an individual adopts from the previous generation and which one transmits—usually in modified form—to the next generation" (Klausen, 1976, 10).

We are dealing here with a set of shared codes that is meaningful to the tradition bearers and gives coherence and identity to their culture. This is also true for the culture of children and their oral forms of communication

---

Original title: "Sangaktivitet som sosio-musikalsk prosess i barnekulturen. En presentasjon av enkelte problemstillinger, metodespørsmål og resultater." Published in *Sumlen. Årsbok för Vis- och Folkmusikforskning*, 1982.

(Enerstvedt, 1976). For children, spontaneous singing constitutes a shared code which they understand and apply systematically within the limited framework of their own culture. It is not the purely musical structure which gives meaning to this code, but an implied reference beyond the music itself to something within the culture of which it is a part (Meyer 1974). The main thesis of this study can thus be formulated as follows. There is a systematic relationship between the act of spontaneous singing and its musical form, based on a musical-linguistic code (Figure 1).

Our model takes the form of a continuous triangle: the song's social context, its specific use, and its form are mutually dependent quantities, discrete parts of a sociomusical whole. The form of the song is shaped by a culture-specific musical code and a range of musical structures and tacitly understood references employed systematically by the child.

From early childhood on, melody and rhythm are important elements in communication not only in singing but also in ordinary speech. Throughout grade school, communication through singing builds on musical formulas and structures transmitted by children to children. These formulas and structures are so firmly integrated with socioculturally determined contexts of meaning and application, that we can characterize children's singing as a kind of mother tongue. Support for the above can be demonstrated by theoretical models in psycholinguistics; the scope of the present article, however, does not permit me to further explore this question here. Instead I will focus on methods of field work and analysis employed in documenting the "musical mother tongue" among children.

A preliminary survey demonstrated that children sing in various situations: while running around, reading a book, playing with dolls or cars, and so on. The type of activity involved is not in itself sufficient to determine categories of song use. What is decisive, however, is how singing functions in the context of each activity. The following functions can be identified:

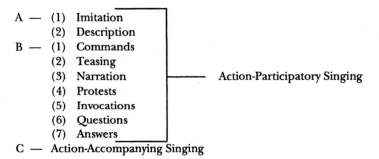

Concrete examples of children's singing are numerous and striking; they could fill a whole article by themselves. Anyone who has spent time with children at play will recognize the exuberant reality behind the system of categories. Category A includes imitative or descriptive singing as part of some

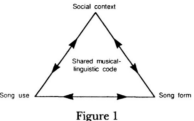

Figure 1

ongoing activity, such as when children imitate the sound of sirens while playing with a toy police car or ambulance. Here singing becomes an instrument of the play-activity (Figure 2).

Dy-de-li, dy-de-li, dy-de-li, dy-de-li

Figure 2

In category B, singing is part of a speech act; here the element of communication is dominant (Figure 3).

Dum-me, dum-me de-re

Figure 3

In category C, singing is not integral to an ongoing activity: it accompanies the activity without necessarily being part of it. For example, the child puts on its overalls while singing "Baa, baa, little lamb!" (Alice Tegner). Here a reflective, introspective element often dominates. Needless to say, in some instances the different categories blend into each other.

In delineating functional categories the following distinction proves to be analytically significant: To what degree are A, B, or C employed to establish or maintain a sense of community among the children, and on what levels? Which of the three categories has, socially speaking, the most pragmatic function? (see Bateson, 1972, 85). "A" contributes to the instrumentality of an activity or game and is thus socially constructive. "A" is also socially effective to the degree that the singing promotes a sense of community among several children involved in the same activity.

"B" is obviously socially constructive since the act of singing establishes contact with others in the group. Singing in this category may be specifically directed to another individual, or to a more or less undefined group. The social constructiveness of "B" will thus vary with the context.

"C" may also function to create a sense of community, such as when the same song is picked up by children drawing at a table. More typically, however, category C singing occurs when the child is alone. The normally introverted character of category C contrasts strongly with the extroversion of "A" and especially of "B." In this respect, "C" has little or no direct social significance.

We can schematize the social-pragmatic function of categories A, B, and C as follows:

B - Highly socially constructive in a given situation

A - Somewhat socially constructive in a given situation

C - Least socially constructive in a given situation

Before proceeding, it is important to define the term "singing." For the purposes of this study, singing is defined as sound produced by the human voice in regular vibrations. "Singing" thus covers a wide spectrum of vocal expressions—from a single sound to songs sung in their entirety with text and melody. In previous scholarship, traditional songs have not usually been included under the label of "spontaneous singing." In the present study any children's singing that is not prompted by adults is considered spontaneous. The distinction spontaneous/non-spontaneous is thus based on social rather than musical criteria.

Concerning categories of musical form, it must be emphasized that form here is not defined in traditional musical terms (thematic structure, periodicity, parts, and so forth). For children, singing assumes a specific form in relation to the social and emotional milieu of which it is a part. In the present study, categories of musical form thus refer only to characteristics of melodic interval and rhythm. The following categories of children's singing can be distinguished:

- Flowing/amorphous singing
- Formulaic singing
- Ready-made songs

"Flowing singing" does not exhibit any fixed formal structure in terms of interval (micro-intervals, glissandi), melody, or rhythm. (Also, textually speaking, such singing tends to improvised.)

"Formulaic singing" exhibits a firmer structure. Intervals are characterized by half or full tones, allowing for gliding effects often in the form of falling thirds on the threshold between small and large thirds. Interval combinations are few and fixed to the point of appearing formulaic. This type of singing arises from language rhythms, but usually its rhythmic core is so pronounced that it can be described in traditional notation.

"Ready-made songs" include compositions by known or anonymous adults, or by the children themselves, that are transmitted in a well-defined basic form. These songs are fixed in terms of interval, melody, rhythm, form, and text, and thus contrast to "flowing/amorphous" singing. Although this type of singing is indisputably based on ready-made songs, we must bear in mind that children do not necessarily sing these songs all the way through—or necessarily "correctly" in strictly musical terms—but rather use the songs as frameworks for their own inventions and variations.

Scandinavian children belong to a culture group whose music is dominated by the major/minor tonal system. However, children's use of the major/minor system is usually much less specific and firm than that of adults. We see this especially in their "flowing/amorphous" singing. "Formulaic" singing, by contrast, represents a transition in the children's gradual adaptation to the dominant tonal system of the surrounding culture. It is in the "ready-made" songs that we recognize the major/minor system most clearly, although here, too, children take a less defined stance than most adults. Even if the above categorization of spontaneous singing among children is analytically useful, this does not mean that the same categories are clearly distinguished by the children themselves, as we can see by their use of combinations and transitional forms.

This study examines "spontaneous singing" among children from the perspective of an external and systematic variable: the influence of adult singing in nursery schools. The three nursery schools in question show markedly different degrees of such influence:

Nursery School East   - Minor adult influence
Nursery School Center - Major adult influence
Nursery School West   - Moderate adult influence

I recorded what and how much the adults sang, thus making it possible to investigate how a given cultural form (that is, adult norms) shaped the children's musical mother tongue on various levels: how adult influence manifested itself, and which adult elements children rejected and which they adopted.

My field work covered an eight-month period. At each of the three nursery schools, I studied groups of fifteen to twenty children between four and six years of age. In order to minimize interference, I used no technical equipment such as a tape or video recorder. When studying singing in a social context, it is important that the social and emotional continuum not be disturbed. Technical apparatus can register data, but it can also affect the observed phenomena—hence, the old problem of finding a balance between validity and verification. Practical experience suggests that in studying singing as part of an ongoing social and cultural activity, the field workers are in fact best served by relying on their own senses sharpened by professional training. For the purposes of the present study, I adopted the role of passive participant and observer. I was with the children all the time, but without actively influencing their playing or singing. Paper and pencil were the only tools I had with me. I had formulated the following range of questions beforehand:

- What was sung (music and/or text)?
- Who sang?

- Who started the singing?
- Who picked up on the singing?
- Who was present without singing?
- What was the social situation or the type of activity in which the singing occurred?
- Where did the singing occur?
- When did the singing occur?

Figure 4 illustrates the method used in recording my observations as data. Erik is listed first because he started the singing. The arrow pointing to Henrik signifies that he picked up on the singing. Roy is listed in parentheses because he was involved in the activity but did not participate in the singing. The type

"Center"
2/14/74   11:32
Round table in main room, three children, coloring.
Erik → Henrik (Roy):

(No one dares climb up!)

Figure 4

of information noted here is determined by the thesis and intention of the present study. The data concerning musical form, text, and social context, are directed toward illuminating the postulated language of children's singing, its structure, use, and function. The data concerning who was singing touch on whether children's singing is related to gender or other patterns of collective behavior. The data concerning where the singing took place record external conditions for the activity. Finally, the date is important for tracing the development of children's singing over time.

Is it possible to demonstrate a complementarity of form and function in children's singing? "Formulaic singing," because of its standardized character, presumably represents a code generally shared by children. On the other hand, because of its non-standardized character, "flowing/amorphous singing" presumably does not represent a widely shared code. "Ready-made songs," too, represent a shared code, but it must be assumed that the last type of singing is less common in a direct communicative context, precisely because it builds on "prefabricated" melodies and texts.

Given the above considerations, we can restate our main hypothesis in the form of the following secondary hypotheses: (1) The more socially constructive/pragmatic children's singing is, the more it takes the shape of "formulaic singing." (2) By contrast, the less socially constructive/pragmatic children's singing is, the more it takes the form of "flowing/ amorphous singing." (3) The less socially constructive/pragmatic children's singing is, the more it takes the form of "ready-made" songs.

Table 1. Distribution of Song Forms

East:	"Flowing"	"Formulaic"	"Ready-Made"	Total
A	18.1%	72.4%	9.5%	100.0%
B	8.6%	89.0%	2.4%	100.0%
C	75.5%	9.0%	15.4%	99.9%
Center:				
A	21.6%	50.0%	28.4%	100.0%
B	12.1%	77.2%	10.7%	100.0%
C	33.3%	3.6%	63.1%	100.0%
West:				
A	26.7%	38.7%	34.7%	100.1%
B	12.5%	72.9%	14.6%	100.0%
C	48.1%	6.5%	45.3%	99.9%

The data collected in the three nursery schools (East, Center, West) show the following distribution of song forms within each category of function (A, B, C) (Table 1). The given data support the main hypothesis of the present study: there is a demonstrable correlation between the form of children's songs and the function of their singing. Furthermore, the secondary hypotheses are also confirmed: "formulaic" songs dominate in functional category B, less in category A, and least in category C. In all three nursery schools "flowing/amorphous" singing dominates in functional category C in contrast to A and B. Correspondingly, "ready-made" songs are more prominent in category C than in A or B.

In all three nursery schools it was also demonstrated that the correlation between the form and function of children's singing changed over time, irrespective of the type or degree of adult influence. The more socially constructive/pragmatic children's singing is to begin with, the more its use increases as the children in each group get to know each other. Inversely, the less socially constructive/pragmatic children's singing is initially, the more its use decreases as the children get to know each other. Statistically, this development can be represented as shown in Figure 5.

The same pattern has been confirmed in nursery schools elsewhere. In children's culture, singing is inextricably tied to the social context. Furthermore, it appears that children intuitively use fixed musical forms to express certain specific meanings. This is evidenced clearly in children's "formulaic" singing: each of the children observed in the present study consistently employed a repertoire of approximately fifteen formulas to express the same type of intentional context. In other words, children possess a shared, culturally determined musical code, a genuine musical mother tongue that is at least as important and expressive as their verbal mother tongue.

The song culture of children stands in a dynamic relationship to adult culture. How children between four and seven years of age are shaped by adult influence but at the same time develop individuality and personal taste, is a

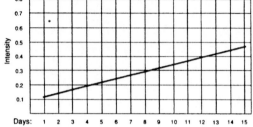

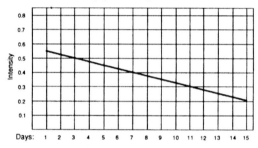

Figure 5

fascinating topic which we cannot fully explore here, but I will touch upon one of its aspects: the question of a child's musical aptitude. Here it is helpful to distinguish the two concepts "use" and "function" (Merriam, 1964). In the present article I have defined "use" as the directly observable employment of singing by children. "Function," on the other hand, relates to the underlying role or significance singing has for children in the context of their own culture. This concept of function is of fundamental importance when discussing musical aptitude on the children's own cultural premises.

Most adults think of children as musical if they have a nice voice and can carry a tune. But from the children's perspective, these considerations are irrelevant. What matters to the child is that singing serves as a distinctive mode of expression in the context of daily activities. Singing has an emotional function: it expresses feelings, communicates feelings, arouses feelings, often in situations where words are not adequate. Singing provides an emotional outlet, it is affective, spanning a range of feelings from giddy joy to sadness and despair. What does it matter if the sound is off-key?

One of the emotional functions of singing is to contribute to the resolution of conflict within an individual child and within groups of children. Tensions are given an outlet, balance is restored, reconciliation is achieved. Singing then has a therapeutic function expertly employed by the children themselves. The

fact that singing serves as a special language within children's culture means that it shares certain central functions of verbal language:
- to convey information
- to establish contact
- to define personal identity

Children's singing, then, does not merely facilitate interpersonal contact by mediating various feelings. "Formulaic" singing in particular conveys concrete information with striking precision. By creating contact and conveying information, children's singing defines the identity of those involved on a number of levels. First of all, in children's culture, singing which exhibits a high degree of uniformity contributes to the formation of cultural identity. Furthermore, the sense of solidarity in children's singing enhances the consolidation of group identity. Finally, singing functions as a defining force in the formation of gender and individual identities.

It is important to emphasize the function of singing in the socialization of children. Through play, in which singing has a central role, children are confronted with the whole range of questions and problems raised in their own lives. Play and song are therefore central to the child's development in the context of the society into which he or she is being integrated.

Another aspect of the socializing function of singing among children has to do with latent ritual. Like adults, children surround death, for example, with a framework of singing. I observed children play "dead" after a train crash and solemnly bury each other in big pillows. We are here talking about ritual tendencies rather than fully developed ceremonies. In a culture where singing is so much part of social reality, it makes little sense to speak of musicality strictly in terms of musical aptitude. However, that is precisely what we do in our daily contact with children, at home as much as in school, with only the faintest comprehension of the consequences.

Old John Bell did not have a very good voice; he bellowed more than he sang, they said. And still, if you listened carefully, you would hear that old John Bell's singing was incredibly beautiful and expressive. The well-known American composer Charles Ives described it this way:

> Once when Father was asked: "How can you stand to hear old John Bell (who was the best stoneman in town) bellow off-key the way he does at camp meetings?" his answer was: "Old John is a supreme musician. Look into his face and hear the music of the ages. Don't pay too much attention to the sounds. If you do, you may miss the music. You won't get a heroic ride to heaven on pretty little sounds. (Cowell, 1955, 23f.)

We can take the same attitude toward singing among children—if only we learn to listen and understand.

The musical mother tongue of children is in essence sociomusical. We must therefore look at children's musicality in sociomusical terms, based on a thorough understanding of the nature and function singing has for children.

For children singing is a way of life, a way of grasping and expressing their sense of reality. Only from this perspective does it become meaningful to talk about children's musicality. Only on this basis can we begin to understand the qualities of children's singing that are specific to our own culture in Scandinavia.

Folklore and Society

THE WHORE IN RURAL SOCIETY

Jonas Frykman

In rural Sweden during the nineteenth century, sexual licentiousness was regarded not only as a social and moral problem, but as a medical one. A person suspected of promiscuity was considered dangerous because he or she was believed to cause rickets in infants. The concept of "whore rickets," as it was called, is one of the most remarkable of the popular beliefs connecting childhood disease and sexual immorality.

Rickets—Infant Disease and Social Behavior

Rickets, medically known today as rachitis, is caused by a deficiency of Vitamin D, a calcium nutrient converted from sunshine, which is essential to healthy bone development. The rachitic child suffers from a softening and deformation of the skeleton. The disease manifests itself in a number of ways, but the most frequent symptoms include a disproportionately large and square head (flattened laterally and in front); lateral bones being noticeably soft; hair loss; and compression of the rib cage, which pushes the breastbone forward. Rachitis is rarely congenital and most often occurs between the ages of six months and three years. In most instances the disease regresses spontaneously, but often leaves permanent deformations, such as curved legs or back and stunted growth. At times the disease is severe enough to cause death. Naturally, the physically weakened child is often subject to secondary illnesses.

Today rachitis is rare in Sweden; a century ago it was the most common of serious childhood diseases. This disparity is due not to medical advances, but to differences in child care: it is clear that the very practices intended to keep the child safe were themselves the cause of the disease. Children, like everybody else, have built-in defenses against vitamin D deficiency by virtue of the skin's ability to convert sunshine into the needed vitamin. This mechanism, however,

Original title: "Horan som samhällsfara." Published in *Horan i bondesamhället*, 1977.

was consistently nullified by the practice of "protecting" the child from the dangers of the out-of-doors. Infants were kept inside the house or, if they had to be outside, were swaddled and covered from top to toe. During the first year, children frequently suffered from rachitis, not recovering until they learned to walk and could expand their range of activity. Folk narratives consistently associate a "cure" for the disease with this second stage of a child's development—but, as we shall see, for a very different reason. In analyzing rickets, we must not be trapped into using the classifications of modern medical science, but rather should examine how the disease was regarded a century ago, and ask what the phenomenon can tell us about the society in which it occurred.

The rural population of nineteenth-century Sweden had a highly differentiated concept of rickets. However, the various forms of the disease were not usually distinguished in terms of symptoms, as they would be in modern medicine, but according to the supposed source. A list from Småland, for example, contains nine different types of the disease distinguished by origin (Tillhagen, 1958, 290). Another list from Skåne dating from 1795 contains twenty-two types (Bringéus, 1951, 90f.), while an informant from Blekinge states that people there distinguished twenty-four forms of the illness (LUF 2759). The magic number nine often occurs in such classifications, as do multiples of the number three.

In the case of "whore rickets" the child usually contracted the disease postnatally. One of the other categories of rickets was diagnosed if a child was affected in the fetal state; it was then assumed that the mother had broken one of the many taboos surrounding pregnancy (cf. Weisser-Aall, 1968). For example, if she left the house on a clear night without covering her head, the child might get "star rickets." The foundation of this belief was the dress code requiring all married women to cover their hair. If a pregnant woman walked through a gate, the child could get "gate rickets," a sanction which effectively limited the mobility of married women in the village. Or, if a woman crossed her legs in church, her child might get rachitis affecting the hips (Fredén, 1974, 39ff.). In each of these examples, beliefs concerning the causes of rachitis enforce various rules governing the proper behavior of pregnant women. In other instances the underlying sanction is less explicit, as in the belief that such women must not witness the slaughtering of animals, must not touch or even see a dead person, must not cross a grave, and so forth.

Many of the prescribed cures for rachitis are not clearly tied to the cause of the disease. For example, one might treat a child afflicted with rickets by applying ointments, or by pulling the child through a specially prepared opening in the ground, or between two trees that have grown together, or through a harness. In other instances, the "diagnostic procedure was to identify the person who had caused the illness, because he or she was also the key to the cure" (Tillhagen, 1958, 291). Thus people healed "cadaver rickets" by having the child touch the dead body, "gate rickets" by leading it through the particular gate, "whore rickets" by making the child drink from the shoe of the person suspected of immoral behavior. These cures confirm the diagnosis and are more closely tied to the perceived cause of the disease.

The preceding examples demonstrate that rachitis was not considered a disease in a medical sense, but rather a symptom of a social threat: "In the old days rickets was not considered a disease or, more precisely, an insufficiency, that could be healed by an ordinary physician. Rickets was a supranormal phenomenon caused by witchcraft, envy or the evil eye" (EU 39136). Given that view, it made little sense to look to a physician for help. In the rural milieu, however, there were specialists who knew how to cure the illness because they understood the underlying causes. These specialists were the so-called "wise folk." They were the people the mother would turn to if she was not able to discover the source of the illness or did not know how to deal with it. From the folk's point of view the traditional forms of treatment were quite effective. The "wise folk" dealt with the whole spectrum of behaviors of which the illness was one of potentially numerous symptoms. The condition of the child usually improved—with or without treatment. More than anything else the prescribed treatment cured a social disorder, and its efficacy depended on locating the source of the illness, usually someone within the community.

"Whore Rickets" and the "Whore"

Under what conditions did someone become "dangerous"? Specifically, what wrong must someone have committed for people to suspect that he or she could harm the child? In the Swedish language the term "whore" is used in various combinations to describe illicit sexual acts from adultery and fornication to prostitution. While today "whore" means primarily a prostitute, that is, a person offering sex in exchange for money, in nineteenth-century rural Sweden the term included any unmarried woman who gave birth to a child or was suspected of having sexual relations with a married man. But in spite of the term "whore rickets," the tradition suggests that men suspected of adulterous behavior could also cause the disorder. In the following story, dating back to the 1890s when the informant was growing up in the parish of Abild in Halland, a man is said to be "dangerous" because he lives with a married woman whose lawful husband has abandoned her:

> When I was a child there was a tailor in our neighborhood, and he had a man working for him. This man had a child with a married woman whose husband had left her and gone to America. But it was kept a secret that he was the child's father. Now I had a newborn brother at that time. And whenever that man came over to our place my mother always hurried to put clothes on my little brother if he wasn't already dressed. I asked my mother why, and then she told me about the man's relation to the married woman, and that my little brother might get "whore rickets" if the man saw him naked. (IFGH 4417)

Another narrative in the form of an anecdote throws further light on the role of the adulterous man in causing or curing "whore rickets." This is one of the few direct documentations of the parallel between adultery and "whore rickets," and here it is the offense rather than the offender upon which the story focuses. As far as I know, the cure described is unique in tradition—but suggestive:

> There was an old man in Almundsryd (in Småland) called Pika-Sven. He walked from farm to farm peddling needles, licorice, fly poison (arsenic), and so on. He also claimed that he was able to cure rickets in infants who couldn't walk. Once he came to a place where they had a child like that, a little over a year old. Sven checked the infant over and said: "It's whore rickets. It's caused by adultery and you get rid of it by adultery. You've got to pretend that you're committing adultery, and then the child will get well." There was nothing else but for the child's mother, who was somewhat gullible, to lie down in bed and for Sven to "pretend" that he was committing adultery. Whatever he was doing, the woman finally said: "That's not pretending!" But Sven was unfazed: "It came from adultery and you get rid of it through adultery." So there was no more to be said about that. (EU 22106)

The total number of texts selected for this study does not exceed 125. The intention is not to make an exhaustive survey of all aspects of "whore rickets," but to analyze the structure of beliefs surrounding the disorder. With this reservation in mind, we can make certain observations regarding the relative frequency of female vs. male "whores." Our study shows seventy-seven "dangerous" women in comparison to fifteen such men. If we include young girls in this category, eighty-six of all "whores" are female. We must therefore conclude that it was primarily females who became "dangerous" through extramarital intercourse. It stands to reason that an equal number of men would qualify for the same role, but it is apparent that traditionally males were more rarely identified as the cause of "whore rickets."

Thus, in looking upon the alleged cause of rickets as a form of social control, we must conclude that women were subject to this form of control to a much higher degree than men. We also find that groups not discussed so far, for example, "secret whores," as well as other categories of people not directly associated with sexual immorality, such as gypsies, horse-flayers, or murderers were connected with "whore rickets." Why?

The "Secret Whore"

The abusive term "whore" did not distinguish between a prostitute and any young girl who had been seduced. But was the village prostitute more "dangerous" than the unmarried mother? The question is central because it relates directly to the structure of society at the time. If socially marginal individuals are suspected of being "dangerous," then beliefs surrounding rickets and those surrounding "uncleanliness" have the same function: to define different social categories and maintain their separation in society (Douglas, 1966).

Belief in the dangerousness of the "secret whore" demonstrates another aspect of the tradition concerning rickets, relating not to social categories but to the moral order. Blaming rickets on "secret whores" (rather than known offenders), served to clarify morally ambivalent situations and define standards of proper behavior. In this instance the concept of "whore rickets" served to exercise moral control in society. "Secret whores" were women who were suspected of "sinning in the flesh" although there was no definitive proof such as pregnancy or the birth of a child. The birth of a child precipitated religious sanctions; the mother was required to submit to confession and absolution, thus signaling that her offense had been discovered and become public knowledge. Society responded to the acknowledged "whore" with the same code as that applied to prostitutes. People knew how to deal with the potential danger surrounding her and took their precautions. But how could one protect oneself against the "secret whore"?

The fear of what is unknown and therefore dangerous is clearly shown in the older sources. Rääf writes that "secret whores" cause rickets in children (2166) and Hyltén-Cavallius informs us that "fallen women" whose offense remained secret were generally believed to be highly "unclean" (1863, 377ff.). But while these older examples demonstrate the special position of the "secret whore," they say nothing about how the latter is regarded in relation to individuals whose sexual immorality is public knowledge. Recently collected data provide a more complete picture here.

In cases where the same informant compares a "secret whore" to a "known whore," the latter appears to be relatively harmless. The following example comes from Enslöv in Halland: "A woman who looks at her illegitimate child won't do it any harm, because everybody knows about it. Only the women who concealed that they were 'whores' were dangerous" (IFGH 4584).

An item collected in Högsby in Småland in the 1920s makes a similar comparison. If a servant girl had a secret sexual relationship with one of the workers there, the farmer's children were in danger of getting rickets. However, if she openly admitted the relationship and perhaps even had a child by the man, then there wasn't any danger (ULMA 3132).

We know that in rural society any woman known as a "whore" was mercilessly condemned to a marginal existence. By giving birth to an illegitimate child she was excluded from membership as an equal in the community. The fear that she might make children ill effectively prevented her from rejoining the community and forced her to retain her marginal status. The notion that the horse-flayer was unclean functioned in precisely the same way. Who would dare expose themselves to the unclean? The accusation that someone was causing rickets thus served to maintain the existing social structure.

While there existed a clear model for dealing with the "known whore," the situation was more ambiguous in the case of the "secret whore." She pretended to the role of an "honest woman" without being entitled to that status. What made her dangerous is precisely that she continued living in the community of "honest" people, even though she deserved to be expelled. She was sailing under a false flag. The "secret whore" represented an anomaly and—given the intolerance of ambiguity in rural culture—this was unacceptable. The fact that the "secret whore" was more feared than other moral offenders provided a weapon against her, a stamp of dangerousness that was used to clarify morally ambivalent situations.

It is important to distinguish the two functions of the belief in "whore rickets"—the expulsion vs. the discovery of the "dishonest" individual. To confuse these two would be the same as confusing the functions of prison and the police in contemporary society. The secret offender was expected to assume her role as "whore," and the appearance of rickets was actively used to bring secret offenses to light. We begin by looking at what presuppositions were implied by the claim that someone had caused rickets.

Rickets could be healed by involving the person who had supposedly caused the illness. Who that might be was discovered by scrutinizing the conduct of the people who had come to the house recently. From the woman—or in rare instances from the man—who was suspected, it was common to steal some piece of clothing, burn it, and feed the ashes to the child as medicine. Other methods were to weigh or let the child sleep in some of the woman's clothing, make the child drink urine from her shoe, and so on.

If the child got better it proved that the cure had been effective. And how could it be effective unless the owner of the clothing used in the remedy was "dishonest"? Thus the cure for rickets was employed to achieve certainty when suspicion had been aroused. The accusation was like a servant who told the master what the latter already knew.

An excellent example of the step-by-step discovery of a person suspected of living "in sin" has been recorded in Vederslöv in Småland. The informant, a woman born in 1872, relates what her mother had told her about the incident:

> I think rickets must have been quite common in the old days. I didn't get it when I was little, but my brother who was born in 1867, he had rickets. My mother told me about it. By the time he wasn't quite a year old, my mother noticed that he didn't develop the way he was supposed to. He had weak joints, his stomach was too large, and when he was learning to walk, his legs wouldn't carry him and they were bent like bows. And his head grew until he looked all deformed.
>
> Well, then, one day the tailor's wife, Stina, came to visit. She was married to a neighbor living in a cottage nearby. When my mother talked about how my brother wasn't developing normally, Stina said: "Are you really so ignorant that you don't understand what illness the boy has? Any fool can see that he's got rickets." "God help me," my mother said, "that's not easily cured, is it?"
>
> But Stina comforted her and said that everything would be fine if she did the

right thing. There were two kinds of rickets children could get, either "dead rickets" or "whore rickets." It wasn't easy to find out which kind it was because the symptoms were the same.

Stina asked my mother whether she had come near a dead body when she was pregnant. But she hadn't; no one in the family had died, and she hadn't been to any funeral either.

"Well," Stina said, "then the boy obviously has 'whore rickets.' He's been sitting on the lap of a 'secret whore,' you can be sure of it."

"That's impossible," my mother answered. "I'm sure there hasn't been anybody else here than Blomgren's sister Tilda. And she couldn't be a 'secret whore!'"

"But you can see for yourself that the boy's got rickets. And you haven't been near anybody dead. Tilda has got to be a 'secret whore.' No use doubting it. This illness here proves it. If Tilda had been 'honest,' this boy wouldn't have rickets. It's hard to tell how many men she's had, but you can't trust her. But don't worry about the boy. There is a sure way to cure him. You've got to weigh the boy in a pair of pants belonging to the 'whore,' or in a pair belonging to a 'dishonest' man who sleeps around."

My mother didn't for a moment question what Stina had said. The boy had rickets and Tilda was a "secret whore." It wasn't so easy to get hold of a pair of her pants. But Stina assured her that if she couldn't get any pants, it would work just as well with an undershirt. And if she couldn't get that either, Stina would borrow pants belonging to Anton, the tailor's helper. That would do it too. Everybody knew he ran around with all kinds of women.

What could my mother do but get a pair of pants or underwear when Tilda would hang out her wash? When Tilda finally did her spring wash and hung it out to dry, my mother kept watch that night. She couldn't get hold of any pants—women mostly didn't have pants in those days—but she got hold of some underwear.

She quickly went home and weighed the boy in it and took it right back. She was in luck: nobody saw her, and Tilda probably never found out what happened, and she would have been mad if she had. It wasn't pleasant for people to think that you were a "secret whore."

I remember my mother talking about this many times. And she always said that my brother got better right away. It was in spring he was weighed and by fall he was like a different person. Tanned and strong and his legs had begun to straighten up and get stronger. I also remember my mother's telling me that Stina said to her, when she saw that the boy had been cured: "I'm so glad that he is better. But it's awful to think that Blomgren's Tilda is a 'secret whore.' I've always suspected her; but now that he's better, we know for sure." (LUF 5820)

The child's illness and recovery conveniently confirmed what Stina had suspected for a long time. Thus the ground was prepared for future sanctions, though it is not known whether any sanctions were actually applied. Tilda "luckily" never found out about the mother's manipulations involving her underwear. Perhaps this says more about the relationship between the two

women than about the relationship of the "secret whore" to the community as
a whole. If and when circumstances required it, Tilda could easily be put in her
place using her alleged "dishonesty" as a tool.

There is no reason to doubt the possibility of sanctions when a woman's real
or alleged immorality was revealed. The local historian Per Söderbäck describes
in his book about life in Kristdala, Småland, how a servant girl was let go when
one of the children in the family fell ill:

> . Not long ago there was a family with a child that began showing signs of rickets.
> They consulted a "wise woman" and were told—as they had suspected all
> along—that someone "dishonest" must have kissed the child. Their suspicions
> focused on the servant girl in the house. It so happened that when they looked
> into it they found out that the girl was not living "honestly." Of course she was
> blamed for the child's illness, and they let her go immediately. (1921, 32f.)

Söderbäck's description demonstrates the importance of considering the
problem of sanctions in the context of specific individuals and their relationship to each other. In the previous example we know the name of the person
concerned (Tilda), but her relationship to the child remains obscure. It appears
that the mother had no occasion to make anything of Tilda's new and
dangerous status. The contrary is true of the servant girl in Söderbäck's
example. She represented an immediate threat to the child's well-being. It was
possible to eliminate her, and evidently that is precisely what was done.

In the absence of a direct and formal relationship as between master and
servant—or, if you will, patron and client—people nevertheless could "get at"
someone whose moral behavior they did not approve of. Sanctions such as
gossip, rumor, and contempt were effective means by which to enforce social
control in a tightly knit rural community.

The following text, recorded in Torsby, Bohuslän, describes how it worked.
The two central characters in this drama are women, one of them married to
a soldier, the other engaged to a soldier. The event took place sometime during
the second half of the last century:

> My father used to tell the story about how one day he was visiting with Torn and
> his wife, "Torna"; Torn was a soldier from our district. Then "Tornella," the
> fiancée and housemate of a soldier by the name of Tornell, came by. When she
> went inside all hell broke loose. The two women came running outside; they were
> fighting, and hair was flying all over the place. The only thing my father could
> hear was that when "Tornella" got to the gate, she shouted:
>
> "You're a whore yourself; or you wouldn't say that about other people!"
>
> The reason for the fight? Torn and "Torna" had invited Tornell and his fiancée
> over one Sunday. The fiancée had taken their one-year-old boy out of the cradle
> and played with him. That evening, after the guests had left, the boy got sick,
> and it turned out he had rickets. There was no doubt at all that "Tornella" had
> made the boy ill. But "Torna" got very angry and went from house to house
> complaining about "Tornella." (IFGH 967)

The attack on "Tornella" was based on the fact that the boy got rickets. Of course, the relationship between the two women must have been strained even before this happened. Otherwise there wouldn't have been any compelling reason for the mother to explain the child's illness as "whore rickets." The symptoms of the boy's illness could just as easily have been diagnosed as some other form of the disease. The example shows how the diagnosis was employed to break with a person with whom the mother or other women in the community had a strained relationship. From the mother's perspective this means being freed from any future contact with the "secret whore." In this respect the accusation of having caused rickets functions precisely like the accusation of witchcraft in other cultures. Victor Turnbull has shown how such accusations were used to end unwanted relationships (cf. Douglas, 1970, XXI). In the case of the soldier's wife, her child's illness provided her with a socially acceptable means of breaking contact. For the accused, the charge of having caused rickets through her immorality proved devastating. She was labeled a "whore," perhaps cut off from most social contacts, certainly excluded from any home where there were infants.

The sources' insistence on the greater dangerousness of "secret whores" indicates that they had access to social situations from which acknowledged "whores" were excluded as a matter of course. Once her moral status was known, the "whore" was never allowed to enter anyone else's house, touch (or even look at) a child. What made the "secret whore" dangerous was precisely that she played a false role. In this context it is interesting to note from the sources that certain nonsexual behaviors were also morally ambivalent and therefore capable of causing rickets. Rääf observes that if a child sees a murderer or someone who has not been punished for a crime he committed, the child will be afflicted with rickets (2166). And in Hyltén-Cavallius' work we read that rickets is caused by a criminal seeing the child (1863, 378).

From the parish of Narum in Västergötland it is reported that people believed that if a man killed someone but was not punished for it, he could cause "murder rickets" (IFGH 2811). The corresponding belief that a hidden crime could stigmatize the criminal is reflected in one of the earliest records in ULMA. This text, from 1875, comes from Västergötland: "When someone who has committed a murder or some other serious crime comes into house where a child lies without clothes on, the consequence will be that the child gets rickets" (ULMA 25).

Here, as in the beliefs concerning "whore rickets," we encounter on the one hand fear of the acknowledged criminal, and on the other fear of the ambiguous, secret crime. If we are to believe the sources, fear of the latter does not appear to have precipitated reactions that would parallel the persecution of the "secret whore." However, there are clear examples of how suspected murderers were stigmatized in popular opinion. The following text from Agnetorp, Västergötland, describes a family who were obviously familiar with the dubious status of the supposed murderer:

We had twins at home, and they were about six months old. One Sunday my
mother was bathing the children when a man from Perstorp in Acklinga came
in. He had killed a man and sworn a false oath. Yes, when he came in he saw the
children. One of the boys fell ill. He got rickets so bad, his legs were bent like a
cross. (ULMA 2626)

The man had gotten off by swearing that he was innocent. The fact that there
was no legal proof of his crime did not keep popular opinion from condemning
him. The child's being afflicted with rickets was proof enough: although the
courts had found the man innocent, the child bore witness to the man's guilt
in the eyes of the community.

The study of situations in which a child's rickets is caused by contact with
someone who has a crime on his or her conscience shows that this concept
served not only to discover and isolate the offender, but also as a corrective, an
effective means of bringing the offender back into conformity with the accepted
norm. One example of this function is the idea that the child's illness reveals
sexual immorality, that is, adultery, on the part of the parents. The married
state potentially provided a cover for a man or a woman involved in an illicit
sexual relationship. The man was generally protected by the patriarchal family
structure; the woman was protected in the sense that if she got pregnant
through adulterous intercourse, this fact would be hidden by her own marriage.
But in terms of contemporary moral norms, adultery was unacceptable. In this
context children functioned as the accusers of their own parents. A text
recorded in Korsberga, Västergötland, for example, it says that a child's illness
could be blamed on the sexual escapades of its father: "People firmly believed
that if a father had "dishonest" relationships with other women, he would cause
rickets in his own child by merely looking at its naked body" (EU 21806).

Knowing what tragedy might befall the child functioned to keep fathers on
the straight and narrow. The assumption of adultery as the cause of rickets in
children was also made in regard to mothers. A note from Ålghult in Småland
indicates that the child would be afflicted with rickets if the mother was
"dishonest" and unfaithful to her husband. To be sure, the same source
indicates that it was equally dangerous to the child if the husband had sexual
relations with another woman at the time the child was conceived (LUF 5910).

Was knowledge of a father's or mother's immorality used to brand such a
person in the eyes of the community? Here the sources are silent; but there is
documentation that such knowledge was employed to restore order in a
marriage and bring the offender back into conformity with existing norms. A
text from Tving in Blekinge, for example, tells of a husband who had cheated
on his wife and caused his child to get rickets, and who then put everything
right by confessing his crime (LUF 723).

These examples demonstrate how the concept of rickets was used to accomplish two things: to enforce moral conformity, and to articulate the right
(or wrong) context for sexual activity. But what do we make of the information

that rickets might even be caused by sexual activity within marriage, between husband and wife? From Berga, Småland, a woman who was born in 1879 reports the following in 1938: "My grandmother used to tell that if people had intercourse while their child was in the same bed with them—and children frequently shared their parents' bed—it was believed that the child would get rickets" (LUF 6639).

Similarly, in 1937 Gotfrid Wagner noted in his book *Smålandska folkminnen* (Folk Traditions from Småland): "If a married couple had a child in their bed while making love, the child would get "whore rickets." A child that had gotten "whore rickets" this way was healed by giving it something to drink from the father's shoe" (1938, 136).

By contemporary standards, neither of the parents had done anything wrong by making love. Why, then, was the child harmed? The two texts provide a whole new perspective on the concept of rickets. In these instances it is not illicit intercourse but intercourse per se which is dangerous. It appears that anyone having intercourse becomes unclean for a certain time, during which he or she is considered dangerous. This attitude has been documented in other cultures, too. Douglas, for example, writes about the Lele in Kasai that after intercourse one must avoid contact with anyone who is ill, otherwise the illness will be aggravated further. Newborn children can actually die from such contact (1966, 151).

I have not been able to find additional documentation that sexual intercourse was considered unclean or dangerous in older Swedish rural culture. Popular attitudes toward sexuality were less focused on the act itself than on the social context. Thus, one way we can explain the above beliefs is to read them as suprasocial sanctions aimed at controlling borderline behavior. In what context might even marital intercourse be looked upon as immoral?

Even within marriage there existed certain restrictions upon sexuality. Intercourse was of less importance here than the circumstances in which it occurred. Did the child get rickets because it witnessed something it was not supposed to know about? Sexuality and reproduction belonged to the adult world, and the child was supposed to be spared knowledge about these matters until it had reached the age of sexual maturity. There existed an extensive arsenal of pseudo-explanations used by parents when children asked where their siblings had come from. The stork had brought them; the midwife had brought them in her handbag; mother had traveled to Germany and bought them there, or she had found them in a swamp. Every one of these fictions is designed to hide a body of knowledge that does not belong in the world of the child. In this context it would be considered immoral to allow the child to be present during intercourse. The threat of illness that might befall the child served to uphold this code.

But it is possible that we are dealing with an infraction of another type. After delivery, marital intercourse was forbidden until the mother had been "churched." This interim period usually lasted five to six weeks (Gustavsson

1972, 22f.). Any intercourse during that time was considered an infraction against church rules and thus against the popular notion of sexual morality.

So far we have seen how the charge that someone had caused a child to fall ill with rickets was used to identify certain offenses and the offenders. Another dimension of this complex of beliefs concerned the mechanisms by which the "whore," once identified, was isolated from the community.

There were other individuals in rural society who were assigned the same kind of dangerous characteristics as the "whore." Horse-flayers, gypsies, and beggars were all thought to pose dangers to the child. A number of recorded texts suggest that it was believed that the child would fall ill when a horse-flayer came into the house. Even more numerous are texts describing the mother's fear of gypsies, who often came to the house begging or asking for a place to sleep. In contrast to the "whore," the gypsies commanded active powers of witchcraft. A gypsy might inflict rickets upon a child in revenge for having been mistreated. If a band of gypsies came to the house and did not get what they pointed to, they would take revenge by casting a spell on the child. They possessed, as one informant from Saleby in Västergötland put it, the "evil eye" (IFGH 4330). In other words, gypsies actively used their dangerous reputation as a means of extortion. On the whole, most beggars were unwelcome in people's homes. The widespread resentment against them was based on the general fear that they might harm the children. The same threat was posed by any and all strangers. The type of stranger might differ, but from the mother's perspective they all shared the characteristic of not fitting her image of what was familiar and therefore safe.

Engström writes that all outsiders—even the midwife—were regarded as a threat to the child during the time between birth and baptism (1903, 126). In many parts of the country there exist a great many devices designed to protect mother and child during the sensitive and vulnerable interlude before the child's baptism. The fear of the anomalous and unfamiliar reached almost hysterical levels during this period. The mother even feared visits from her own relatives (Burjam, 1917).

The nearly undifferentiated fear of anything and anybody from the outside is quite understandable. The risk of the child's dying during the first few weeks after birth was considerable. During the middle of the nineteenth century, every sixth child failed to survive its first birthday. People hurried to get the child baptized because baptism was considered a ritual protection against lurking dangers. But in contrast to interdictions designed to keep people out of the nursery, those aimed at individuals believed to be able to inflict rickets on the child continued in force, even after baptism.

ALTERNATIVE MEDICINE IN TODAY'S SOCIETY

Bente G. Alver and Torunn Selberg

The health care system includes both official and nonofficial health care (Kleinman, 1980, 49ff.). The official health care sector in Norway is one of the best developed in the world, and few contemporary Norwegian institutions have experienced such marked expansion. During the period 1950–76, this sector's share of the gross national product more than doubled—from three and a half to eight percent. In the same period, the number of health care personnel more than tripled, to nearly one hundred thousand (Hansen, 1979, 233). We find, however, that despite the prominence of the official health service in Norwegian society, there is widespread interest in alternative forms of treatment.

If, for the moment, we define alternative therapy as that which is practiced by nonauthorized, nonprofessional personnel, we find good cause to regard it as widespread. A national survey in 1977 showed that one out of every five Norwegians had made use of one or more forms of alternative treatment, and that two-thirds would consider accepting such treatment under certain circumstances (Brusgaard and Efskind, 1977, 1385). A survey conducted in 1979 by the Central Hospital in Østfold showed that, out of a group of one hundred cancer patients, fifty-seven had made use of one or more forms of alternative treatment. Out of a group of one hundred admitted to the hospital with different diagnoses, forty-nine had made use of alternative therapy in some form (Gjemdal, 1979).

In 1981, a study at the Telemark Central Hospital showed that out of a group of 235 rheumatics, sixty-one percent used some form of alternative treatment (Lønning and Kogstad, 1981). The same year, a study based on a sample from the Oslo Sanitetsforenings Rheumatism Hospital showed that, out of a group of 775 patients, thirty-eight percent had used or were using alternative forms of treatment (Larsen, Alver, and Munthe, 1984, 50–53). These studies were all

Originally published in *Temenos*, 1984.

done by physicians in order to determine the extent of use of alternative medicine, the possible measurable results, and possible harmful effects. In the present article we wish to present another perspective. As folklorists, we perceive nonofficial medicine as part of people's knowledge: an aspect of their belief system concerning illness and its treatment. This has long been an area of study within folklore, and the material, which covers a long period, demonstrates continuity in people's concepts and use of this form of medicine (Skjelbred, 1983a).

At one time, the science of folklore considered folk tradition to be a historical expression of culture; information about it was found in archives. Today, we consider it a dynamic expression of culture which adapts itself to a changing society. The questions we pose, as well as our perspectives on the present material, are the result of knowledge about tradition, its structure and content. Analysis of the interplay between historical reconstructions and contemporary material is characteristic of the working methods of folklore.

For the purposes of this article, we have divided nonofficial health services into categories, according to the place they have in society's health care system. We then describe alternative medicine as it exists in Norway today, and present a picture of its users through their own descriptions and explanations. We also discuss some of the factors which cause folk medicine traditions to be active in a society which has a comprehensive, scientific health care system.

Our material was collected through interviews with folk therapists, their patients, and groups of sick and healthy people. We have used a qualitative method and a form of interview which attempts to gain familiarity with the informant's view of reality. By allowing informants to speak freely, we are better able to grasp the relationships between their opinions and the underlying value system. The informant usually answers a general question with a story about an experience. It is in these case histories that we find people's understanding of what it means to be ill. Attitudes toward illness and treatment are often difficult to discover with a standardized questionnaire (Larsen, Alver, and Munthe, 1984, 45–88).

Alternative Treatment

Alternative medicine is "marginal" in that it exists alongside a medical system which has a formal monopoly, established by law, on setting criteria regarding illness and treatment (Wallis and Morley, 1976). The definitions of medical science set official boundaries for the patient's choice of treatment (Freidson, 1970).

Individuals who provide treatment alternative to official medicine are called folk therapists. There are two forms of alternative treatment: nature medicine and folk medicine; these two categories have unequal status in the health care system. Therapists in nature medicine are called "nature doctors" (naturopaths), whereas those who work in folk medicine are known as "wise folk" (healers). In examining these two categories, we can distinguish (1) how a folk therapist acquires knowledge and skills, (2) the folk therapist's place in society, and (3) what gives the folk therapist legitimacy.

The naturopath's theories about illness and treatment can be acquired through books and are taught in school courses. Many naturopaths have a formal education and belong to a community of fellow therapists. Their position is closer to official health services than that of folk healers. They can be located through the Yellow Pages, newspaper advertisements, and business signs. Some of them belong to professional organizations, and their activities take place within a formalized framework of appointments, office hours, and fixed fees. Legitimacy comes partly from the endorsements of their patients and partly from their education.

The activity of folk healers is based on the fact that they and their local community consider them to be mediators of a special power and to have special abilities. Their knowledge about illness and treatment comes partly from folk tradition and partly from the patient's own interpretation of his or her sickness. Their activity has a less formal framework than the naturopath's; it is not so much a "job" as a way of relating to their surroundings.

Information about folk healers belongs mostly to the private sphere and is relayed through family and acquaintances. The folk healers occasionally written about in popular magazines are only a few of the number actually practicing. Their legitimacy is established by having patients.

People generally have their own way of distinguishing between physicians and folk therapists. Folk healers and naturopaths are grouped together because their approach to sickness and therapy differs from that of medical doctors. However, people also distinguish between naturopaths and folk healers. In the case of naturopaths, patients relate to their methods; in the case of folk healers, patients relate to the person (Larsen, Alver, and Munthe, 1984, 112ff.).

Folk Medicine and Folk Healers

Because nature medicine has a more prominent position in society than folk medicine, information about its categories is more readily available (see Schjelderup, 1974; Staugaard, 1979; Hill, 1981). Therefore this essay will concentrate on a general picture of folk medicine and its practitioners.

Folk medicine has no place in official definitions of sickness and treatment; it is part of another reality. For example, in daily newspapers, professionals, not the people themselves, debate the use of folk medicine (Skjelbred, 1983a). Hidden realities, which can be only partly expressed, are subject to the public's interpretation and belief: it is claimed that ignorant people use folk medicine, that everyone involved in folk medicine is drawn to the occult, that folk medicine is on its way out, that its users come from the older generation. Several analyses of folk medicine have been based upon such assumptions (see Broch, 1980). Folk medicine has few official channels through which to express itself. It is, in the main, available only through a system of folk communication.

The folk healer perceives him- or herself, and is perceived by the community, as someone with special abilities and as an intermediary of supranormal powers. These powers are variously explained by different categories of folk healers in accordance with their belief systems and world views.

Folk healers today fall into three main categories: (1) those who transmit the powers of nature through plant medicine; (2) those who transmit divine powers through word, thought, and touch; and (3) those who transmit "universal" energies through thought and touch. All three function as mediums, and we can trace through history the concepts according to which they work. We most often find these categories in combinations rather than in pure form. Those who transmit universal energies and those who convey divine power are often grouped together; the folk term for such therapists is "layers-on of hands."

Plants

The use of plants in the treatment of sickness involves both lay knowledge and the knowledge of a specialist. Both the lay person and the specialist know the relationship between plants and certain diseases, but the specialist also knows when and where herbs are most effective, as well as rituals concerning how and when they must be picked and used. Folk healers consider much of this knowledge to belong to them; it is secret knowledge, not to be passed on until they no longer wish to practice. Knowledge about plants belongs to a larger context of beliefs about nature and its gifts and powers; "nature" and the "natural" are values in themselves. A folk therapist from western Norway said this about his work:

> My basic theory about what I do may seem simple, but I think there is something to be said for it; I believe that people are just like the earth we are made of and from which we take our nourishment and life. Just as the earth can suffer from deficiencies and become sick, so the body can suffer from deficiencies and become sick. I believe that many more sicknesses than you imagine come from such deficiencies. When the earth is pining for something, we give her what she needs. To put it simply, when the body gets what it craves, it gets well, the balance is restored. (Hauge, 1978, 51)

We find the same thoughts expressed by a patient:

> My confidence in God, in Jesus' name, is great because it ought to be the natural way for all people. I believe He has made medicines for all kinds of sickness if people would only open their eyes to it. But we prefer to take artificial medicine instead of going to nature. That doesn't mean I would do away with medical science, it's just that true science should be first sought in nature; but unfortunately, all too often people don't see the forest for the trees. (EFA:EMP)

Recruitment to the group of folk healers who use plants is limited, and apparently such therapy is on the way out in Norway. One of the reasons may be that naturopaths, especially homeopaths and health-food specialists, have taken over the field. Because most people think that homeopathy is plant medicine, they often choose homeopathy as an alternative to herbal folk medicine. Homeopathic compounds, health foods, and herbal medicines overlap in people's thinking. Another reason naturopaths are replacing folk healers could be that the former have a greater degree of public exposure. We do know that people sometimes find it difficult to get in touch with folk healers.

Although traditional specialist knowledge is waning, lay knowledge thrives. Plants are used extensively in the treatment of sickness today, and this is stimulated by the amount of literature on the subject. Behind the widespread use of plants in self-treatment is the ideology that the "natural" is something good in itself, a positive counterweight to "synthetic" medicine. In a broader perspective, the idea of what is healthy and natural plays an important role in modern life.

Words

Since ancient times, magic words, or formulas, have been important in Norway, in both specialist and lay knowledge (Johnsen, 1979). We find both written and spoken magic words. A general rule of formula lore is that when used, the formula must be spoken or written exactly as tradition prescribes, or it will not be effective. Therefore the formula tradition is conservative (af Klintberg, 1965). The formula or magic word must not be used without due cause and must not be taught to someone else unnecessarily: otherwise its power will disappear. The sanction for breaking this rule lies with whomever or whatever the power is received from. These restrictions make it difficult to ascertain which formulas are actually in use. We know that there are therapists who use an old, traditional formula vocabulary. But if this group were to give us insight into their knowledge of formulas, it would mean that they were not serious about their use, or that they regarded us as their heirs.

The largest group in Norway using words in their treatment today are practicing Christians. This group is part of the Christian lay movement. The Christian God is believed to inflict illness for the purpose of testing those who are stricken and those who heal with divine power. Christian belief is of central importance for this group of therapists, and it is through the word that God manifests His power. They see themselves as a medium for God's power, and make this known by asking their patients to thank God, not them, when they recover. But the prayer, like other formulas, is a power in its own right:

> One word, says the Lord, is enough to heal all sickness. This word is a word of power which He, by His grace, gives to the one He chooses to be His instrument in performing His magnificent deeds. Since God in a wondrous way has given

me to know His word of power, I can witness with my whole heart that the word of the Evangelist is true. (Schei, 1947, 85)

We do not know how prayer is composed in the therapy situation. Practitioners use personal prayers and traditional prayers like the "Our Father." They often pray quietly or *sotto voce* so that only occasional words are understood, and their patients tell us that they do not know or cannot remember the content of the prayers. For the patient, the function of the prayer, not its form, is important. Not all of those who seek out a religious therapist are themselves Christians, but many are. For them, faith is central in the common frame of reference between the therapist and the experience of God's healing power:

When I came into his room, it was so full of people. It was just crammed, but there was an empty seat on the sofa; someone else was already sitting there, but there was room for me, so I sat down. But then I was in such pain that I didn't know how to sit. Then I saw a Bible lying there on the table; I picked it up and I was praying all the time, and I opened the book and came to the place where it says: "The body belongs to the Lord." "Thank you, dear Jesus," I said, "my body is yours. So, you can do whatever you want with this body. If you want this body to get well, then it will get well. If you will that his body should be sick, then it will be sick." I didn't know anything about whether I would get well or not get well, but then, all of a sudden, I felt such peace, such blessed peace. But then there was a voice which said: "Read it one more time." So I opened the book and read, "He shall do it and none other." He shall do it. . . "Yes, you, Jesus, and nobody else." And then I laid the book down, and then faith just flowed through me. I understood it. The others sitting there—they disappeared—then suddenly I heard somebody say my name. "You can come in now!" Well, I stood up and went in and he said, "Please, sit here." But I didn't tell him anything about what was wrong with me—absolutely nothing. But I had a description of what was wrong with me from both my own doctor and the district doctor. So, he took the Bible out and he said, "Do you believe in God?" "Yes, I believe in God, and I am a Christian." "All right," he said, "that's fine. Do you believe that God can heal you?" "Yes," I said, "I believe it." So he stood up. Then he stroked down over my body like this, first once, then twice—and the third time he stopped. "You have calcifications in the neck," he said. "Here, between the shoulder blades and they go down over here, is that right?" Exactly as I would have told him—he told me . . . then I felt how it burnt through—I felt heat going through my whole body, there as he drew his hands down over it. Then he got down on his knees in front of me, he stroked and then he asked me to stand up and then he started again and then he said, "Out, in Jesus' name. Let these pains go out in Jesus' name." Then he didn't say anything else. I felt the contact of his hands—that the power flowed through them as he stroked down over me. "You may go now," he said, "But you can just come again if it won't go away, because it often happens that you have to come two or three times before it'll let go." I thanked him and went out. When I got out to the sidewalk, I felt suddenly as if everything just broke and there was a warmth which flowed through me—just as if I was being lifted up. It felt so light, just like when you carry a heavy burden and then it's lifted from you; exactly like when you've been going around with a heavy sack and then you put it down and then you feel that you are free. Well, I was so glad—so I thanked Jesus—and so I went . . . "Thank you, dear Jesus." I went to the doctor again afterwards, and I said that I was going to start work again. So, he said that it was on my own responsibility. "Yes," I said, "I'm going to do it." So, I started working. I went and carted beef carcasses around. I was a butcher. I went and carted them around as if I had never been sick. And the X-rays. They couldn't see any of the scars, the breaks and all that. It was gone. They couldn't find it again. (EFA:EMP)

Although faith in God is crucial to religious therapists, they do not all demand that their patients say whether or not they believe in God. Still, their work as therapists is considered part of missionary activity. They convince the sick of God's strength through healing. One of western Norway's major therapists formulated it as follows: "God has many ways of bringing people to Him. One of them can be this: that the sick non-Christian has a chance to see and experience God's power and omnipotence through his own healing and thus give himself to God" (Schei, 1947, 47).

Over a period of time, religious therapists demonstrate the greatest uniformity with respect to the form and content of treatment and the complex of ideas surrounding sickness. The principles of their work are already established by Christian ideology.

Touch

Therapists who use touch are best known as "the ones with warm hands." They transfer energy to the sick through touch. They talk about their abilities and the powers they transmit in terms of modern technology, calling the power magnetism, electricity, or current, and talking about sickness and health as a deficiency or overabundance of energy; they refer to "charging" the sick person or tapping him or her for power:

People are really quite electric; our brains work electrically; the impulses go from the brain to all parts of the body. Many ailments, I believe, are caused simply by impulse errors in the body's nerve network, and I think that the impulse errors are caused by all the electrical impulses in the atmosphere. A little transistor radio is capable of receiving radio stations from all over the world right through thick walls; what the human body mustn't have to stand of intruding impulses! . . . What my hands do, is hard to say, but I really feel that I can fix the electrical disturbances in the body. In other words, my function is more or less the same as that of a trouble-shooter at a power plant. (Møller, 1975, 23)

The injection of energy affects the blood circulation of the sick person so that the organism is stimulated and becomes well: "I magnetize a person with current, just like a battery. Then the current goes through the pituitary or brain, opens the points in the brain and stimulates them so that they make themselves become well" (EFA:EMP).

These therapists, like the others, are concerned with the quality of the power, and they tell how it feels to transmit it:

> It flows through my fingers. It flows out—violently. And then the fingers get hot and I just go over to people, they can cry out from the heat: "God!" Then it flows through all at once. Some days it can be ten times stronger than it usually is. I have noticed that. Then I have to have a patient, to get rid of some of it. Sometimes the patient will say something like: "There is a terrible difference from the last time I was here." "Such power," they say. "Yes," I say. "It's strong today." It is on such a day I feel this kind of increase. (EFA:EMP)

The idea is often expressed that this power is not constant—it is sometimes stronger and sometimes weaker. The treatment of certain illnesses can be experienced as a greater drain on energy than the treatment of others. Likewise, lengthy treatments or too many patients are a strain. The practitioner has to stop for a few hours to get charged again:

> I have been in contact with people who were really sick. It has a tremendous effect on me. I wouldn't say that I get sick, but I feel it as a tremendous inner tension, and I become tired in my body; it's obvious that these people have pulled too much out of me, so I have to produce an awful lot of new magnetism to get on top again. (EFA:EMP)

Usually the power is transmitted by touch. These practitioners explain that they can find the pain with the palms of their hands. This is difficult for them to put into words—they describe it, for example, as an intense warmth or cold, felt as a pole in the palm of their hand:

> It feels so different. It depends on what it is. For example, if it's cancer, I might jerk my hand away again, because I can't stand to hold it there for so long; it starts to hurt. With infections I can feel some really bad pains, but not to that degree. If it's cancer, it goes right through me like a jolt. A heat effect. It has its own heat effect—I mean, it flows when there's not anything wrong. But then it enters the hand in its own way. I can feel it right away. It's really difficult to describe, you understand, because we've got used to these different feelings. (EFA:EMP)

These therapists regard their abilities as real and the power they transmit equivalent to energy or current, but there is a call behind their practicing which they explain nonrationally, as a call from another world, from God or Providence. Such people may know from an early age that they have a special ability, but only if they are "called" to help the sick do they expand their circle of clients beyond family and friends. The call often takes the form of experiences or events which they themselves interpret as a command to use their gifts. They often feel that it is a heavy responsibility, but the call means that, as the chosen, they feel stronger in the therapeutic situation (Alver/Selberg, 1980).

These folk therapists say that in their treatments, they transfer energy to the sick. Their patients feel that they become warm, their skin and joints prickle, the blood flows better, and their bodies become supple and light:

> I noticed his hands right away when I greeted him. Yes, they radiated warmth. They were such oddly warm hands. It is something you don't often think about, but, when you notice it, well, then you certainly know it. . . . So I was a little tense about what was going to happen. Then he started making a diagnosis by examining my hands. I mean, I was really surprised that he was able to diagnose right off that it was rheumatism that I had, just by examining my fingers. Well, I thought he was on the wrong track, because my fingers were, in any case, one of the places where I didn't feel anything. So, we sat down on a chair there in the room where he started to examine my arms and asked me to say whether I couldn't feel a warm blood-flow after he held me under the armpits. Well, I felt it more or less. What I noticed was in my left arm; there I noticed a warm blood flow. . . . Then he took the other arm and then the knees. I could feel in both arms how the blood circulation got better and I noticed how it all sort of softened up. Although I couldn't have said right off that I felt stiff, if anyone had asked, I could feel the difference. I certainly knew that I had been more stiff before than I had been aware. My legs too. When I stood up, it felt as if I had taken off a backpack, that I had become lighter and that everything softened up. (EFA:EMP)

Although these therapists usually want to have very close contact with their patients, the power of the therapist can be transmitted through another person or an intermediary object. This makes it possible for the power to be transmitted over great distances, when the sick person has no way of coming to the therapist.

The Patients

"Ignorance breeds prejudice. Better health knowledge is probably the best vaccine against the epidemic of medical charlatanism which seems to be spreading in the population" (Fugelli, 1978, 1359). So writes Doctor Per Fugelli about the use of folk medicine today, which, according to him, is the result of insufficient education. The knowledge he advocates is based on medical science. But folk knowledge about illness does not always concur with medical science and, for this reason, many people seek help outside the established health services.

It is by now clear that it is not lack of knowledge that causes people to choose alternative methods, but rather their not receiving the help they expected from their doctors. Patients hope to get help from the folk therapist, and many believe that they do get help—but it is not measurable by the criteria of medical science.

As a rule, the road to the folk therapist is via the doctor, and the patient often goes back to the doctor, at least for a check-up. The doctor has the first and last word. Not many doctors are aware of this, because the relationship between doctor and patient is often such that patients will not or dare not tell their doctors that they have been to a folk therapist. Often the patient seeks treatment from a medical doctor and a folk therapist at the same time. Beginning with the fact that people do not feel that they get enough help from the doctor, we find that those who seek alterative therapy fall into three groups (cf. Rørbye, 1980, 176ff.): (1) the terminally ill, (2) those who, according to the doctor, are not ill or cannot be clearly diagnosed, (3) those with long-term or chronic ailments. Not all people who fall into these groups choose alternative treatment; many would never consider it. Beliefs about alternative medicine often suggest that people with terminal illnesses most commonly become patients of folk therapists, because this form of treatment is considered the "last hope." But this is in fact the smallest group. However, these are the cases we encounter most often in the narratives told by folk therapists to legitimize their work to us and to their patients, and the group most often covered in popular magazines. These reports become part of the stereotype that forms around folk healers. People who are chronically ill usually visit folk therapists because they are not satisfied with the medical treatment they have received, and they hope to get well through another form of treatment. During a long illness, they may have tried—and become afraid of—many different medications, and are motivated to try a more "natural" therapy. There is widespread belief that nature's means are free from side effects. In cases where there are side effects, people seem to have greater tolerance for them than for side effects from synthetic medicines. The largest group consulting folk therapists consists of people who, according to the doctor, are not ill. They suffer from many different complaints and ailments that are often called psychosomatic. Many have been told that there is nothing wrong with them. They feel that they are ill, but cannot get a clear diagnosis. The patient's experience does not fit the doctor's definition of illness. For the folk therapist, the patient is ill precisely because he or she says so. The patient's own experience and interpretation are not questioned.

The Sick-Role

Illness can be defined as deviant, asocial behavior in that the sick person withdraws from normal obligations to work, family, and society. When someone has the status of sick person or patient, he or she is also given the role of sick person, which is accompanied by the implication that this person is relieved of responsibility. There are other rights, too, such as the right to care and nursing, but also the duty to seek help and get well as soon as possible (Coe, 1970, 100).

Sickness behavior differs from other kinds of deviant behavior in that society excuses it and assigns responsibility to something outside the will of the sick person (Young, 1976). Patients whose deviant behavior is not interpreted as illness find themselves in a no-man's-land between sickness and health. They are unable to obtain a diagnosis which makes the sickness socially acceptable. When the doctor, as the officially sanctioned disease-therapist, does not confer this status, the patients may seek out a folk therapist in order to get confirmation of their sickness. Among the patients who go to folk therapists, those with long term or chronic illnesses are on the border between "sick" and "well," and are therefore motivated to seek out a folk therapist to get a diagnosis and have the illness accepted. Patients lacking a diagnosis have failed to fulfill the requirements for a sick-role: they have not gotten well. The sick-role has become permanent for them, rather than temporary as it is supposed to be. This group, like the former one, is socially problematical. People in it are not sick according to accepted definitions, and this may cause problems with their milieu, problems such as a lack of acceptance, which can lead to isolation.

Society's expectations of a good patient are such that many sick people fall outside the accepted pattern, which gives them additional reason to seek alternative help. The social environment helps motivate the person to seek this help; therefore folk medicine has a place in people's awareness as an alternative to official medicine. A diagnosis from a folk therapist will be accepted and alternative medicine seen as a way for the sick person to fulfill his or her duty to become well. Family and friends may even put pressure on them:

> One summer, my father had trouble with his balance. It happened all of a sudden. He had worked a little too much—and it was quite hot. Well, mother wanted him to go to her. Yeah, yeah, he didn't believe in any of that. "Yes, but for my sake, can't you give it a try?" she said. Well, that was okay. So I went with him the same evening on the bus. When we got to town, I said, "Let's walk over there." "No," he said, "I can't make it; we'll have to take a cab." "All right," I said. We got the cab and drove out. So, he was in there—well, I guess it must have been a quarter of an hour. She talked with him and asked if he believed in it. "No," he said, "but on account of my wife; I promised her that I would give it a try." "Well, I'm going to get you to believe it," she said. . . . After a quarter hour, he came out again. So I asked him, "Can't you ask her to call a cab for us, so that we can get back?" "No, what do we need a cab for?" he said. "I am completely all right." He had got well, he didn't feel anything at all. That was two years ago this Christmas. He hasn't said one word of criticism about such things since. (EFA:EMP)

It is also from the social environment that the sick person gets information about a naturopath or a folk healer. It is through a personal network that people learn about folk therapists, what they can expect from them and what sort of results they have achieved.

Concepts of Sickness and Therapy

At different times there have been different ideas about disease. This is mirrored in the history of folk medical activity. For example, during the 1800s, the widespread disease of rickets was the speciality of many wise folk. The doctors did not know the cause of the disease until the 1900s, when the connection between dietary deficiency and rickets was discovered. Wise folk, on the other hand, had an explanation and treatment for the illness which fit the popular concept (Bø, 1973; Nordland, 1962/63).

In an article dated 1899, we find the following comment about one of the wise folk of the nineteenth century: "It is certain that Hans cured a number of the mentally ill in his own way. Also many other kinds of sick people, who, to no avail, had sought out qualified doctors, were healed by him. This cannot be denied" (Hvidberskår, 1968, 56).

It is still true today that certain types of sickness motivate interest in folk medical knowledge and behavior. Folk therapists' explanations of illness are still in keeping with popular concepts: for example, healers and patients have common ground in the concept of prayer as an expression of power. By the same token, belief in the transfer of energy or the efficacy of herbs and plants expresses a common belief in the powers of nature (cf. Alver, 1982).

Generally, these ideas reflect the concept that illness is caused by an imbalance and that a transfer of power can restore equilibrium. But people's conceptual universe regarding sickness and treatment is more complex than this, because it is influenced by both traditional knowledge and modern science. These are not mutually exclusive, but are activated in different contexts. When a patient is with a folk therapist, the frame of reference which includes traditional knowledge is activated and establishes common ground between them. The help provided by a folk healer cannot be evaluated only according to the measurable effect of the treatment. Sickness has two sides: disturbances in the biological and/or physiological processes, and psychosocial experiences of personal, cultural and social relations. These two aspects can be called disease and illness. Official medicine is oriented toward disease, folk medicine toward illness (Kleinman, 1980). For the folk therapist, a patient's interpretation of the illness is an important part of understanding sickness and treatment. It is in this regard that folk healer and patient find each other. The folk therapist can make a difficult situation more comprehensible for the patient.

Between Therapist and Patient

People's estimation of folk medicine and healers is partly determined by social, cultural, and ethnic ties. Sometimes, people choose a folk therapist because they feel that he or she belongs to their social group, whereas the doctor represents something distant or alien. The relationship between patient and doctor is not equal; it is a meeting of two worlds—the lay world and the professional world—and these are always, if only latently, in conflict (Freidson, 1970).

In our material, that conflict is manifested in statements the patients make: they do not feel they know enough about their illness, they are afraid to ask the doctor questions. They are afraid to use too much of the doctor's expensive time, they feel they do not have personal contact with the doctor, and they do not dare tell him or her about visits to a folk therapist. But many patients experience a different relationship with a folk healer. Patients recount the following:

> He was just completely ordinary. You could imagine seeing him up in the stands of a football stadium. But I must say that I had much more confidence in him than in a doctor. You're facing an individual. You don't have any idea of playing a role when you're with him. It's not just a white coat you meet, it's a person. (EFA:EMP)

> She's so jovial! It's as though you can ask her about anything. You're on the same wavelength with her right away. You know, doctors are so many things. They appear, shall we say, strict, turned in on themselves, sort of. You have so much respect for them, you don't dare ask questions. (EFA:EMP)

> Well, I had my own opinion as to what wise women were like. . . . Thought that it would smell of cat all over the house, and she would be mysterious in one way or another. Quite the opposite, she appeared just like what I was used to at home. Nice and clean in all the corners, well-groomed, clean and shiny, flowers all over the place. It was almost a shock, the difference, and it strengthened my belief. (EFA:EMP)

The relationship between patient and doctor can be formal, distant, strange; the relationship with a folk therapist can be warm, close, meaningful. This is due in part to the form of communication between patient and therapist. They communicate, to a large degree, through stories. The therapist talks about illness and treatment, about the particular illness and its prognosis, through stories about previous patients. The patient will always find that the therapist has treated the illness before, and always with positive results (Alver, 1980). The patient also describes the illness in story form, and through these stories the therapist gets a picture of the patient's sickness and health. Such everyday stories are an important part of communication and a form patients feel at home with (Bausinger, 1977).

The dialogue between doctor and patient, on the other hand, is built on questions and answers directed by the doctor; the illness is discussed in abstract, scientific terms, which can contribute to the patient's estrangement from his or her own situation. Such estrangement can make the sickness seem more frightening. Folk therapist and patient, on the other hand, both talk about illness and treatment in concrete language, which can make the illness more comprehensible, something one can understand and act upon.

Conclusion

Alternative medicine in the Norwegian health-care system includes many different forms of therapy. The fault in most studies of alternative medicine is that the concept is applied to several different fields, which are then treated as a uniform entity. We have divided alternative medicine into two main groups—nature medicine and folk medicine—according to type of knowledge, place in the public eye, and source of legitimacy.

Folk medicine particularly has been perceived in modern society as the survival of curious concepts held by small pockets of the population; and it has been claimed that the use of these concepts is simply the result of ignorance, or that the need for alternative health care is created by the popular press, the "green wave," and the "occult" renaissance. We have pointed out that folk medicine is so vital because the traditional system changes, and its content and functions are modified with time. It is activated in situations determined by prevailing ideas about illness, individual needs, and the relationship of the environment to alternative treatment.

The social environment is important in several ways for the choice of alternative treatment, in both motivation and acceptance. The sick hear about the folk therapist through the same channels. Stories about successful results are the lifeline of folk medicine traditions. Ideas about the abilities of folk healers, their status in people's awareness, and expectations of alternative treatment all change as ideas about sickness change. By discussing this and showing which groups of patients go to folk therapists, we have isolated the factors playing a part in activating folk medical knowledge. What characterizes the patients of folk therapists is that they fall outside society's expectations of a good patient: that a clear diagnosis can be made and that the patient will get well. The folk therapists' patients have either not acquired the social sick-role, or they have not been able to get rid of it.

Official and alternative medical systems function in different ways. When people find they can get help from the folk therapist, it shows certain deficiencies in the official system, but it also shows that alternative health care actually is an alternative for many people and that it cannot be replaced by the official health care system as it functions today.

THE FUNCTION OF RIDDLES

Leea Virtanen

In Finland today, rumors and short jokes pass quickly from person to person. Stories come into fashion and sink into oblivion. Riddles have become the tradition of school children and have changed into short sallies and parodies. Many traditional genres required a socio-cultural milieu different from modern times, one in which personal relationships were stable and of long duration. The old riddle lore, too, was the product of prolonged development, during which it took on its specific stylistic characteristics. What was the social base of the genre, and what factors caused the riddling tradition to be forgotten during the last decades?

The information collected in the folklore archives of the Finnish Literature Society makes it possible to describe the social background of the Finnish riddling tradition. A technique widely used in Finland during the last century was the publication of questionnaires in magazines, in which readers were asked to send in information on various traditions and types of folklore, among them riddles. The contributors were asked to record lore "just as they heard it from the mouth of the folk." This way the archives collected some 110,000 riddles from people living in a rural milieu: farmers, their wives, foresters, and teachers. The performance contexts of the riddling tradition described by the informants explain why this once-common Finnish genre disappeared.

Riddle games were traditionally played in the home: "Children and adults posed riddles in the evenings or on Sundays when there were many folk of all ages gathered together" (First competitive inquiry, Folklore Archives of the Finnish Literature Society, 1966). Such evenings were popular during the first half of this century, especially in the teens and twenties. Riddle collectors point out, however, that modern mass culture has eliminated the kind of evening which fostered the old pastimes: "There weren't any newspapers, so you had time to tinker about." "When you watch the boob tube, it takes your time and your thoughts into its own world." "In almost every house and cottage nowadays

Original title: "On the Function of Riddles." Published in *Arvoitukset—Finnish Riddles*, 1977.

[1966], there is at least a radio and in some even a television to provide entertainment, so other hobbies aren't needed any longer."

The peasant milieu and self-sufficient economy in Finland changed with industrialization: spinning, churning, seine fishing, and ploughing disappeared; pothooks, stills, bakers' peels, spits, carding combs, sieves, quill pens, sleigh runners, scythes, and millstones became obsolete. Central heating and electricity replaced fireplaces and fir torches. It was no longer taken for granted that people had head lice, that everyone ate porridge from a common bowl, that pigs could wander in the living room. Everyone learned to write. Riddles, more than any other tradition genre, are tied to material culture and reflect it; their topics and themes are drawn from objects, animals, and activities common to a community. The uniformity of material culture in the agrarian milieu created a uniform tradition; therefore, the changes in Finnish economy and lifestyle made riddles obsolete. Their adaptation to contemporary life would have required a period of vigorous creativity and total renewal.

The introduction of mass-produced clothing and household goods ended evening spare-time work, whose significance for oral communication cannot be overemphasized. Women continually spun, knitted, sewed, and patched; men carved spoons, resoled shoes, mended harnesses, and wove seines. Monotonous work kept people tied down for hours at a time, and word games lightened the labor and provided amusement—in this way, material and spiritual culture were interdependent. A major change in social patterns resulted from the introduction of electric light, for it eliminated the twilight hours when people used to sit in the dusk in order to conserve fuel. The work pause was a time for riddling games. Twilight hours have generally been important for the transmission of oral tradition; more riddling was done during the autumn, winter, and Christmas holidays, for example, because the shorter days precluded working outside.

Urbanization also altered the composition of the family, which was one of the important conditions for riddling evenings. Riddling games flourished in homes in which there were "many folk of all ages" but foundered in the modern, nuclear family. Today, only sporadic riddling occurs, and frequently it is children who pose riddles learned in school to their parents, whereas in the past, tradition was transmitted from the older generation to the younger.

The extended family, in which sons and their families lived with their parents, was a favorable milieu for the preservation of all folk knowledge; in order to maintain a riddle tradition, a community had to be fairly large. Väinö Salminen has said, "Ancient poetry and especially wedding 'runes' don't flourish where people live in solitary backwoods cottages in families of a few souls" (1945, 580). The same is true for riddles. The community also had to have sufficient contacts to the outside world (such as servant girls, farm hands, wandering craftsmen) so that new riddles could enter the repertoire. While folk songs, tales, and legends can bear repetition, the riddle game requires new stimuli.

The obsolescence of riddle lore was hastened by its archaic meter and

Kalevalan style. As Matti Kuusi has noted, the birth of Kalevalan poetry during the Finno-Baltic period was the most important turning point in thousands of years of the development of the Finnish language; on the other hand, for countless years, people had contented themselves with composing lyric poetry, epics, incantations, ceremonial "runes," proverbs, and riddles in the same Kalevala meter, which gave these products a certain primitiveness. The Kalevalan meter is primarily that of sung "runes." Even after Kalevalan songs disappeared almost completely from western Finland, riddle lore, like part of the tradition of proverbs, still reflected the Kalevalan model. An international genre was thus expressed using four-foot trochaic lines, alliteration, and complex parallelism. This style added to the popularity of riddles; but it also caused this tradition to die out in the twentieth century with the arrival of new trends. That is to say, people have generally preferred the "rune" form to prose form; Kalevalan metrics have been regarded as a means of stylistic intensification introduced, for instance, in the middle of a prose story. The poetic, metaphorical phraseology and exotic expressions of old-style riddles have given esthetic satisfaction to tradition bearers and enhanced the value of this genre. At the same time, the archaisms have become a double-edged sword from the perspective of the tradition's survival.

The humor in old-style riddles is generally obscure to urban dwellers. A riddle image may seem obscure to an adult city resident but obvious to a child. For example, to a child the riddle image of the "red moose" that cannot be driven away is clearly the red, rising sun (Potter, 1950, 138). The drawing of parallels between two incompatible concepts—for example, the depiction of the living as lifeless and vice versa—is humorous from the perspective of a preliterate person or culture. The meter and style of sexual riddles often appear to be of more recent date than those of other riddles. However, these too could not survive in the present day if detached from their genre background.

Like folksongs and narratives, riddling existed as an evening pastime. Riddles were posed in the twilight when people began to gather inside, but before they lit candles; once lights were struck, people returned to work. Riddles were performed primarily in fall and winter, since summer was a period of hectic outdoor work. They were performed most often on holiday evenings, during name-day celebrations, or whenever people wanted to pass the time. Riddles included features of both play and joking.

The Trip to "Smileville" or "Numskull Place"

A riddle game frequently ends with teasing the person who is "caught." He or she might have to do something unpleasant—go out in the cold to get a glass of water or chop wood, for example. In Greek riddle games, the victim had to drink wine mixed with salt water (Ohlert, 1912, 70). In the games of the Buryats a player who lost was auctioned off with a traditional derogatory verse, in which the price was gradually reduced from a camel to a broken needle or fringeless scarf (Castren, 1857, 228–29). Sometimes local, farcical references characterized the teasing ceremonies (Hart, 1964, 57–60). In Finland, the riddle game included a popular drama in which the unsuccessful guesser was sent to Hyvölä, Himola, or Hymylä (Smileville), or to Huikkola or Hölmölä (Numskull Place). Participants would agree ahead of time how many unsuccessful guesses were allowed before the loser had to leave "to get some wits." In the preface to his riddle anthology (1783), Christfrid Ganander says:

> To this day even little children say to the one who cannot answer three riddles, "Fie, fie, (you go) to Smileville, Smileville's dogs will bark, go you girl to see what's coming from there! Yes, she'll turn into a tattered girl, in rags, in ra-ags, a mouse as her horse, a scoop for her sleigh, etc." The rhyme is chanted in sing-song, scornfully dragged out, all joining in.

The victim who is "a boy out of kilter," "a wife's old wretch," or "Toivonen's fool, snot on his nose, ice on his beard, eyes popping out of his head" arrives in rags on a nonsensical conveyance. Apparently the unsuccessful participant was actually dressed in comical clothing and sent into the courtyard, entryway, or kitchen corner. Some of the players then pretended to be "Smileville" folk who discuss the arrival of the stranger and answer questions. At the destination the guesser is offered the most repulsive food and left-overs. He or she is made to "wash" in a tar barrel and dry with feathers. Treatment of the "stranger" differs. When, in Kiikka, a stupid guesser arrives in "Smileville,"

> There on the floor a small boy drinks pap from a dish. The guesser asks about other folk of the house and receives, in answer, the remainder of the pap right in his face. Then comes the lady of the house, and the boy or girl asks for water to wash with. The lady offers, instead, a bucket of dregs and a horse blanket. Then the folk of "Smileville" ask about recent news, but the stranger can tell them nothing but the unsolved riddles. Then the people laugh at such a witless fool, and send the stranger back.

The following is also from western Finland:

> Thus the girl was soon ready for "Numskull Place." She was dressed in the oddest "billygoat" (nuuttipukki) fashion and sent out of the living room. Then the guessing began about how she would be received at "Numskull Place." Someone says that the dogs are barking, and the children go to investigate; they report the arrival of an old woman, dressed in rags with horns on her head, drawn by a cat in an upside-down sleigh. The "Numskull Place" housewife takes fright and, just as she is salting the butter, throws in ashes instead of salt, overturns the milk pail onto the hearth and lights the fire with her Sunday dress. The daughter of the house throws a slop bucket over the stranger. When the latter asks to wash she is given a tar bucket and ordered to dry herself with bedding straw. When she is asked for news of the world and can only respond with the unsolved riddles, the

poor creature is pitied and given chaff mixed with buttermilk, the heads of last year's herrings and the holes of ring bread to eat.

After this, the visitor is considered sufficiently punished. She is invited to come into the living room and tell about her journey. Now imaginations soar, and people invent whatever bizarre details they can—about children in the cowshed, calves in the cradle, etc. This was the most delightful part of the game, as people tried to top each other's inventions.

The explaining of the riddles usually takes place in "Smileville" or "Numskull Place." They are explained one at a time, "while taunts resound" and the loser is reproached for being ignorant. The next act of the farce takes place at "home," when the victim returns and recounts the journey. The success of this part of the game depends upon the respondents' inventiveness, with which they can compensate for earlier failure by making the listeners laugh at new inventions. They tell the news "out of their own heads," "whenever and whatever comes to mind." The absurdities can be carried on without end:

Boys yelped on the farm; dogs ate at the head of the living room. Daughters grunted in the pigsty, and, in the chambers, pigs looked at themselves in the mirror. Porridge was mixed with an axe, wood was chopped with a large spoon; churning was done with a club, and cut grain was threshed with a needle.

The same motifs appear in condensed form in the *Kalevala*-metered "rune" "Hämeen ihmeet" (The Wonders of Häme). During the first half of the nineteenth century in Lapland, Jacob Fellman recorded the following account of a "dumbbell" who had visited Häme:

Wonders I saw when I visited Numskull Place: Pigs stirred, cows baked, sheep distilled, dogs practiced law; snow buntings chopped wood, swallows cut shingles, a titmouse wove sticks, a baby squirrel carved beams. Cooking was done with an axe, chopping with pots; a wolf mixed, his tail slept; a hare ground flour, her head trembled. A log drew the plow, an ox shook; the sleigh endured, the road fell apart.

This passage contains international "impossibility" motifs, an ancient formula. The poetry of the Middle Ages, for example, teems with role reversals. According to Martti Haavio, the purpose of "contrariness" is the affirmation of in-group norms: the world has turned evil, anything could happen (Haavio, 1959). The one who fails in the riddle game belongs to this topsy-turvy world. When wishing to extend the game, people borrowed from "The Wonders of Häme." At the end,

People at home are fearful when the visitor to "Smileville" receives permission to come into the company of others. All sorts of gestures and words indicate how frightful the newcomer looks with feathers on his or her tarry face. (Fellman)

The *Kalevala*-metered rhyme by which the loser is "conjured away" to "Smileville" is reminiscent of an incantation. The loser is treated like a disease; he or she is ordered out of the community. The transportation is amusing and trifling, a parody of the horse of Hiisi "with iron reins along its flanks, an iron sleigh behind." The incantational nature of the "Smileville" recitation is echoed in the charm used for treating a sore: the sufferer spits on the sore and says, "Fie, fie, (you go) to Smileville, Smileville's dogs will bark." In the "rune" the stranger is seen through a window, and the mistress of the house sends her servant to find out why the dog is barking. This scene echoes a heroic epic of the *Kalevala*, in the *Kilpakosintaruno* (Competitive Courtship Rune). The rhyme is apparently derived from Kalevalan epic poetry, and there does not seem to be an equivalent for this form of the riddle game in other traditions, although there is a single notation from southern Estonia reminiscent of the Finnish tradition, and other points of convergence which have not been accounted for (Virtanen, 1960, 179–80).

The competitive riddling game was uncommon in Estonia, but riddling was related to magic. It was widely believed that the observation of twilight hours could affect "luck" in raising livestock. Sheep were said to produce motley (rather than white) lambs if women and girls posed riddles to each other before Christmas. However, when the women solved the riddles well, lambs and calves were born without difficulty. Riddling prevented tablespoons and other household items from disappearing and food from running out. The observation of the twilight hour was thought to promote the healthy birth and development of lambs and calves. There are similar commands and prohibitions in Lettish tradition. Riddling may be mandatory during certain seasons: during distribution time in Estonia, between Christmas and the time animals bear their young in Setumaa, from St. Martin's Day until Christmas among the Letts. From Finns who moved to Sweden during the seventeenth century comes the saying, "Mottled lambs are born when riddling is done at Christmas." The importance of riddling is not otherwise emphasized in Finland, although there is a proverb, still recited in jest today, connecting a daily work break with the fertility of cattle: "He who doesn't lie on his side after eating won't have his pigs multiply, won't have lambs from his sheep" (Virtanen, 1960, 182–89). Generally speaking, the magical implications of riddling in Estonia are absent from the game in Finland, where the emphasis is clearly on merrymaking.

The riddle game has sometimes been played as a game of forfeits. The unsuccessful guesser is sent from the room while the other players decide on a penalty, which is usually "work, money, or bodily suffering." Bodily suffering was the most common penalty, and at the end of the game, there was "malicious laughter and noise and even physical harm the old folks did not consider proper"; in other words, the game frequently became so rowdy that older people had to put a stop to it.

As one collector notes, the riddle game was an information contest, and failure was considered a disgrace. It was believed that true riddles measured

intelligence and that riddling helped children become "quick-witted and wise."
Players would respond to a performance with praise or reproach:

> Those who guessed quickly were admired. People sometimes shouted, "The
> rutabaga cuts! The head shines! The sawdust in his head has just been changed!
> There's no rag in his head!" Someone who did not guess correctly might be called
> "Dim attic, to Smileville with you! Talks like a rotten sheephead!"

An unsuccessful riddler might be comforted with:

> "Even horses with their four feet make mistakes, not to speak of a human with
> two." But the one who had guessed right—especially a child—was praised:
> "Indeed, it is from buds you grow the crop." Or it might be said that the child
> who guessed right was becoming like his aunt, uncle or godparent.

It is clear that, for all of its playfulness, the unsuccessful guesser's being sent
to "Smileville" was humiliating. It might be said to a poor guesser, "I now
pronounce sad words for you, 'cause you got ten (wrong) guesses, I now order
you out; you ain't fit to be in this group." According to some memoirs, "the trip
to 'Smileville" was so frightening that it was liable to disturb one's sleep later
in the evening." The riddle game was sometimes avoided because it offended
people's dignity. In any case, "people tried hard to remember (the riddles) so
that there'd be no trip to "Smileville"—that was considered a disgrace."

Communal excitement, rewards and punishments conferred by the social
group, were essential parts of riddling evenings. It was considered a demonstration of superiority to pose a riddle that no one could solve, even if the solution
were extraordinary or artificial. Only the poser knew the answer, and the
community expected the wisdom of the riddle to be presented in a traditionally
approved manner. It is important to recall that the content of riddles was
relevant to daily life, unlike the kind of question posed on quiz shows today,
which requires the recall of trivia or isolated bits of information from diverse
fields. Riddles were supposed to be learned, not contrived, just as round dances
were supposed to be traditional, even though they might be improvised on the
spot. The thought of conscious invention was foreign to a tradition bearer. The
preservation of tradition was more important than originality and inventiveness. It was said in Ostrobothnia that

> We stick strictly to that, that riddles must be "right," that is, the poser isn't allowed
> to invent (them) unless he knows how to invent such a good (rune-metrical) one
> that others don't recognize that it is made up. Someone might try during a riddle
> game to make a riddle, and if it turned out well, people tried to find the solution,
> and it was accepted. Usually, the riddler revealed only afterwards that the riddle
> was his own. And in this way the riddle found its way to others and then it was
> often said whose riddle it was.

But creating riddles was rare, and they had to conform to traditional imagery and style. Riddle repertoires were usually limited to under three hundred, and inventors of riddles were less renowned than those who knew many riddles and could pose them cleverly.

Occasional Use

It was not only during riddling games or on special evenings that riddles were posed: like proverbs and anecdotes, they could be posed any time, by anyone: "[Riddles were asked] at any time, when somebody remembered a riddle he'd heard." "The time and the place made no difference." "At any time for passing the time." They might be posed by "anybody who knew." "They could be asked by whoever knew and answered by whoever was fast enough." Riddles could be posed to while away the time and might be suggested by an appropriate occasion. A woman spinning wool might be asked: "A hairy thing lies on the thigh, waiting to get into the hole." To the woman the phrase was offensive because she did not realize that the answer was innocent: "There it (the wool) is in your lap." People were also eager to share new riddles and would pose them, just as we would tell a new joke, at any possible time to any appropriate audience: "When somebody heard a new riddle, he posed it anywhere: at work, on a walk, sitting in the courtyard, at home, on social calls." Like the *Kalevala*-metered lyrics and epics which flourished during twilight hours but could be recited any time, riddles were common on all occasions. Both genres were appropriate to the extended family or work community. Short sallies and jokes can be told between casual acquaintances, but the imagery, style, and world view reflected in the riddle game are less easily internalized.

Suggestive Riddles

According to many accounts, suggestive or erotic riddles were usually not posed "in a party at dusk." The twilight tradition does not generally include sexual folklore or sexual motifs: although songs and belief legends in the *Kalevala* tradition approach the problems of human life drastically, sexual topics are deliberately avoided. This was mainly due to the composition of the group—usually one or more conjugal families, among whom it was considered inappropriate to arouse sexual feelings lest sexual competition destroy the cohesiveness of the group. Another reason was the competitive nature of the game, whose purpose was to test the knowledge and attitude of the players. The purpose of erotic or suggestive riddles, on the other hand, was to create an erotically charged atmosphere, beguile the guesser's thoughts and in the end embarrass the respondent because the answer to the riddle was finally innocuous. The behavior of the riddler indicates the differences in intended usage: the poser of true riddles tried to keep the answer to himself as long as possible, whereas in suggestive riddles, like contemporary short jokes, the questioner wanted to deliver the punchline as quickly as possible. As a school child remarked, "Some people just all of a sudden ask in class, 'How does an elephant get down from a tree?' and answer straightaway, 'They go on a leaf and wait for autumn until the leaf falls down. You sure don't know much!'"

Erotic or suggestive riddles might form part of a riddling evening under certain circumstances, however. For one thing, a large number of riddles is required for a single evening if there are many participants. Some members of the group may think that "fun is missing from the game if only tame and tidy riddles are asked." And, too, the atmosphere might turn more erotic and boisterous as the evening wears on, especially if many young people are present. According to one informant, "Often that game ended when my late grandma said, 'That's enough now. That sort of thing shouldn't be asked with children listening.'"

The presence of children was an important factor in censoring riddles; the posing of sexual riddles when children were listening was sternly rebuked by older people because provocative riddles were considered unfit for the ears of children. However, the presence of children might provoke the introduction of ambiguous riddles: people who disapproved of riddles whose answer was openly obscene might ask children riddles in which the question appeared dubious but the answer was innocuous, such as, "The woman's on the ground, the man is in the tree, she has his 'balls' in her mouth." Mention is made of people whispering "unclean" riddles in order to safeguard the children. Although adults attempted to keep matters pertaining to sexual life secret from children, their lack of knowledge was considered comical. The answers to riddles with sexual themes were not disclosed to them; adults would "just laugh and say that it has to be guessed, not told." A sexual riddle presented by a child in innocence made the adults laugh uproariously. The attitudes toward sexual riddles reveal an ambivalence toward sexuality in general. As one collector observes, "It was attempted to conceal from children everything having to do with sexual life; indeed, a mother didn't even tell her grown-up daughters about these matters."

If children could not obtain information from their peers, they might remain, by modern standards, surprisingly ignorant. Of course, among themselves children might ask sexual riddles they had heard. The possession of secret knowledge enhanced the status of the questioner, and secretiveness added to children's interest in the riddle genre.

Adults do not explain their reticence on the grounds that talking about sexual matters can be dangerous, as they explain their tabu against mentioning the names of the dead and of the Evil One, though that may be the reason on the most basic level. The transmission of sexual folklore has been avoided in recent times for pedagogical reasons: childhood innocence is valued. Veikko Ruoppila states in his book on the popular rearing of children that, just as regards childbirth, one ought to say as little as possible about sex. In rural areas, gender differences were not explained to children (Ruoppila, 1954, 97).

Sexual riddles were posed, however, in settings other than the extended family and the "twilight" audience, in age, gender, and occupational groups. Collectors have noted the following milieus of ambiguous riddles: they were presented, for example, by boys in their own gangs, by mature boys at evening parties of young people, by loggers among themselves, by men at their place of work; granny poses them to the maids during free time, boys tease girls with them. This riddling tradition has its own virtuosi; mention is made, for example, of the itinerant loggers.

The atmosphere was freer in job situations because children were not present. There is mention of suggestive riddles being asked during smoking breaks and at workmen's barracks. Presenting sexual folklore strengthened the cohesiveness and feeling of solidarity in a gender group, and inhibitions were reduced. In the peasant community there has been a tradition of avoiding material considered "too coarse for women's ears." If this kind of lore is nevertheless presented with women listening, it has that much more significance in creating a boisterous or erotic atmosphere.

"Riddles sounding a bit risqué" were presented in husking bees or other work in outbuildings. V. E. V. Wessman mentions that in Swedish Finland, malting houses and distilleries offered a place for the performance of ambiguous riddles. Girls did the work, but boys hastened to amuse them. A favorite amusement was to pose riddles which led the girls' minds to something other than a matter-of-fact solution (Wessman, 1949, VII). Malting houses and saunas were also favorite places for young people to gather in the evenings to sing, play, and pose riddles. In Sweden as well as Finland, erotic riddles are associated with the gathering places of the young.

Ambiguous riddles, because of their suggestive nature, were well-suited to the erotic teasing between boys and girls; one could always accuse the respondent of having improper thoughts. The following description is from the Karelian Isthmus:

> A boy asked a girl, "What's black on top and red inside?" The girl starts to scold the boy, "Shame on you, the things you ask!" "Don't 'shame' me. It's only galoshes. But what's this: red inside and black on top?" "Well, galoshes, of course." "No, it isn't. It's what you meant a little while back."

The boys present the riddles in these cases, and the girls provide the bashfully giggling audience, roles which reflect the different sexual attitudes considered appropriate to each group. Boys were allowed to be sexually curious, but girls, however curious they might have been, were expected to be modest and shy. At mixed gatherings of young people—during riddling evenings or social events—riddling took on a sportive tone, and ambiguities were presented eagerly. A boy could pose such riddles "that a girl didn't answer, but was perplexed and looked like she'd have liked to sink into the earth." So the girl was ready to be sent to "Numskull Place." Riddles are comparable in this milieu to other sexual lore, in that their presentation is an indication of sexual awareness and maturity.

During the last decades, riddles have passed into children's folklore in Finland. Some of the old riddles were intended specifically for children; they were said to be "shorter and cleaner" than adult riddles. Children's riddles appeared in Sakari Topelius's reader *Maamme* (Our Country), which circulated widely in Finland. Children's riddles do not seem to have become rooted in folk tradition merely through print, but did change in form to fit the models in books.

In the 1960s many old riddles, usually those learned from readers, survived in oral tradition alongside elephant jokes and absurd riddles. By the 1980s, however, the old riddles had been forgotten. Children's riddles in Finland now follow international riddle types, usually based on puns or plays on words ("What's a gardener's professional hazard? — Corns"). Children's interest in pictorial riddles indicates the importance of visual messages in Western culture. Instead of adults asking children riddles, children ask adults or each other.

The favorite riddles of school-age children parody methods of assessment in school. Children today are placed in competitive situations and therefore enjoy stumping someone or beating them in word games. Current riddling is based on word games or jokes, while old riddling was like a puzzle concealing a familiar object behind a screen of misleading information.

STORIES OF DEATH AND THE
SOCIALIZATION OF CHILDREN

Reimund Kvideland

The expanding research on children's culture and socialization has largely overlooked the children's own role and their use of traditional genres. Parents in the nuclear family, adult friends and relatives, the school system and mass media are considered the principal agents in the socialization process of children. However, it has been asserted by some sources in recent sociological and ethnological research that these agents have ceased fulfilling their duties in important areas. A typical characteristic is the father's physical or psychological absence (Mitscherlich, 1963). It has been claimed that the nuclear family is a pathogenic situation for children because of "the emotionally overburdened seclusion of privacy" (Dreitzel, 1973, 9–12). Although the distance between parents and children is nothing new, the problem is that today parents are often the child's only contact. The crisis comes when that contact becomes difficult or broken. Socialization provided by the school system is excessively oriented toward the social status quo (Dreitzel, 1973, 311–33). This lack of alternatives must be compensated for, and the peer group is one of the few possible agents. As a result, children's own traditions increase in quantity and intensity. Verbal statements—songs, games, rhymes, word play, jokes, and stories—have an important role in the socialization process. Children actively adopt material from adult tradition, and develop new categories and new types.

The material for this study was collected during the period 1969–1978 in and around Bergen, Norway, and included several thousand items, some written down by the children themselves, some supplied through tape recordings or notes from interviews. The interviews were conducted at school without the teacher present, or at playgrounds and gathering places in residential areas. The data show quite clearly that children's traditions play an important role in several aspects of the socialization process, including the acquisition of lan-

Originally published in *Folklore on Two Continents: Essays in Honor of Linda Dégh*, 1980.

guage competence, shared standards, roles, norms, and values. The social importance of children's traditions manifests itself in various forms, including songs, jokes, and stories.

Gorer claims that by the early 1940s, perhaps earlier, psychologists were noting that "death had superseded sex as a taboo subject" (Anthony, 1971, 8). The French cultural historian Phillippe Ariès has suggested the background for this change in his analysis of Western attitudes toward death (1976). He claims that death was formerly considered a natural and accepted conclusion to life. It was the thought of dying unprepared, without the necessary ceremonies, that was frightening. Death was conquered, in a sense, if one was warned of its approach and could prepare for its arrival. The whole family, including the children, would be gathered at the deathbed.

According to Ariès, a revolution in the attitudes toward death has occurred in the last thirty to forty years. Death has become a taboo subject, something shameful. The dying person must be spared the solemnity of the occasion, and relatives and close friends an unnecessary emotional experience. Death is embarrassing. It does not correspond with the ideal of eternal youth and happiness. The burial ritual has been moderated, and sorrow is suppressed, particularly in public.

Certain tendencies indicate that this view is changing again, but it has nevertheless strongly influenced both children and adults. The question here is how children react to the death taboo. Can children compensate for the socialization of which adults have deprived them? If so, how? Even though society attempts to obliterate all reminders of death, children still quickly discover that death exists, but they do not receive adult help in discussing it. Over thirty years ago the Hungarian psychologist Maria Nagy published a groundbreaking analysis of children's responses to death. She found three stages in its development:

1. Up to age five, death is perceived as a separation, but it is not considered final.

2. Between five and nine, children personify death as an individual or a dead person.

3. At nine and ten, death is final and unavoidable. (1973, 3–27)

Kastenbaum and Aisenberg claim in their introduction that the concept "you are dead" is developed earlier than the more introspective "I will die." "You are dead" implies that you are absent, and I am thus deserted, leading to the common feeling of separation. The small child has no idea of time or the future and cannot distinguish a short, temporary absence from a permanent one. This situation is further complicated when children develop a sense of the cyclic pattern in their own lives. The declaration "I will die" involves an understanding that death is final (1969, 20–24).

A recent Swedish study shows that children do think about death; among ten-year-olds, ninety percent said that they think about death, while one-fourth wanted to talk about it. Before the age of eight, children associate death with concrete events, while older children associate death with the cessation of vital bodily functions (Johansson and Larsson, 1976). Sylvia Anthony found similar results in her study in England (1971).

Parents often explain death away, as a long journey or as sleep. Children are nevertheless confronted—both through television and in nature—with a different image of death, which they must incorporate into their cognitive systems. Such understanding is achieved in part through individual reflection; but peer groups also play an important part, similar to the one they have been shown to play in the acquisition of sex roles and knowledge about sex (McCandless, 1973, 791–820).

Because it is difficult to discuss or even speak about death, children make use of stories and jokes about death, death warnings, murder, and ghosts. These stories are told mainly by children between the ages of five and fifteen. I have focused here on the ten-to-twelve age group. The material analyzed here is quite homogenous. There are about twenty different tale types, and they illustrate various aspects of children's thoughts about death. The examples presented below were chosen from a large body of items.

Children are concerned with advance warnings of death. In one story a boy will not help a skeleton up from a coffin and the skeleton takes revenge:

> There were once three boys in a cemetery. Suddenly they heard someone who called for help. In an old coffin with a half-lid lay a corpse. They couldn't see what it was because it was only a skeleton. Then they heard the voice again. They opened the half-lid. Then the voice said, "Help me up from here." But then one of the boys slammed the lid on again. Then the voice said, "One day when you are crossing the street with your mother you will die." One day when he and his mother were crossing the street he stopped and couldn't cross, but his mother pulled him along. When they came to the middle of the street he fell dead. (Informant 1)

Another story tells of a light that appears and moves about in the cemetery. When it comes to the church door it shows the face of the one who will die:

> There were two boys. One was following the other home. On the way they had to go past the cemetery. It was a dark night. As they went past the cemetery they saw a light, but nobody was holding it. So the one asked if he knew what it was. He said that it was a light which came every time someone was going to die. The light went among the graves and when it came to the church door it showed the face of the one who was going to die. The other didn't believe it, and wanted to go over and see. He went and stood by the church door and he saw the light come nearer and nearer, but there was nobody holding it. When it came to the church door he saw a face, and he knew he recognized it, but couldn't remember who it was. He got scared and ran home. A week later he was sick and got pneumonia. He asked for his friend to come and told him that now he knew which face he had seen. It was his own. He had seen that he would die himself. (Informant 2)

A third story tells of a boy who sat on his mother's grave. He heard a voice: "Tonight at midnight I will come and get you." The story can also end in an anticlimax with the father frightening the boy in bed. Here children have adapted the traditional death warning to their own circumstances.

In both the Swedish study and Anthony's study, the data show that six- to eight-year-olds consider death to be a result of violence. Ten- to twelve-year-olds are aware of other causes of death, but for children up to the age of fourteen, violence still plays a role in explaining death, and the importance of this role is reflected in the stories told by these children. They describe slit throats, knives in the heart, and coffins full of blood. An element of anxiety is prominent in many of these stories. Studies have shown that ten- to twelve-year-olds are particularly afraid of dying. The scene is often set in the basement, on a dark and stormy night.

> There was once a girl who was going to spend the night with her grandmother. There was a storm outside, and the wind howled. In the room in the attic where she lay it creaked terribly. Then she heard a voice which said that it would happen at midnight. She went down to her grandmother and told her, but she only laughed and said that they could change rooms. The next morning she found her grandmother with her throat slit and blood running everywhere. (Informant 3)

> There once was a little girl, she was going down in the basement to get the dessert. She heard a voice that said "Blood on the steps, blood on the steps." She ran up to her mother and told her. "Nonsense," said her mother. The girl went down again. She heard the same, "Blood on the steps, blood on the steps." She ran up again. The girl told her mother. "Nonsense." The girl went down once more, then she didn't hear anything. She took the dessert and went up again. Then she saw her mother lying with a knife in her stomach." (Informant 4)

Parents, grandparents, and uncles are given roles as murderers. Is this a result of ignorance concerning the realities of dying? Or is it a technique for decreasing fright by associating it with someone who—however threatening—is at least familiar?

> Yeah, there was once—there was once a—a girl who was going up to the attic and hang up clothes for her mother. And so she didn't dare go up and so her grandmother followed her up. And so—and so they came up and so that grandmother said, "Open up that coffin." So there were three coffins there, so that grandmother said, "Can't you open one of them up?" So there lay her mother with a knife in her heart. And so—there was another—was another coffin. And so her mother opened up—no, the grandmother opened it up. And there lay her father with a knife in his heart. So—the girl was going to open up the next one and there was nobody lying there. So she said—so she said, "Who is going to lie here?" So—that—that grandmother said, "YOU." So she stabbed her in the heart with a knife. (Informant 5)

Can there be reassurance in dying together with one's parents so that one is not alone in death? The Johansson/Larsson study showed that children associate death with loneliness. These stories express children's fear of betrayal by those who are closest to them. Relatives die, are killed or disappear, or they pose a threat, giving shape to a previously formless anxiety about death.

Fear is also the theme in stories about cemeteries, death, and ghosts. One tale type with many variants concerns a dead person who appears before a living relative or close friend and asks if the relative will follow him—to the cemetery, into the grave, then into the coffin. But when the dead person asks the living relative to close the coffin lid behind them, the story is concluded with a loud "NO!" Another story tells about two boys riding in a car with a man. He stops at a cemetery and asks the boys to wait. The waiting becomes interminable, so they venture into the cemetery and discover him down in a grave. There he sits chewing on an arm.

Stories of this kind help to locate death in a child's world view, but they tend to increase, rather than decrease, anxiety. This tendency is furthered by the narrative situation. Stories are no longer told in the family circle, where adults offer reassuring protection. The contemporary narrative situation typically features a peer group outside in the dark, in an apartment house stairwell, or in a child's room in the evening. Children therefore use several narrative techniques in order to prevent anxiety from becoming too strong. Stories can be concluded with an anticlimax, can be told as parodies, or can release anxiety through a loud shriek (Virtanen, 1978, 73). The narrator might begin "Blood on the Steps" in a dramatic tone:

> There was blood on the steps, all the way up, there was blood on the steps, blood on the steps all the way up, on all the steps—and at the top was [with a light and happy voice] a blood orange [an orange with a reddish pulp]. (Informant 6)

A child is frightened by a voice that says that at midnight tonight she will die:

> There was once a girl who was home alone because her mother and father were at a party. At seven o'clock a voice said, "At eleven o'clock you must go up to the attic and open up the old trunk. If you don't you will be killed." It was ten o'clock, ten-thirty, and finally eleven. The girl shook as she went up the stairs at eleven o'clock. She opened the trunk and there was a voice which said, "BOO!" (Informant 7)

A common story with many variants tells of a boy or girl who is supposed to wash the blood out of a piece of clothing by midnight:

> There was once a woman who was at home. Her husband was away on vacation. One day she took an afternoon nap. When she woke, she saw in a closet a sheet covered with blood, and it said, "Must be washed before midnight." That evening she was at a party, and came home at ten-thirty. Then she remembered the sheet, so she went down in the basement and scrubbed and scrubbed. The sweat ran.

> Eleven o'clock, eleven-thirty, one minute before midnight, then she heard steps behind her and a voice said, "BLENDA WASHES WHITER." (Informant 8)

The many variations of "The Man from the Gallows" (AT 366) also belong in this context:

> There was once a girl who was going to buy liver for her mother. Before she went her mother said that if the butcher didn't have liver, "I will kill you." When she came to the butcher, he didn't have any liver. But then she went up to the attic because she knew there was a trunk full of liver there. She took what she needed and went home with it. When they were eating dinner they heard a voice from the attic which said, "Who took my liver?" Her father went up, but he didn't see anything. When he came down again they heard the same thing. This time her mother went up. But she didn't see anything either. When she came down again they heard the same thing and the girl went up but she didn't see anything. When she was going down again she heard a voice which said, "YOU TOOK MY LIVER." (Informant 9)

Black humor is particularly common among teenagers, but certain forms of it are also used by younger children:

> A boy came running in to his mother and said, "Mother, mother, papa has hung himself in the attic." "Oh, no, what do you mean, has he hung himself in the attic?" She ran up but came down right away and said, "You are lying, boy. He hasn't hung himself in the attic." Then he said, "April Fool, Mother, he hung himself in the basement." (Informant 10)

In both age groups black humor serves to explain death and to provide the necessary distance from it.

The results of this continuing project can be tentatively formulated as follows: By talking about death in a very concrete manner and tying death and its causes to loved ones whom he or she least desires to die, the child employs a therapeutic principle which takes the sting from the fear of death.

Children have created or partially adopted fixed-form narrative types as frameworks for communication about death. There are undoubtedly many reasons for this use of narrative: one of the most important is that the form provides both the desired distance from death and the proximity needed to incorporate it into the child's world view. Children thus express a form of internal protest, or perhaps also a symbolic protest against adults' indifference or inability to help.

BIBLIOGRAPHY

Aarne, Antti. 1910. *Verzeichnis der Märchentypen*. Helsinki (FFC 3).
Aarne, Antti, and Stith Thompson. 1961. *The types of the folktale. A classification and bibliography*. 2nd rev. ed. Helsinki (FFC 184).
Abrahams, Roger D. 1970. *Deep down in the jungle*. 1st rev. ed. Hatboro.
_____. 1976. Genre theory and folkloristics. *Studia Fennica* 20, 13–19.
Ala-Könni, Erkki. 1953. Melismat eli niekut Lapuan seudun herännäisveisuussa (Melisma and melodic decorations in the songs of the awakened in the area of Lapua). *Kalevalaseuran vuosikirja* 33, 26–31.
_____. 1974. Nurmon herännäisveisuu (The singing of the awakened in Nurmo). *Nurmon kirja*, 191–225.
Allardt, Anders (ed.). 1917–20. *Sagor i urval*. Helsingfors (Finlands svenska folkdiktning 1B:1–2).
Allardt, A., and P. Perklén (eds.) 1896. *Nyländska folksagor och -sägner*. Helsingfors (Nyland 6).
Allport, G. W., and L. J. Postman. 1947. *The psychology of rumor*. New York.
Alver, Bente Gullveig. 1971. Conceptions of the living human soul in the Norwegian tradition. *Temenos* 7, 7–33.
_____. 1978. "Du skal gå frisk herfra": En etnomediciner og hans patientbehandling. *Tradisjon* 8, 27–36.
_____. 1980. Andreas. In B. G. Alver et al. 1980. 119–54.
_____. 1982. Folk medicine as an open medical system. In T. Vaskilampi and C. P. MacCormack (eds.), 1982, 124–39.
Alver, Bente Gullveig, et al. 1980. *Botare. En bok om etnomedicin i Norden*. Stockholm.
Alver, Bente Gullveig, and Torunn Selberg. 1984. Alternative medicine in today's society. *Temenos* 20, 7–25.
Alver, Brynjulf. 1962. Historiske segner og historisk sanning. *Norveg* 9, 89–116.
_____. 1967. Category and function. *Fabula* 9, 63–69.
_____. 1980. Nasjonalisme og identitet. Folklore og nasjonal utvikling. *Tradisjon* 10, 5–16.
_____. 1980a. *Studiet av folkekulturen*. Bergen.
Amundsen, Svein Schrøder, and Reimund Kvideland. 1975. *Emigrantviser*. Oslo (Norsk folkeminnelags skrifter 115).
Anderson, Walter. 1934–40. Geographisch-historische Methode. *Handwörterbuch des deutschen Märchens* 2, col. 508–22.
Anthony, Sylvia. 1971. *The discovery of death in childhood and after*. London.
Apo, Satu, et al. (eds.). 1974. *Strukturalismia, semiotiikkaa, poetiikkaa*. Helsinki.
Apollon, Daniel, et al. 1981. *Djevleutdrivere. Eksorsisme i Norge*. Oslo.
Arewa, E. Ojo, and Alan Dundes. 1964. Proverbs and the ethnography of speaking folklore. *American Anthropologist* 66, 70–85.
Ariès, Phillippe. 1976. *Essais sur l'histoire de la mort en Occident du Moyen Age à nos jours*. Paris.
Arvastson, Gösta. 1986. Arbetslivets berättelser. Exempelstudier och tolkningsdiskussion. *Tradisjon* 16, 35–44.
Bäckström, P. O. 1845. *Svenska folkböcker* 1–2. Stockholm.
Bælter, Sven. 1783. *Historiska anmärkningar om kyrkoceremonier*. Stockholm.

Bang, A. Chr. 1901–02. *Norske Hexeformularer og Magiske Opskrifter.* Oslo (Det norske videnskaps-akademi i Oslo. Skrifter 2, hist.-filos. klasse. 1901:1).

Barnes, D. R. 1966. Some functional horror stories on the Kansas University campus. *Southern Folklore Quarterly* 30, 305–12.

Bascom, William R. 1965. The forms of folklore: Prose narrative. *Journal of American Folklore* 78, 3–20.

Bascom, William R. (ed.). 1977. *Frontiers of folklore.* Washington, D.C.

Basgöz, Ilhan. 1972. Folklore studies and nationalism in Turkey. *Journal of the Folklore Institute* 9, 162–76.

Bateson, Gregory. 1972. *Steps to an ecology of mind.* 4th printing. New York.

Baughman, E. 1945. The cadaver arm. *Hoosier Folklore Bulletin* 4:2, 30–32.

———. 1945a. The fatal initiation. *Hoosier Folklore Bulletin* 4:3, 49–55.

Bauman, Richard. 1983. The field study of folklore in context. In R. M. Dorson (ed.), 1983, 362–68.

Bausinger, Hermann. 1968. *Formen der "Volkspoesie."* Berlin.

———. 1969. Zur Algebra der Kontinuität. In H. Bausinger and W. Brückner (eds.), 1969, 9–30.

———. 1977. Alltägliches Erzählen. *Enzyklopädie des Märchens* 1, col. 323–30.

———. 1977a. Zur kulturalen Dimension von Identität. *Zeitschrift für Volkskunde* 73, 210–15.

———. 1980. On contexts. In N. Burlakoff and C. Lindahl (eds.). 1980, 273–79.

Bausinger, Hermann, and Wolfgang Brückner (eds.). 1969. *Kontinuität? Geschichtlichkeit und Dauer als volkskundliches Problem.* Berlin.

Beardsley, R. K., and R. Hankey. 1942. The vanishing hitchhiker. *California Folklore Quarterly* 1, 303–35.

———. 1943. A history of the vanishing hitchhiker. *California Folklore Quarterly* 2, 13–26.

Ben-Amos, Dan. 1973. A history of folklore studies. Why do we need it? *Journal of the Folklore Institute* 10, 113–24.

———. 1976. The concept of genre in folklore. *Studia Fennica* 20, 30–43.

Ben-Amos, Dan, and Kenneth Goldstein (eds.). 1975. *Folklore, performance, and communication.* The Hague (Approaches to semiotics 40).

Bergstrand, Carl-Martin. 1956. *Frimurarna och hundturken.* Göteborg.

Bjersby, Ragnar. 1964. *Traditionsbärare på Gottland vid 1800-talets mitt. En undersökning rörande P. A. Säves sagesmän.* Uppsala (Dialekt- och folkminnesarkivet. Skrifter. Serie B 11).

Bjørkvold, Jon-Roar. 1979. *Barnas egen sangbok.* Oslo.

———. 1979a. *Barnesangen - vårt musikalske morsmål.* Oslo.

———. 1982. Sangaktivitet som sosio-musikalsk prosess i barnekulturen. En presentasjon av enkelte problemstillinger, metodespørsmål og resultater. *Sumlen,* 124–33.

———. 1985. *Den spontane barnesangen - vårt musikalske morsmål: en undersøkelse av førskolebarns sang i tre barnehager i Oslo.* Oslo.

———. 1988. *Canto—ergo sum. Musical child cultures in Norway, United States and the Soviet Union. Developmental and pedagogical implications.*

Blehr, Otto. 1974. *Folketro- og sagnforskning.* Oslo.

Bø, Olav. 1973. *Folkemedisin og lærd medisin. Norsk medisinsk kvardag på 1800-talet.* Oslo.

Boberg, Inger M. 1953. *Folkemindevidenskabens historie i Mellem- og Nordeuropa.* Copenhagen (Danmarks folkeminder 60).

Bødker, Laurits (ed.). 1962. *Nordisk seminar i folkedigtning 1.* Copenhagen.

Bogatyrev, Pjotr, and Roman Jakobson. 1929. Die Folklore als eine besondere Form des Schaffens. In *Donum natalicium Schrijnen.* Nijmegen/Utrecht, 900–13.

Borchgrevink, Louise Storm. 1956. *Frå ei anna tid. Folkeminne frå Nordfjord.* Oslo (NFL 78).

Boström, H. J. 1929. Kuolemantuomioista ja niiden täytäntöönpanosta Suomessa enne vuotta 1826 (Office of death records and vital statistics in Finland before 1826). *Defensor Legis* 163–96.

Bregenhøj, Carsten. 1969. Svigermor i bagagerummet. *Folkeminder* 14, 9–14.

Bremond, Claude. 1964. Le message narratif. *Communications* 4, 4–32.

———. 1970. Morphology of the French folktale. *Semiotica* 2, 247–76.

Bringéus, Nils-Arvid. 1951. Uppteckningar om vidskepelser i Lunds stift 1795. *Arv*, 84–95.

———. 1976. *Mäiskan som kulturvarelse*. 2nd ed. 1981. Lund.

Brix, Hans. 1935–38. *Analyser og problemer*, vols. 2 and 4. Copenhagen.

Broch, Ole-Jacob. 1980. *Naturmedisin og legekunst*. Oslo.

Brusgaard, Dag, and Lasse Efskind. 1977. Befolkningens syn på bruk av folkemedisin. *Tidsskrift for Den norske lægeforening* 97, 1385–88.

Büchmann, Georg. 1937. *Geflügelte Worte. Der Zitatenschatz des deutschen Volkes*. 28th ed. Berlin.

Buckner, H. T. 1965. A theory of rumor transmission. *Public Opinion Quarterly* 29, 54–70.

Burjam, F. 1917. *Den skandinaviska folktron om barnet under dess ömtållighetstillstånd i synnerhet före dopet*. Helsingfors.

Burlakoff, Nikolai, and Carl Lindahl (eds.). 1980. *Folklore on two continents: Essays in honor of Linda Dégh*. Bloomington, Ind.

Byström, A. 1973. *Pizzerior*. MS. Institutet för folklivsforskning, Stockholm.

Calame-Griaule, C., et al. (eds.). 1984. *Le conte. Pourquoi? Comment? Actes des Journées d'études en littérature orale. Analyse des contes. Problèmes de méthodes, Paris. 1982*. Paris.

Campbell, Åke. 1925. Rec. of Halländsk bygdekultur, studier red. av D. Arill et al. Göteborg. 1925. *Folkminnen och folktankar* 12, 31–47.

Castrén, M. A. 1857. *Versuch einer burjätischen Sprachlehre*. St. Petersburg.

Cederlöf, J. 1964. *Ekenäs stads historia*. 3: 1810–1930. Ekenäs.

Celander, Hilding. 1925. Julen som åringsfest. *Folkminnen och folktankar* 12(3), 6–18; 12(4), 1–38.

Christiansen, Reidar Th. 1946. *Eventyr og sagn*. Oslo.

———. 1958. *The migratory legends. A proposed list of types with a systematic catalogue of the Norwegian variants*. Helsinki (FFC 175).

Coe, Rodney M. 1970. *Sociology of medicine*. New York.

Cowell, Henry. 1955. *Charles Ives and his music*. New York.

Dal, Erik. 1956. *Nordisk folkeviseforskning siden 1800*. Copenhagen.

Dasent, G. W. 1858. *Popular tales from the Norse*. London.

Dégh, Linda. 1968a. The boyfriend's death. *Indiana Folklore* 1, 101–106.

———. 1968a. The hook. *Indiana Folklore* 1, 92–100.

———. 1968b. The runaway grandmother. *Indiana Folklore* 1, 68–77.

———. 1969. *Folktales and society. Storytelling in a Hungarian peasant community*. Bloomington, Ind.

———. 1971. The "belief legend" in modern society. In W. D. Hand (ed.), 1971, 55–68.

———. 1975. The study of ethnicity in modern European ethnology. *Journal of the Folklore Institute* 12, 113–29.

———. 1976. The postulative proto-memorate. *Studia Fennica* 20, 48–57.

Dégh, Linda, and Andrew Vázsonyi. 1971. Legend and belief. *Genre* 4, 281–304.

———. 1973. Sägen och tro. In B. af Klintberg (ed.), 1973, 83–113.

———. 1975. The hypothesis of multi-conduit transmission in folklore. In Dan Ben-Amos and K. Goldstein (eds.), 1975, 207–52.

Dorson, R. M. 1959. *American folklore*. Chicago.

Dorson, Richard M. (ed.). 1983. *Handbook of American folklore*. Bloomington, Ind.

Douglas, Mary. 1966. *Purity and danger. An analysis of concepts of pollution and taboo*. London.

Douglas, Mary (ed.). 1970. *Witchcraft. Confessions and accusations.* London (ASA monographs 9).
Dreitzel, Hans Peter (ed.). 1973. *Childhood and socialization.* New York and London.
Dröge, F. 1970. *Der zerredete Widerstand. Zur Soziologie und Publizistik des Gerüchtes im 2. Weltkrieg.* Düsseldorf.
Dundes, Alan. 1964. *The morphology of North American Indian folktales.* Helsinki (FFC 195).
_____. 1971. On the psychology of legend. In W. D. Hand (ed.), 1971, 21–36.
_____. 1982. The symbolic equivalence of allomotifs: towards a method of analyzing folktales. *Arv* 36, 91–98.
Dundes, Alan (ed). 1965. *The study of folklore.* Englewood Cliffs, N.J.
Egardt, Brita. 1962. *Hästslakt och rackarskam. En etnologisk undersökning av folkliga fördomar.* Stockholm (Nordiska museets handlingar 57).
Eike, Christine N. F. 1980. Oskoreia og ekstaseriter. *Norveg* 23, 227–309.
Ellekilde, Hans. 1938. Det sidste Neg i angelsk Folkeoverlevering. *Folkminnen och folktankar* 24, 180–95.
Enerstvedt, Åse. 1976. Om barnekulturen. Et forsøk på å se dens særtrekk som kulturform. *Forskningsnytt.* 1976:5, 22–26.
Engström, T. 1903. *Öland, dess historia, land och folk.* Kalmar.
Eriksson, Kerstin, Inger Lövkrona, and Per Peterson. 1973. "Varulven finns, gör den inte?" *Tradisjon* 3, 13–30.
Eskeröd, Albert. 1947. *Årets äring. Etnologiska studier i skördens och julens tro och sed.* Stockholm (Nordiska musets handlingar 26).
_____. 1964. Needs, interests, values, and the supernatural. In *Lapponica. Essays presented to Israel Ruong. = Studia Ethnographica Upsaliensis* 21, 81–98.
Espeland, Velle. 1979. Voggeviser og viser om vogging. *Sumlen,* 72–79.
Eurajoen nuottipainos (The Eurajoki notebook). 1963. Pieksämäki.
Evans-Pritchard, E. E. 1965. *Theories of primitive religion.* Oxford.
Fältarbete. 1968. Synpunkter på etno-folkloristisk fältforskning. Helsingfors (NEFAs publ. 1).
Faye, Andreas. 1833. *Norske Folkesagn.* 2nd ed. Oslo. 1844, 3rd ed., 1948 (NFL 63). Arendal.
Feilberg, H. F. 1904–08. *Ordbog over jyske Almuesmål* 3. Copenhagen.
Festinger, L., et al. 1948. A study of a rumor: its origin and spread. *Human Relations* 1, 464–86.
Flatin, Kjetil A. 1930. *Tussar og trolldom.* Oslo (NFL 21).
Forde, Daryll. 1962. Death and succession. An analysis of Yakö mortuary ceremonial. In M. Gluckman (ed.), 1962, 89–123.
Frandsen, Ernst. 1929. Det 16. Aarhundredes Elskovslyrik. *Edda,* 225–69.
_____. 1954. Middelalderlig lyrik. *Danske studier,* 75–108.
Fredén, L. 1974. *Havandeskapet i svensk folktro.* Stockholm.
Freidson, Eliot. 1970. *Profession of medicine: A study of the sociology of applied knowledge.* New York.
Fritzner, Johan. 1954. *Ordbog over det gamle norske Sprog* 3. Oslo.
Frykman, Jonas. 1977. Horan som samhällsfara. In Frykman, J.: *Horan i bondesamhället.* Lund, 25–54.
Fugelli, Per. 1978. Naturmedisin. *Tidsskrift for Den norske lægeforening* 98, 1359–60.
Funk and Wagnalls. 1949–50. *Standard dictionary of folklore, mythology and legend* 1–2. New York.
Ganander, Christfrid. 1783. *Aenigmata Fennica. Suomalaiset Arwotuxet/Wastansten kansa.* Vaasa.
Gasparov, Boris. 1974. Taron semioottinen koulukunta (Tartu semiotic school, fundamental conception and current trends). In S. Apo et al. (eds.), 1974, 25–42, 240–41.

Georges, Robert A. 1969. Toward an understanding of storytelling events. *Journal of American Folklore* 82, 313–28.

Gjemdal, Torbjørn. 1979. Pasienters bruk av naturmedisiner. *Tidsskrift for Den norske lægeforening* 99, 883–86.

Gladwin, T., and Wm. C. Sturtevant (eds.). 1962. *Anthropology and human behavior.* Washington, D.C.

Gluckman, Max (ed.). 1962. *Essays on the ritual of social relations.* Manchester.

Goslin, D. A. (ed.). 1973. *Handbook of socialization theory and research.* Chicago.

Götterberg, Tore. 1976. Säfrua och Junis. Sädesandar i svensk och baltisk tradition. *Rig* 59, 105–14.

Granberg, Gunnar. 1935. Memorat und Sage. Einige methodische Gesichtspunkte. *Saga och sed,* 120–27.

———. 1935a. *Skogsrået i yngre nordisk folktradition.* Uppsala (Skrifter utg. av Gustav Adolfs Akademien 3).

Grande, A. 1931. "Korsen" i Leksvik. *Årbok for Nordtrøndelag historielag,* 51–56.

———. 1932. Kjempehaugane på Leksviksneset. *Årbok for Nordtrøndelag historielag,* 65–68.

Greimas, A. J. 1966. *Sémantique structurale.* Paris.

Grimstad, Edvard. 1953. *Etter gamalt. Folkeminne frå Gudbrandsdalen* 3. Oslo (NFL 71).

Grobman, Neil R. 1973. Eighteenth-century Scottish philosophers on oral tradition. *Journal of the Folklore Institute* 10, 187–95.

Grundtvig, Svend (ed.). 1854–56. *Danmarks gamle folkeviser* 2. Copenhagen.

Grüner-Nielsen, Hakon. 1912–31. *Danske Viser fra Adelsvisebøger og Flyveblade 1530–1630.* 1–7. Copenhagen. Facs. ed. Copenhagen. 1978–79.

———. 1927–28. *Danske skæmteviser.* Copenhagen.

Gunnlaugs saga Ormstunga. Sigurdur Nordal and Gudni Jonsson (eds.), 1938. Reykjavik (Islenzk fornrit 3).

Gustavsson, Anders. 1972. *Kyrktagningsseden i Sverige.* Lund (Skrifter från Folklivsarkivet i Lund 13).

———. 1976. *Forskning om folkligt fromhetsliv.* Lund.

———. 1979. Folklore in community conflicts. Gossip in a fishing community. *Arv* 35, 49–85.

Haapalainen, T. Ilmari. 1979. *Suomalaisten kansansävelmien lähdetutkimuksia* (Source studies in religious folk melodies in Finland). Helsinki.

Haavio, Martti. 1942. *Suomalaiset kodinhaltiat* (Finnish house sprites). Porvoo.

———. 1959. *Essais folkloriques.* Porvoo (Studia Fennica 8).

———. 1959. The upside-down world. *Studia Fennica* 8, 209–21.

Hackman, Oskar. 1911. *Katalog der Märchen der finnländischen Schweden.* Leipzig (FFC 6).

Hackman, Oskar (ed.). 1917–20. *Sagor. Referatsamling.* Helsingfors (Finlands svenska folkdiktning 1A:1–2).

Hall, G. 1975. *Den farliga tanten.* MS. Institutet för folklivsforskning, Stockholm.

Hammarstedt, Nils Edvard. 1923. Svensk forntro och forsed. Ett jamförande utkast. *Hävd och hembygd* 1, 53–64.

———. 1927. Seder vid åkerbruk och boskapsskötsel som härleda sig från jakt- och fångstriter. *Fataburen,* 40–50.

Hand, Wayland D. (ed.). 1971. *American folk legend. A symposium.* Berkeley, Calif.

Handwörterbuch des deutschen Märchens. 1–2. Berlin/Leipzig. 1934–40.

Hansen, Finn Henry. 1979. Helsesektoren i velferdsstaten: kjempevekst og fordelingskrise. *Tidsskrift for samfunnsforskning* 20, 219–40.

Hardar saga ok Holmverja. Gudni Jonsson (ed.), 1945. Reykjavik.

Hart, Donn. 1964. *Riddles in Filipino folklore.* New York.

Harva, Uno. 1948. *Suomalaisten muinaisusko* (The ancient religion of the Finns). Porvoo.

Hasslöf, Olof, et al. 1970. *Sømand, fisker, skib og værft.* Copenhagen.

Hauge, Alfred. 1978. Vistemannen personleg. *Tradisjon* 8, 47–54.
(Heilfurth, Gerhard.) 1969. *Kontakte und Grenzen. Festschrift für G. Heilfurth.* Göttingen.
Heimann, Walter. 1977. Zur Theorie des musikalischen Folklorismus: Idee, Funktion und Dialektik. *Zeitschrift für Volkskunde* 73, 181–209.
Hermundstad, Knut. 1955. *I kveldseta. Gamal Valdres-kultur* 6. Oslo (NFL 75).
Herranen, Gun. 1984. A blind storyteller's repertoire. In G. Calame-Griaule et al. (eds.), 1984, 511–25.
Herranen, Gun (ed.). 1978. *Tradition, dokumentation, arkiv. NIF's andra nordiska folkloristiska arkiv- och dokumentationskonferens.* Åbo (NIF publications 6).
_____ . 1981. *Folkloristikens aktuella paradigm.* Åbo (NIF publications 10).
Herranen, Gun, and Lassi Saressalo (eds.). 1976. *NIFs andra nordiska folkloristiska ämneskonferens.* Turku (NIF publications 5).
_____ . 1978. *A guide to Nordic tradition archives.* Turku (NIF publications 7).
Hildeman, Karl-Ivar. 1950. *Politiska visor från Sveriges senmedeltid.* Stockholm.
Hill, Ann (ed.). 1981. *Alternativ legekunst.* Oslo.
Hodne, Bjarne. 1973. *Personalhistoriske sagn. En studie i kildeverdi.* Oslo.
Hodne, Ørnulf. 1979. *Jørgen Moe og folkeeventyrene. En studie i nasjonalromantisk folkloristikk.* Oslo.
Holbek, Bengt. 1974. The ethnic joke in Denmark. *Unifol,* 45–55.
_____ . 1979. Stiltiende forudsætninger. *Norveg* 22, 209–21.
_____ . 1981. Moderne folkloristik og historisk materiale. In Herranen (ed.), 1981, 129–49.
_____ . 1982. Kunsten at hente prinseser ned fra glasbjerge eller tolkning af trylleeventyr. In *Folksagor och barnlitteratur* 1. Nordens Biskops-Arnö. 1982, 24–43.
_____ . 1983. Nordic research in popular prose narrative. *Studia Fennica* 27, 145–62.
_____ . 1987. *Interpretation of fairy tales. Danish folklore in a European perspective.* Helsinki (FFC 239).
Holmberg (Harva), Uno. 1913. *Die Wassergottheiten der Finnisch- ugrischen Völker.* Helsinki (Mémoires de la Société Finno-Ougrienne 32).
Holst, Elling. 1901. Gamle ulvehistorier. *Julehilsen,* 20–21.
Honko, Lauri. 1962. *Geisterglaube in Ingermanland* 1. Helsinki (FFC 185).
_____ . 1963. Itkuvirsiruunous (Finnish laments). *Suomen kirjallisuus* 1, 81–128.
_____ . 1964. Memorates and the study of folk belief. *Journal of the Folklore Institute* 1, 5–19.
_____ . 1964a. Siirtymäriitit (The rites of passage). *Sananjalka* 6, 116–40.
_____ . 1965. Finnische Mythologie. In *Wörterbuch der Mythologie* 1, 261–371. Stuttgart.
_____ . 1965a. On the functional analysis of folk-beliefs and narratives about empirical supernatural beings. *Laographia* 22, 168–73 = G. A. Megas (ed.). 1965. International Congress for Folk-Narrative Research in Athens, 1964.
_____ . 1968. Genre analysis in folkloristics and comparative religion. *Temenos* 3, 48–66.
_____ . 1969. Role-taking of the shaman. *Temenos* 4, 26–52.
_____ . 1970. Der Mythos in Religionswissenschaft. *Temenos* 6, 45–52.
_____ . 1973. Tradition barriers and adaptation of tradition. *Ethnologia Scandinavica,* 30–49.
_____ . 1976. Genre theory revisited. *Studia Fennica* 20, 20–25.
_____ . 1977. The role of fieldwork in tradition research. *Ethnologia Scandinavica,* 75–90.
_____ . 1978. Folkmedicin i utvecklingsperspektiv. *Tradisjon* 8, 1–26.
_____ . 1979. Forskarens ideologi. *Norveg* 22, 253–61.
_____ . 1979a. A hundred years of Finnish folklore research: A reappraisal. *Folklore* 90, 141–52.
_____ . 1979b. Perinteen sopeutumisesta (On the adaption of tradition). *Sananjalka* 21, 57–76.
_____ . 1979/80. Methods in folk narrative research. *Ethnologia Europaea* 11, 6–27.

_____. 1981. Four forms of adaption of folklore. *Studia Fennica* 26, 19–33.
_____. 1981a. Traditionsekologi - en introduktion. In L. Honko and O. Löfgren (eds.), 1981, 9–63.
Honko, Lauri, and Pekka Laaksonen (eds.). 1983. *Trends in Nordic tradition research*. Helsinki (Studia Fennica 27 = NIF publications 13).
Honko, Lauri, and Orvar Löfgren (eds.). 1981. *Tradition och miljö. Ett kulturekologiskt perspektiv*. Lund (Skrifter utg. av Etnologiska sällskapet i Lund 13 = NIF publications 11).
HSHL. 1966. Siion virret ja Halullisten Sieluin Hengelliset laulut (The religious songs of the awakened souls. Orig. 1790). Rauma.
Hultkrantz, Åke. 1953. *Conceptions of the soul among North American Indians*. Stockholm. (The Ethnographic Museum of Sweden. Monograph Series 1).
_____. 1968. "Miscellaneous beliefs": Some points of view concerning the informal religious sayings. *Temenos* 3, 67–82.
_____. 1973. *Metodvägar inom den jämförande religionsforskningen*. Stockholm.
_____. 1977. History of religions in anthropological waters. Some reflections against the background of American data. *Temenos* 13, 81–97.
Hvidbergskår, A.-S. 1968. *Kvakksalvere og folkemedisin på Agder*. Kristiansand (Kristiansand museum. Småskrifter 8).
Hyltén-Cavallius, G. O. 1863. *Wärend och Wirdarne. Ett forsök i svensk ethnologi* 1. Stockholm.
Hymes, Dell. 1962. Ethnography of speaking. In T. Gladwin and Wm. C. Sturtevant (eds.), 1962, 13–55.
Ibsen, Henrik 1857. Om Kjæmpevisen og dens Betydning for Kunstpoesien. *Illustreret Nyhetsblad* 6, 89–91, 97 = Samlede skrifter 15 (1902) 350–72.
Illich, Ivan. 1973. The breakdown of schools: A problem or a symptom? In H. P. Dreitzel (ed.), 1973, 311–33.
Jöckel, Bruno. 1939. *Der Weg zum Märchen*. Berlin/Steglitz.
Johannesen, Georg. 1980. Hva er en folkevise? Fortellingen om en 200 år gammel oversettelsesfeil. *Basar* 2, 41–46.
Johansson, Birgitta, and Gun-Britt Larsson. 1976. *Barns tankar om döden*. Stockholm.
Johnsen, Birgit Hertzberg. 1980. Her Ulve Mand har revet Aar Seksten Hundred Tolv. Tradisjon, miljø og verdirelatering - en sagnstudie. *Norveg* 23, 155–94.
Johnsen, Marit Hauan. 1979. ". . . om Gud vil det": Litt om fire religiøse helbredere i Nord-Norge. *Nord-Nytt* 6, 17–20.
Johnsen, Marit Hauan, and Stein Mathisen. 1979. Hjemme-alene-fest. Tenåringenes festmønster. *Tradisjon* 9, 53–65.
Jolles, André. 1929. *Einfache Formen*. Halle.
Jonsson, Bengt R. 1956. Balladdiktning. *KLNM* 1, col. 316–21.
Kastenbaum, Robert, and Ruth Aisenberg. 1976. *The psychology of death*. 3rd ed. Swedish transl. 1969. New York.
Keesing, Roger M., and Felix M. Keesing. 1971. *New perspectives in cultural anthropology*. New York.
Kienhardt, Godfrey. 1961. *Divinity and experience: the religion of the Dinka*. Oxford.
Kivekäs, Pekka. 1963. *Halullisten Sieluin Hengelliset Laulut*. Spiritual songs of the awakened souls. Unpubl MS. at the University of Helsinki.
Klausen, Arne Martin. 1976. *Kultur - variasjon og sammenheng*. 5. oppl. Oslo.
Kleinman, Arthur. 1980. *Patients and healers in the context of culture. An exploration of the borderland between anthropology, medicine and psychiatry*. Berkeley, Calif.
af Klintberg, Bengt. 1965. *Svenska trollformler*. Stockholm.
_____. 1968. "Gast" in Swedish folk tradition. *Temenos* 3, 83–109.
_____. 1971. Varför har elefanten röda ögon? *Fataburen* 125–42.
_____. 1972. *Svenska folksägner*. Stockholm.

_____. 1974. Råttan i pizzan. *Expressen* 26.1, 4–5.

_____. 1976. Folksägner i dag. *Fataburen,* 269–96.

_____. 1976a. Sprutan på tunnelbanan. *Förr och nu.* 1976:2, 44–46.

_____. 1980. Hejnumkjerringen. In B. G. Alver et al., 1980, 9–52.

_____. 1986. *Råttan i pizzan. Folksägner i vår tid.* Stockholm.

af Klintberg, Bengt (ed.). 1973. *Tro, sanning, sägen.* Stockholm.

Klusen, Ernst. 1969. *Volkslied. Fund und Erfindung.* Cologne.

Kommerel, Max. 1933. Das Volkslied und das deutsche Lied. *Jahrbuch des Freien Deutschen Hochstifts. 1922/33* = Max Kommerell. *Dame Dichterin und andere Essays.* Munich, 1967.

Krohn, Ilmari. 1899. *Über die Art und Entstehung der geistlichen Volksmelodien in Finland.* Helsinki.

_____. 1938. Hengellisten kansansävelmiemme syntyvaiheista (Concerning the origin of our religious songs). *Kalevalaseuran vuosikirja* 18, 63–76.

Krohn, Kaarle. 1926. *Die folkloristische Arbeitsmethode.* Oslo. (Institutt for sammenlignende kulturforskning. Serie B: Skrifter 5).

_____. 1971. *Folklore methodology.* Austin, Texas.

Kurki-Suonio, Erkki. 1952. *Hengelliset kansansävelmämme koraaleina* (Our religious folksongs in musical notation). 1. Helsinki.

Kuusi, Matti. 1956. Virolais-suomalainen Maailmansyntyruno (The Estrian-Finnish poem of creation). *Kalevalaseuran vuosikirja* 36, 49–84.

_____. 1963. Varhaiskalevalainen runos. (The early Kalevala poetry). *Suomen kirjallisuus* 1, 129–215.

_____. 1974. "The bridge and the church": an anti-church legend. *Studia Fennica* 18, 35–75.

Kvideland, Reimund. 1973. Det stod i avisa! *Tradisjon* 3, 1–12.

_____. 1973a. Folkeleg songtradisjon som brukspoesi. In E. Prøysen (ed.), 1973, 97–103.

_____. 1975. Emigrantviser - propaganda og nostalgi. In S. S. Amundsen and R. Kvideland (eds.), 1975, 9–35.

_____. 1976. Barnetru: Ein faktor i den kulturelle innlæringsprosessen. *Fataburen,* 233–54.

_____. 1980. Stories about death as a part of children's socialization. In N. Burlakoff and C. Lindahl (eds.), 1980, 59–64.

_____. 1981. Folkloristikkens nye paradigmer: Performans. In G. Herranen (ed.), 1981, 55–74.

_____. 1983. Folk ballad and folk song. *Studia Fennica* 27, 177–83.

Kvideland, Reimund, and Henning K. Sehmsdorf. 1988. *Scandinavian folk belief and legend.* Minneapolis, Minn.

Laboulaye, Edouard. 1867–68. *Blå sagor.* Stockholm.

Landstad, Magnus Brostrup. 1853. *Norske Folkeviser.* Oslo.

Landtman, Gunnar. 1922. Hustomtens förvantskap och härstamning. *Folkloristiska och etnografiska studier* 3, 1–48.

Lantz, Monica. 1980. *Sjömansvisor.* Stockholm.

Larsen, Øyvind, Bente Gullveig Alver, and Eimar Munthe. 1984. *Hjelp meg - jeg har gikt. Holdninger og forventninger til skolemedisin og alternativ medisin.* Oslo.

Launonen, H., and K. Mäkinen (eds.). 1974. *Folklore tänään.* Helsinki.

Ledang, Ola-Kai. 1975. Folkemusikkforsking - intellektuelt spel eller målretta kulturarbeid. *Tradisjon* 5, 1–12.

Lehtipuro, Outi. 1974. Trends in Finnish folkloristics. *Studia Fennica* 18, 7–36.

Lehtonen, Aleksi. 1931. *Kirkon pyhät toimukset* (Holy activities of the church). Porvoo.

Leino, Pentti. 1981. Folklorens textteori: Behövs strukturalismen i folkloristiken? In G. Herranen (ed.), 1981, 103–24.

Lévy-Bruhl, Lucien. 1922. *La mentalité primitive.* Paris.
Lévy-Strauss, Claude. 1955. The structural study of myth. *Journal of American Folklore* 68, 428–44 = Sebeok. 1958, 81–106.
_____. 1960. L'analyse morphologique des contes russes. *International journal of Slavic linguistics and poetics* 3, 122–49.
Lid, Nils. 1928. *Joleband og vegetasjonsguddom.* Oslo (Det norske videnskaps-akademi i Oslo. Skrifter II. Hist.-filos. klasse. 1928:4).
_____. 1931. *Wilhelm Mannhardt og hans samling av norske folkeminne.* Oslo (NFL 24).
_____. 1933. *Jolesveinar og grøderikdomsgudar.* Oslo (Det norske videnskaps-akademi i Oslo. Skrifter II. Hist.-filos. klasse. 1932:5).
_____. 1935. Innleiing. *Nordisk kultur* 19: Folketro, 1–2. Oslo.
_____. 1935a. Magiske fyrestellingar og bruk. *Nordisk kultur* 19, 3–76.
Liestøl, Knut. 1915. *Norske trollvisor og norrøne sogor.* Oslo.
_____. 1922. *Norske ættesogor.* Oslo.
_____. 1937. *Norsk folkedikting.* 3rd ed. Oslo.
_____. 1949. *Moltke Moe.* Oslo.
_____. 1963. *Segner.* Oslo. (Norsk folkedikting 3. 2nd ed.).
Lindeman, Ludv. M. 1850. Indberetning. *Norske Universitets- og Skoleannaler.* 2. Række 5, 481–500 = *Tradisjoninnsamling frå 1800-talet* (NFL 92), 89–123. Oslo.
Lindqvist, S. 1936. *Uppsala högar och Ottarshögen.* Stockholm.
Littleton, C. Scott. 1965. A two-dimensional scheme for the classification of narratives. *Journal of American Folklore* 78, 21–27.
Löfgren, Orvar. 1975. Fetströmming och lusmörtar. Folktro och kognitiva system i två kustbygder. In *Sista lasset in. Studier tillägnade Albert Eskeröd,* 321–42. Stockholm.
_____. 1976. Peasant ecotypes. Problems in the comparative study of ecoclogical adaptions. *Ethnologia Scandinavica,* 100–15.
Lønning, Per Eystein, and Odd Kogstad. 1981. Naturmedisin og reumatiske sykdommer. *Tidsskrift for Den norske lægeforening,* 314–16.
Lord, Albert B. 1964. *The singers of tales.* Cambridge, Mass.
Lore and Language. 1973 to date. Sheffield.
Lotman, Jurij M. 1964. Sur la délimination linguistique et littéraire de la notion de structure. *Linguistics* 6, 59–72.
Louhivuori, Jukka. 1978. Halullisten sielujen hengelliset laulut 1–26. Rakenneanalyysi ja toisintojen vertailu (The religious songs of the awakened souls, 1–26. A structural analysis and a comparison of variants). Unpubl. MS. at the University of Turku.
_____. 1979. Siionin virret ja Halullisten Sielujen Hengelliset Laulut työn alla: Uuden nuottilaitoksen toimitustyön erityispiirteitä (Zion's chorales and the religious songs of the awakened souls edited: criteria for editing the new notation). *Kirkkomusiikkilehti, joulukuu.* 1979, 14–18.
Lowenfeld, Berthold. 1964. *Our blind children. Growing and learning with them.* Springfield, Ill.
Lund, Jens. 1975. The legend of the king and the star. *Indiana Folklore* 8, 1–37.
Luomala, K. 1972. Disintegration and regeneration: the Hawaiian phantom hitchhiker legend. *Fabula* 13, 20–59.
Lüthi, Max. 1947. *Das europäische Volksmärchen. Form und Wesen.* Bern.
McCandless, B. R. 1973. *Childhood socialization.* In D. A. Goslin (ed.), 1973, 791–820.
Malinowski, B. 1954. *Magic, science, and religion, and other essays.* New York.
Maranda, Elli Köngas, and Pierre Maranda. 1971. *Structural models in folklore and transformational essays.* The Hague (Approaches to semiotics 10).
Maranda, Pierre (ed.). 1974. *Soviet structural folkloristics.* The Hague/Paris.

Marret, R. R. 1920. *Psychology and folk-lore*. London.
Mathais, T., L. Lynch, and B. Miller. 1972. The vanishing hitch-hiker. *Journal of the Ohio Folklore Society*, n.s. 1, 48–50.
Mathisen, Stein. 1979. "Resande Toivonen och hans kamrat Pekka." Vitser om finner i Norge. *Tradisjon* 9, 15–29.
Mattson, Christina. 1974. "Vad säger svenska folket när dom får en sup? - Jo, jag tackar." En studie i 1900-talets supvisetradition. *Tradisjon* 4, 51–70.
Mauland, Torkéll. 1934. *Folkeminne fraa Rogaland*. 2. Oslo. (NFL 26).
Meletinskij, Eleazar. 1969. Problemy strukturnogo opisanija volšebnoj skazki. Trudy po znakovym sistemam 4, 86–135. = Problems of the structural analysis of folktales. In P. Maranda (ed.), 1974, 73–139.
_____. 1971. Structural-typological study of the folktale. *Genre* 4, 249–79.
Merriam, Alan P. 1964. *The anthropology of music*. Evanston, Ill.
Meyer, Leonard B. 1974. *Emotion and meaning in music*. Chicago.
Mitscherlich, A. 1963. *Auf den Weg zur vaterlosen Gesellschaft: Ideen zur Sozialpsychologie*. Munich.
Mo, Ragnvald. 1952. *Soge og segn. Folkeminne frå Salten* 3. Oslo (NFL 69).
Moe, Moltke. 1924. *Folkeminne frå Bøherad*. Oslo (NFL 9).
_____. 1927. *Samlede skrifter* 3. Oslo.
Møller, Arvid. 1975. *Solveigs hender*. Oslo.
Møller, J. S. 1940. *Moder og barn i dansk folkeoverlevering*. Copenhagen (Danmarks folkeminder 48).
Morin, Edgar. 1971. *Ryktet i Orléans*. Stockholm.
Mullen, Patric B. 1970. Department store snakes. *Indiana Folklore* 3, 214–28.
_____. 1972. Modern legend and rumor theory. *Journal of the Folklore Institute* 9, 95–109.
Nagy, M. 1973. The child's view of death. *Journal of genetic psychology* 4, 3–27.
Nenola-Kallio, Aili (ed.). 1982. *Folktradition och regional identitet i Norden*. Åbo (NIF publications 12).
Nergaard, Sigurd. 1925. *Hulder og trollskap. Folkeminne fraa Østerdalen* 4. Oslo (NFL 11).
Neuland, Lena. 1977. *Jumis die Fruchbarkeitsgottheit der alten Letten*. Stockholm (Stockholm studies in comparative religion 15).
Nikander, Gabriel. 1916. Fruktbarhetsriter under årshögtiderna hos svenskarna i Finland. *Folkloristiska och etnografiska studier* 1, 195–315.
Nilsson (= Eskeröd), Albert. 1936. Interessedominanz und Volksüberlieferung. Einige überlieferungs-psychologische Gesichtspunkte. *Acta ethnologica*, 165–86.
Nilsson, Martin Persson. 1921. Julkärven, sista kärven och julklappen. *Folkminnen och folktankar* 8, 57–70.
Nordbø, Halvor. 1928. *Ættesogor frå Telemark*. Oslo (Det norske videnskaps-akademi i Oslo. Skrifter II. Hist.-filos. klasse. 1928:1).
Nordland, Odd. 1962–63. The street of the "Wise women." *Arv* 18/19, 263–74.
Nyman, Arre. 1974. Oudot liftarit ja grillatut vauvat (Strange tales and grilled children). In H. Launonen and K. Mäkinen (eds.), 1974, 63–73.
Nyvold, Frode. 1979. *Kulturaktivismen i Oksitania*. Oslo.
Ohlert, K. 1912. *Rätsel und Rätselspiele der alten Griechen*. Berlin.
Ohlsson, Hans. 1974. Kycklingen i hatten. MS. Institutet för folklivsforskning, Stockholm.
Oinas, Felix J. 1975. The political uses and themes of folklore in the Soviet Union. *Journal of the Folklore Institute* 12, 157–75.
Olrik, Axel. 1909. Epische Gesetze der Volksdichtung. *Zeitschrift für deutsches Altertum* 51, 1–12. = Epic laws of folk narrative. In A. Dundes (ed.), 1965, 129–41.

Østberg, Kristian. 1925. *Svartboka*. Oslo.

Otto, Rudolf. 1936. *Das Heilige*. 29.-30. ed. Munich.

Paredes, Americo, and Richard Bauman (eds.). 1971. *Toward new perspectives in folklore*. Austin, Texas.

Parochetti, J. S. 1965. Scary stories from Purdue. *Keystone Folklore Quarterly* 10, 49–57.

Paulaharju, Samuli. 1924. Syntymä, lapsuus ja kuolema. Vienan Karjalan tapoja ja uskomuksia (Birth, childhood and death. Strange occurances and beliefs in Karelia). *Kalevalaseuran julkaisuja* 2. Helsinki.

Pedersen, H. 1888. *Vognfundene i Dejbjergs Præstegaardsmose*. Copenhagen.

Pentikäinen, Juha. 1968. Grenzprobleme zwischen Memorat und Sage. *Temenos* 3, 136–68.

———. 1968a. *The Nordic dead-child tradition*. Helsinki (FFC 202).

———. 1969. The dead without status. *Temenos* 4, 92–102.

———. 1970. Quellenanalytische Probleme der religiösen Überlieferung. *Temenos* 6, 89–118.

———. 1978. *Oral repertoire and world view. An anthropological study of Marina Takalo's life history*. Helsinki (FFC 219).

Pentikäinen, Juha, and Tuula Juurikka (eds.). 1976. *Folk Narrative Research*. Helsinki (Studia Fennica 20).

Peterson, W., and N. P. Gist. 1951. Rumor and public opinion. *American Journal of Sociology* 57, 159–67.

Peuckert, Will-Erich. 1938. *Deutsches Volkstum in Märchen und Sage, Schwank und Rätsel*. Berlin.

Peuckert, W.-E., and Otto Lauffer (eds.). 1951. *Volkskunde, Quellen und Forschungen seit 1930*. Bern (Wissenschaftliche Forschungsberichte 14).

Piø, Iørn. 1971. *Folkeminder og traditionsforskning*. 2nd ed. Copenhagen.

———. 1976. De rige og de fattige. Et essay om "Danmarks syngende mand." *Sumlen*, 162–74.

———. 1977. Om at læse sungne ballader. De danske middelalderballader. *Sumlen*, 9–19.

———. 1979. Perspektiver i studiet af Danske Viser fra Adelsvisebøger og Flyveblade 1530–1630. H. Grüner-Nielsen. *Danske viser*, vol. 7. Copenhagen. 1979, 322–42 (= DSLS præsentationshæfte 6).

Piø, Iørn, Gustav Henningsen, and Birgitte Rørbye. 1974. Dansk folkemindeforskning. 1953–1973. *Danske studier*, 115–31.

Ploss, Heinrich. 1911. *Das Kind in Brauch und Sitte der Völker*. 3. Aufl. Leipzig (Völkerkundliche Studien 1).

Popper, Karl R. 1969. *The poverty of historicism*. 2nd ed. London.

Potter, Charles Francis. 1950. Riddles. In Funk and Wagnalls. 1950, 2, 138.

Propp, Vladimir. 1928. *Morfologija skazki*. Leningrad.

———. 1928a. Transformacii volsebnyx skazok. *Poetika* 4, 70–89.

———. 1946. *Istoriceskie korni volsebnoi skazki*. Leningrad.

———. 1958. *Morphology of the folktale*. Austin, Texas.

Prøysen, Elin. 1973. *Folkelige viser*. Oslo (Norsk folkeminnelags skrifter 109).

Qvigstad, Just. 1927–29. *Lappiske eventyr og sagn* 1–4. Oslo. (Instituttet for sammenlignende kulturforskning. Serie B:Skrifter 3, 10, 12, 15).

Rääf, L. F. 1957. *Svenska skrock och signerier*. Red. av K. Rob. V. Wikman. Stockholm (Kungliga Vitterhets, Historie och Antikvitets Akademiens handlingar, filologisk-filosofiska serien 4).

Rank, Otto. 1909. *Der Mythus von der Geburt des Helden*. Leipzig/ Vienna.

Ranke, Kurt (ed.). 1961. *Internationaler Kongress der Volkserzählungsforscher in Kiel und Kopenhagen (19.8–29.8.1959). Vorträge und Referate*. Berlin (*Fabula*. Reihe B. 2).

Rantasalo, A. V. 1919–25. *Der Ackerbau im Volksglauben der Finnen und Esten mit entsprechen-den Gebräucher der Germanen verglichen* 1–5. Helsinki (FFC 30–32, 55, 62).
Rasmussen, Knud. 1931. *The Netsilik Eskimos. Social life and spiritual culture.* Copenhagen. (Report of the fifth Thule expedition. 1921–24. 8:1–2).
Reichborn-Kjennerud, Ingjald. 1928–47. *Vår gamle trolldomsmedisin* 1–5. Oslo. (Det norske videnskaps-akademi i Oslo. Skrifter II. Hist.-filos. klasse. 1927:6, 1933:2, 1940:1, 1943:2, 1947:1).
Richette, C. 1974. Berättartraditioner bland taxiförare. MS. Institutet för folklivsforskning, Stockholm.
Rietz, J. E. 1862–67. *Svenskt Dialektlexikon eller Ordbok öfver svenska allmogespråket.* Lund.
Roberts, Warren E. 1958. The special forms of Aarne-Thompson type 480 and their distribution. *Fabula* 1, 85–102.
Roemer, D. 1971. Scary story legends. *Folklore Annual of the University Association. The University of Texas at Austin* 3, 1–16.
Röhrich, Lutz. 1958. Die deutsche Volkssage. *Studium Generale* 11, 664–91.
Rooth, Anna Birgitta (ed.). 1971. *Folkdikt och folktro.* Lund.
Rørbye, Birgitte. 1976. Den illegale sygdomsbehandling som folkloristisk problem. *Fataburen*, 203–20.
_____. 1978. Nutidig folkemedicin. *Tradisjon* 8, 37–45.
_____. 1978a. Folketroen som begrep og forskningsfelt. *Norveg* 21, 305–17.
_____. 1980. Allmän etnomedisinsk översikt. In B. G. Alver et al., 1980, 155–210.
Ruoppila, Veikko. 1954. *Kansa lastensa kasvattajana* (On the education of the nation's children). Porvoo/Helsinki.
Salminen, Väinö (ed.). 1945. *Suomen kansan vanhat runot* (Ancient poems of the Finnish people) 13:4. Helsinki.
Sande, Olav 1892. *Segner fraa Sogn* 2. Bergen.
Sanderson, S. 1969. The folklore of the motor-car. *Folklore* 80, 241–52.
Sarmela, Matti. 1969. *Reciprocity systems of the rural society in the Finnish Karelian culture area.* Helsinki (FFC 207).
_____. 1974. Folklore, ecology, and superstructures. *Studia Fennica* 18, 76–115.
Schei, Henrik. 1947. *Overnaturlige helbredende nådegaver.* Bergen.
Schjelderup, Vilhelm. 1974. *Legekunsten på nye veier.* Oslo.
Schmidt, Leopold. 1963. *Die Volkserzählung: Märchen, Sage, Legende, Schwank.* Berlin.
Sebeok, Thomas A. (ed.). 1958. *Myth: a symposium.* Bloomington, Ind.
Sehmsdorf, Henning. 1987. The drama of Peder W. Cappelen and folklore. In Susanne Frølich (ed.), *Papers of the international and interdisciplinary congress on dimensions of the marvellous.* Oslo, 49–57.
_____. 1987a. Eventyr og allegori: Peder W. Cappelens Tornerose, den sovende skjønnhet. In Ebbe Schön (ed.), *Folklore och litteratur i Norden.* Stockholm (NIF Publications No. 17). 134–42.
_____. 1987b. The poetry of Halldis Moren Vesaas and tradition. In Leif Mæhle (ed.), *Halldis Moren Vesaas. Festskrift til 80-årsdagen,* Oslo, 132–40.
_____. 1988. Envy and fear in Scandinavian folk tradition. *Ethnologia Scandinavica,* 34–42.
_____. 1988. Survival, assimilation, adaptation: Norwegian-American traditions in the Pacific Northwest. *Folklore northwest* 70, 1:3–13.
_____. 1989. The romantic heritage: Ibsen and the uses of folklore. In Oskar Bandle et al. (eds.), *Nordische Romantik.* Basel and Frankfurt (Beiträge zur Nordischen Philologie No. 19) (forthcoming).
_____. 1989a. AT 711: The folktale and its socio-cultural context. *Scandinavian Studies* (forthcoming).
Selberg, Torunn. 1979. Å helbrede med elektriske hender. *Nord-Nytt* 6, 32–36.

_____ . 1980. "Marta" - en folkelig helbreder. Om dagens folkemedisin sett gjennom en kloks praksis og selvforståelse. *Budkavlen* 59, 31–39.

Sell, Hans Joachim. 1955. *Der schlimme Tod bei den Völkern Indonesiens*. The Hague.

Shibutani, T. 1966. *Improvised news: a sociological study of rumor*. New York.

Siikala, Anna-Leena. 1978. *The rite technique of the Siberian shaman*. Helsinki (FFC 220).

_____ . 1980. Miina Huovinen. En verbales atiker. In B. G. Alver et al., 1980, 53–82.

_____ . 1980a. Perinneorientaatio ja kertojan persoonallisuus. Kertojat ja kuulijat (Tradition, narrative, audience). *Kalevalaseuran vuosikirja* 60, 83–92.

Simon, Arthur. 1978. Probleme, Methoden und Ziele der Ethnomusikologie. *Jahrbuch für musikalische Volkskunde* 9, 8–52.

Simonsuuri, Lauri. 1961. *Typen- und Motivverzeichnis der finnischen mythischen Sagen*. Helsinki (FFC 182).

Skar, Johannes. 1911. *Gamalt or Sætesdal*. 5. Oslo.

_____ . 1961. *Gamalt or Sætesdal. Samla utg*. 1–3. Oslo.

Skjelbred, Ann Helene Bolstad. 1983. Står det i avisen? Avisen som folkloristisk kilde. *Tradisjon* 13, 101–109.

_____ . 1983a. *Bibliografi over alternativ medisin og behandling i Norge til og med 1980*. Oslo (Universitetsbiblioteket i Oslo. Skrifter 13).

Smart, J. 1970. We pop the elephant myth. *Small World. For Volkswagen owners in the United States* 9:4, 6–8.

Söderbäck, P. 1921. *Skrock, sed och sägen i en smålandssocken. Anteckningar från Kristdala*. Stockholm.

Solheim, Svale. 1951. Gardvoren og senga hans. *Maal og minne*, 143–58.

_____ . 1952. *Norsk sætertradisjon*. Oslo (Instituttet for sammenlignende kulturforskning. Serie B: Skrifter 47).

_____ . 1962. Historie og munnleg historisk visetradisjon. In L. Bødker (ed.), 1962, 107–25.

_____ . 1970. Historical legend—historical function. *Acta Ethnographica Acad. Scient. Hungaricae*. 19, 341–46.

_____ . 1973. Historisk segn - historisk funksjon. *Norveg* 16, 141–47.

Sørensen, Bjarne. 1979. Gatekrig. *Tradisjon* 9, 1–14.

Spamer, Adolf. 1934. *Die deutsche Volkskunde* 1. Leipzig.

Staugaard, Frants. 1979. *Den folkliga medicinen. Svart magi eller sunt förnuft*. Stockholm.

Steenstrup, Johannes C. H. R. 1891. *Vore Folkeviser fra Middelalderen*. Copenhagen.

Steward, Julian H. 1973. *Theory of cultural change*. Urbana, Ill.

Stoklund, Bjarne. 1976. Ecological succession: Reflections on the relations between man and environment in pre-industrial Denmark. *Ethnologia Scandinavica*, 84–99.

Strejk. 1972. Strejk! En bok om strejker och strejkvisor från Bageriarbetarstrejken 1873 till Storstrejken 1909. Stockholm.

Strompdal, Knut. 1929. *Gamalt frå Helgeland*. 1. Oslo. (NFL. 19).

Suojanen, Päivikki. 1978. *Saarna, saarnaaja, tilanne* (The spontaneous sermon: Its production and context). Helsinki.

_____ . 1979. Veisuuaktien antropologiaa (The anthropology of hymn singing). *Sananjalka* 21, 97–128.

_____ . 1981. Den religiösa mötessångens gruppdynamik. En etnomusikologisk undersökning av religiös mötessång. *Sumlen*, 9–19.

_____ . 1983. I varje socken sjunger man med en egen melodi. Forskningsmetodologi vid studiet av andlig sång i Finland. *Sumlen*, 94–109.

_____ . 1984. *Finnish folk hymn singing. Study in music anthropology*. Tampere (University of Tampere Institute for Folk Tradition publication 11).

_____ . 1985. Zur Methodologie der Volksliedforschung (Gesangforschung). Bericht über empirische Forschung zum religiösen Volksgesang. *Jahrbuch für Volksliedforschung* 30, 68–80.

Svéréus, B. 1976. *Vår tids rykten bland skolbarn.* MS. Institutet för folklivsforskning, Stockholm.

Swahn, Jan-Öjvind. 1971. Jason och Medea i Kråksmåla. In A. B. Rooth (ed.), 1971, 76–91.

Taylor, Archer. 1964. The biographical pattern in traditional narrative. *Journal of the Folklore Institute* 1, 114–29.

Thigpen, K. A. 1971. Adolescent legends in Brown county: a survey. *Indiana Folklore* 4, 141–215.

Thompson, Stith. 1946. *The folktale.* New York.

Thomsen, Thomas. 1980. *Farvel til Danmark. De danske skillingsvisers syn på Amerika og på udvandringen dertil 1830–1914.* Århus.

Tillhagen, Carl-Hermann. 1958. *Folklig läkekonst.* Stockholm.

_____. 1962. Traditionsbäraren. In L. Bødker (ed.), 1962, 36–47.

_____. 1969. Finnen und Lappen als Zauberkundige in der skandinavischen Volksüberlieferung. In G. Heilfurth, 1969, 129–43.

Torp, Alf. 1919. *Nynorsk etymologisk ordbok.* Oslo.

Torstensson, Inge. 1979. *Signekjerringer i storbyen.* Magistergradsavhandling i folkeminnevitskap, Institutt for folkeminnevitskap, Universitetet i Oslo.

Trankell, A. 1974. Svenskarnas fördomar mot invandrare. *SOU.* 1974, No. 70. Invandrarutredningen, vol. 4. Bilagdel (Appendix), 121–212. Stockholm.

van Gennep, Arnold. 1960. *The rites of passage.* London.

Vaskilampi, Tuula, and Carol P. MacCormack (eds.). 1982. *Folk medicine and health culture: Role of folk medicine in modern health care. Proceedings of the Nordic research symposium 27–28 August 1981.* Kuopio.

Velure, Magne. 1975. *Kniv, sprit och sisu.* Stenc. forskningsrapport, Nordiska museet, Stockholm.

_____. 1975a. Tradisjonsforskaren - frå romantikar til realist. Nye tankar i vesttysk "Volkskunde." *Tradisjon* 5, 13–24.

_____. 1976. Hovuddrag i nordisk folketruforsking 1850–1975. *Fataburen,* 21–48.

_____. 1983. Nordic folk belief research. *Studia Fennica* 27, 111–20.

Virtanen, Leea. 1960. Arvoitus ja sen tehtävä (The riddle and its function). *Suomalaisen Kirjallisuuden Seuran Tietolipas* 17, 144–89.

_____. 1976. Lagom lycka är bäst. Magiska föreställningar i dag. *Fataburen,* 255–68.

_____. 1977. On the function of riddles. In L. Virtanen et al. (eds.), 1977, 77–89.

_____. 1978. *Children's lore.* Helsinki (Studia Fennica 22).

_____. 1980. Contemporary responses to legends and memorates. In N. Burlakoff and C. Lindahl (eds.), 1980, 65–70.

Virtanen, Leea, et al. (eds.). 1977. *Arvoitukset* (Finnish riddles). Helsinki.

von Sydow, Carl Wilhelm. 1944. Folkminnesforskningens uppkomst och utveckling. *Folkkultur* 4, 5–35.

_____. 1948. *Selected papers on folklore.* Copenhagen.

von der Leyen, Friedrich. 1934. Die Volkssage. In A. Spamer (ed.), 1934, 203–15.

VVK. 1963. Vanha Suomalainen Virsi- ja Evankeliumikirja (The old church hymnal). Rauma.

Wagner, Gotfrid. 1938. *Småländska folkminnen* 2. Vetlanda.

Wall, Jan. 1977–79. *Tjuvmjölkande väsen* 1–2. Uppsala (Studia ethnologica Upsaliensis 3 and 5).

Wallis, Roy, and Peter Morley (eds.). 1976. *Marginal medicine.* London.

Waronen, Matti. 1895. *Vainajainpalvelus muinaisilla suomalaisilla* (Worship of the dead among the ancient Finns). Helsinki.

Weber, Max. 1949. *The methodology of social sciences.* Glencoe.

Weiser-Aall, Lily. 1968. *Svangerskap og fødsel i nyere norsk tradisjon.* Oslo (Småskrifter fra Norsk etnologisk gransking 6/7).

Wesselski, A. 1934. Die Formen des volkstümlichen Erzählgutes. In A. Spamer (ed.), 1934, 216–48.
Wessman, V. E. V. 1931. *Mytiska sägner.* Helsingfors (Finlands svenska folkdiktning 2:3).
_____. 1949. *Gåtor.* Helsinki (Finlands svenska folkdiktning 4).
Wikman, K. Rob. V. 1947. Rev. of Albert Eskeröd: Årets äring. *Folkliv* 11, 81–85.
_____. 1955. Finlandssvensk folkminnesforskning. Historia och idéer under ett sekel. *Budkavlen* 34, 1–25.
Wille, Hans Jacob. 1786. *Beskrivelse over Sillejords Præstegield i øvre-Tellemarken i Norge, tilligemed et geographisk Chart over samme.* Copenhagen.
Wilson, William A. 1975. The Kalevala and Finnish politics. *Journal of the Folklore Institute* 12, 131–55.
_____. 1975a. The vanishing hitchhiker among the Mormons. *Indiana Folklore* 8, 80–97.
Wolf, Eric. 1966. *Peasants.* Englewood Cliffs, N.J.
Yoder, Don. 1974. Toward a definition of folk religion. *Western Folklore* 23, 2–15.
Young, Allan. 1976. Some implications of medical beliefs and practice for social anthropology. *American Anthropologist* 78, 5–24.

CONTRIBUTORS

Bente G. Alver is a Professor of Folklore at the University of Bergen, where she has taught since 1973. She is the author of books and articles on witchcraft, magic, concepts of the soul, and folk medicine, as well as contributions to the theory of fieldwork in ethnology and folklore.

Brynjulf Alver has taught folklore at the University of Oslo and the University of Bergen. In 1967–1979 he was Director of the Nordic Institute of Folklore (then located in Copenhagen). Professor Alver's publications include monographs on oral literature, folk music, calendar customs, and folklore theory and methodology.

Jon-Roar Bjørkvold is Professor of Musicology at the University of Oslo. He has published in various fields, including sociology of music, Soviet music history, film music rhetoric, and children's musical culture. He is currently preparing a monograph on cross-cultural studies of children's traditions in the U.S., Norway, and the Soviet Union.

Jonas Frykman teaches ethnology at the University of Lund. Dr. Frykman's major publications analyze sociocultural patterns in rural pre-industrial Sweden, and world view as reflected in middle-class attitudes toward body and sexuality in twentieth-century Swedish society.

Gun Herranen is a research scholar at the Academy of Finland and teaches folklore at Abo Academy, the Swedish-language university in Turku. Her published research concerns narrator-centered studies of folktales, historical legends, and the history of folklore study in Swedish Finland. Since 1984 she has been the secretary of the International Society for Folk-Narrative Research (ISNFR).

Bengt Holbek teaches folklore at the University of Copenhagen, where he has specialized in the study of folktales, proverbs, fables, folk belief, and the history of folkloristics. A major study by Dr. Holbek, *Interpretation of Fairy Tales: Danish Folklore in a European Perspective* (1987), was published in the series Folklore Fellows Communication (FFC) (Helskinki).

Lauri Honko, Director of the Nordic Institute of Folklore (now in Turku), holds a chair in folkloristics and comparative religion at the University of Turku. He is the editor of *Folklore Fellows Communications, Temenos,* and *Studia Fennica,* and co-edits several Nordic, German, and American folklore journals. His many publications include studies on folk medicine, laments, Finno-Ugric mythology and belief systems, and folklore theory.

Birgit Hertzberg Johnsen is head curator at the Department of Folklore, University of Oslo. Her books and articles focus on the sociocultural context of folklore and on feminist perspectives on tradition.

Bengt af Klintberg was formerly curator at the Folklore Archives at the Nordic Museum, Stockholm. He has taught folklore at the University of Stockholm but now works as a freelance folklorist and writer, and has a regular program on Radio Sweden. His many books on Swedish folklore include editions of legends, magic, and children's lore.

Reimund Kvideland, currently president of the Société Internationale d'Ethnologie et de Folkloristique (SIEF) and of the International Society for Folk Narrative Research (ISFNR), has been teaching folklore at the University of Bergen since 1966. He has published widely on children's lore, ballads and folk song, narrative tradition, and folklore theory. He is co-editor of *Norsk eventyrbibliotek* (Norwegian Folktale Library) and edits the folklore journal *Tradisjon*. Together with Henning K. Sehmsdorf, he is publishing a three-volume English-language series on Scandinavian folklore.

Juha Pentikäinen, Professor of Comparative Religion at the University of Helsinki, has published research on arctic cultures, minority studies, the analysis of oral repertoire and world view, and the theory of folkloristics.

Henning K. Sehmsdorf, Associate Professor, teaches Scandinavian and general folklore at the University of Washington, Seattle. His publications include studies on folk belief, folktale, and the relations of folklore, mythology, and literature. He is associate editor of the journal *Northwest Folklore*.

Torunn Selberg, Research Associate in Folklore at the University of Bergen, has published studies on folk belief, ethnomedicine, and popular culture. She is co-author, with Bente G. Alver, of a forthcoming monograph on alternative medicine in Norway.

Päivikki Suojanen is Research Fellow in Folklore and Anthropology at the University of Tampere and holds teaching appointments at several other Finnish universities. Dr. Suojanen has published monographs on folk sermons and hymn singing in religious communities in Finland.

Magne Velure is Director of Maihaugen Folk Museum at Lillehammer. He is the author of studies concerning folk belief, folklore theory, folklorism, and cultural revitalization. In recent years his research has been concerned with the role of cultural-historical museums in collecting and documenting contemporary culture.

Leea Virtanen teaches folklore at the University of Helsinki. Professor Virtanen has published articles and monographs on Finnish, Estonian, and Karelian folklore, including children's traditions, proverbs, urban legends, and supernatural beliefs in contemporary society, as well as a textbook on Finnish folklore and folkloristics.

INDEX

Role: of patient, 216; of sick person, 216
Role theory, 34
Rudbeck, Olaus, 17
Rumor, 8, 71f; and legend, 71; dissemination of, 71

Sagas: as national symbol, 19; Icelandic, 132, 133
Sanctions: against "secret whore," 202
Sarmela, Matti, 8
Såve Nyland (Strong Såve), murderer, 138
Säve, P. A., 7
Schepping, Wilhelm, 171
Scherer, Wilhelm, 12
Scott, Walter, 12
Sehmsdorf, Henning K., 3–11
Selberg, Torunn, 8, 207–20
Sexuality: popular attitudes toward, 205; restrictions upon, 205; views toward, 10
Shadow-soul, 127
Shaman, 125
Sickness: concept of, 218
Siikala, Anna-Leena, 97
Simon, Arthur, 171
Singing: activity, 10, 183; creativity in, 174; hymn, 173; spontaneous, 10
Singing act: definition, 174
Singing event: definition of, 174
Socialization, 232; and the family, 232; and the peer group, 232; and the school, 232; and traditional genres, 232; of children, 232
Solheim, Svale, 6, 9
Solli, Anders: soldier killed, 150–62; Wolf Song, 152
Soul: concept of, 8, 110; dream-soul, 123, 127; free-soul, 127; fylgje, 121; hug, 110; of shaman, 125; placeless, 128; poor, 128; shadow-soul, 127; unstable, 125; vor(d), 121–22
Spencer, Herbert: manistic theory, 93
Stereotype, 8; ethnic, 73–78
Stories: about death, 234; about murder, 234
Storyteller, 7, 8, 42, 61–62, 63–69; blind s., 63–69
Storytelling, 9, 43; among children, 232–37; domestic, 42; public, 42
Strandberg, Julius: broadside producer, 170
Street war, 11
Strömberg, Berndt: blind storyteller, 7, 63–69

Structuralism: linguistic and anthropological, 29; paradigmatic, 30; Russian, 29; syntagmatic, 30
Structure: of folk tales, 43–62
Strunk, Orlo, 175
Suojanen, Päivikki, 10, 173–82
Survival theory, 94
Swedish Literature Society, 4
Symbols, 43–62; polyvalent, in folk tales, 43
Syv, Peder, 13

Taboo subject: death as, 233; and medical doctors, 216
Takalo, Marina, 7
Thompson, Stith, x, 5
Thought: power of, 118
Tradition: ecology, 35; viability of, 160
Tradition ecology, 36; and quantification, 38
Tradition process, 161–62
Transmission: of legend, 155; of tradition, 154
Troll cat: aegagrophilae, 120; hugham of the witch, 120
Turkey, 18

Unwed mothers: sanctions, 202
Urform, 24

Van Gennep, Arnold, 130
Vardøger, 116, 117; warning of death, 117
Vedel, A. S., 13
Velure, Magne, 73
Virtanen, Leea, 221–31
Volkslied, 166
Von Sydow, Carl Wilhelm, 5, 6, 71, 94, 101–103; concept of genres, 101; contrast to Jolles, 103

Walking dead: guilty, 131; innocent, 131
Wall, Jan, 97
Werewolf, 112
Wergeland, Henrik, 13
Wessman, V. E. V., 63, 64
Whore rickets, 196
Wikman, K. Rob. V., 95
Witch: hugdragging, 119
Witchcraft, 118
Wolff, Simon Olaus, 14
World view, 7

Printed in the United States
722600002B